PHILIP GRIERSON

Numismatics

OXFORD UNIVERSITY PRESS
London   Oxford   New York
1975

· C

Oxford University Press, Ely House, London W.1

GLASGOW NEW YORK TORONTO MELBOURNE WELLINGTON
CAPE TOWN IBADAN NAIROBI DAR ES SALAAM LUSAKA ADDIS ABABA
DELHI BOMBAY CALCUTTA MADRAS KARACHI LAHORE DACCA
KUALA LUMPUR SINGAPORE HONG KONG TOKYO

PAPERBACK ISBN 888098 7
CASEBOUND ISBN 885098 0

© OXFORD UNIVERSITY PRESS 1975

FILMSET AND PRINTED IN GREAT BRITAIN BY
BAS PRINTERS LIMITED WALLOP HAMPSHIRE

Contents

List of Figures

Coins and paper money are reproduced natural size unless otherwise indicated in the captions.

Acknowledgements

My chief debt of gratitude is to Ian Stewart, not simply for having read this book in draft and greatly improved it but because of the contribution he has made, over many years of friendship and collaboration, to my knowledge and understanding of coinage. Other friends have been kind enough to read either the whole of this book or those sections where they have special knowledge: Christopher Brooke (all), Michael Crawford and Martin Price (the classical period), Nicholas Lowick (Muslim and Indian coins), and Rose Chan-Houston and Michael Loewe (Far Eastern coins). To all of them I am most grateful, but since I have not always accepted their advice such errors of fact or judgement as readers may discover are imputable to me and not to them. In particular, it was my decision to dispense with virtually all diacritical marks for words in non-European languages, since they seemed to me inappropriate in a book of this nature.

The illustrations of coins are taken from a miscellany of sources, mainly sale catalogues but in some cases involving material in the British Museum, the Fitzwilliam Museum at Cambridge, or the Museum of the American Numismatic Society. I am grateful to the appropriate authorities for permission to use them. For the photographs used for Figs. 26 (Swedish bank note), 49 (touching up a die), 52 and 54 (various coining implements), and 55 (modern coining presses) I am indebted to the keeper of the Royal Coin Cabinet at Stockholm (photo Nils Lagergren ATA), the Director of the Administration des Monnaies et Médailles at Paris, the Director of the Coin Cabinet of the Kunsthistorisches Museum at Vienna, and the Deputy Master of the Royal Mint (photo by Photographic Division, Central Office of Information) respectively.

Note on Weights

The weights of coins are customarily given in grams (abbreviated gm. or g.), but grains (abbreviated gr.) are still widely used in books printed in Great Britain, especially for English coins. 1 g. = 15·43 gr.; 1 gr. = 0·065 g. Conversion tables of grains into grams are included in all British Museum coin catalogues. Grams are used throughout this book, but for English coins the equivalents in grains are given also.

Since it is often difficult to envisage the weights of coins one has not oneself handled, the following weights of current British and American coins may be useful for comparison:

50 Pence	13·50 g.		(Dollar	26·73 g.)
10 Pence	11·31 g.		Half-dollar	11·50 g.
5 Pence	5·66 g.		Quarter	5·67 g.
			Dime	2·27 g.
2 Pence	7·13 g.			
Penny	3·56 g.			
Halfpenny	1·78 g.		Nickel	5·00 g.
			Cent ('Penny')	2·75 g.

1
Introduction

The Scope of Numismatics

Numismatics is defined in the *Oxford English Dictionary* as 'the study of coins and medals, especially from an archaeological or historical standpoint'. The American *Webster* spells out the details more comprehensively: 'The study of coins, tokens, medals, paper money, and objects closely resembling them in form or purpose, including standard media of exchange and decorations.' Both indicate the basic ambiguity of the word. Numismatics grew out of the attempt to understand and put in order what collectors of the sixteenth and seventeenth centuries described as 'medals'. This term had not yet become restricted to its modern meaning, implying something essentially commemorative in character. It covered all kinds of small metal objects bearing inscriptions or designs, whatever their original purposes might have been. Their grouping together under the heading of a single discipline was based on their external appearance, not on their function, but since one of the main functions of 'medals' in the old sense was economic, it has been easy for later scholars to extend the scope of numismatics so that it embraces all more or less portable objects used as means of exchange, from the cowries or brass manilas of primitive societies to the banknotes of economically more developed ones.

How far these extensions are legitimate is a matter upon which numismatists differ. Scholars who consider coins as archaeological objects to be studied in themselves, holding that their purposes and functioning are topics best left to the economic historian, or who are interested in coins primarily as works of art, will be prepared to take account in varying degrees of medals, tokens, jettons, and coin-weights. These for the most part look like coins, and since they have been traditionally regarded as coming within his purview, the numismatist is likely to have acquired some knowledge of them and become accustomed to dealing with them. On the other hand, if the approach of the scholar is primarily economic, he will regard most of them as only marginally interesting, and some he will be inclined to exclude altogether. He will, however, wish to take account of primitive money and paper money, which are not coin at all.

A generous attitude is probably the best one to adopt, since even such objects as amulets, communion tokens, and military medals, although they have no economic significance, are of interest to the historian of society. Of the others, the study of medals is relevant to the history of coin design and the development of manufacturing techniques, that of coin-weights to numismatic metrology and the treatment of coin in circulation, and that of primitive money for any inquiry into the origins of money and the working of colonial coinages. It is also helpful towards an understanding of what happens when, as sometimes occurs, there is a breakdown in an advanced economic system and a reversion to earlier methods of exchange. Paper money and tokens are allowed by even the most rigorous definition to be 'money' if issued by the state, and even when issued by banks, corporations, or private persons are at least intended to perform monetary functions whether officially authorized or not. With both tokens and paper money, however, there is much difficulty in drawing the line between monetary and non-monetary identities. There are tokens which circulate as money without having been expressly created for that purpose, and it is not always easy to distinguish notes and bills which are general instruments of credit from cheques and other negotiable instruments which are not in themselves money but are commonly used for its transfer. One is apt to think of credit as characteristic of highly sophisticated modern societies, but it can in fact play an equally conspicuous role, however different in its details, in societies that have no coin at all. Such societies, indeed, if 'advanced' in other respects, as were the great empires of antiquity, may well make proportionately more use of credit than a society possessing coin requires to do.

Numismatics and the Historian

Coinage is primarily interesting to the historian because, to put it simply, it is part of the evidence. He may learn from it facts about the past that are otherwise unknown, and he will often find that it supplements or corrects his other sources of information. Coins are, of course, archaeological objects, and so cannot be expected to explain themselves in the way that written evidence often does. They have to be interpreted, and the possibility of error is thus in some respects greater than is the case with evidence which can, so to speak, meet the scholar half-way. But coinage has several great advantages. Coins are primary sources and contemporary in character: they do not supply us with information about events at several removes, and often long after their occurrence. They are also official, and thus likely to provide better and more authoritative information than evidence from private sources usually can. Their testimony is not necessarily unbiased and its reliability has to be critically assessed, but at least it will not have been produced with the object of affecting the judgement of posterity. Further, since minting is one of the oldest forms of mass production, its object being to produce thousands of objects as nearly identical as possible, coins provide large-scale evidence about the past which under favourable circumstances can be subjected to statistical analysis. This evidence is moreover of an economic character, whereas the written sources of many historical periods are conspicuously uninterested in such an unheroic aspect of human activity.

This does not mean that the evidence of coins is necessarily true. The purpose of their inscriptions and types is sometimes one of propaganda, not simply a means of identification, and the historian has to ask himself at what level of government they were devised and what message they were intended to convey. They can mislead as a result of the phenomenon known as immobilization, when the name or effigy of a ruler may be retained on the coins for years or even centuries after his death. Their evidence is very uneven: at some periods they can tell us a great deal, while at others the same types or inscriptions are repeated with a minimum of change from year to year, and such deductions as can be drawn from this fact are usually of very limited usefulness. Coins should be most valuable in periods when other evidence, and in particular archival evidence, is in short supply, but it is precisely under such conditions that their testimony is most difficult to interpret. This is particularly true of their economic significance. Since it is usually taken for granted that coins are primarily manufactured with economic purposes in view they should be an important source of monetary history, but their usefulness in this respect, in our present state of numismatic understanding, is severely limited. Many accepted lines of numismatic reasoning were first developed

in the field of ancient coinage, where the correctness of their conclusions could not be easily checked. In the context of the later
Middle Ages and early modern times, when commercial and minting activities are reasonably well documented, these approaches
do not always seem to work. If finds of foreign coins are taken as
evidence of the existence of commercial relations between two
countries, why is the reverse not the case, for there is virtually no
numismatic evidence for such well-documented phenomena as
the English wool trade with Italy in the thirteenth and fourteenth
centuries and the wine trade with Gascony from the fourteenth
century onwards? Where written evidence is available as well, the
study of numismatics can often be of great value to the economic
historian, but where there are coins alone, the range of possible
interpretations is too great for them to be a guide on which he can
very confidently rely. Perhaps, indeed, this is only to be expected,
for coins are made by governments and not by merchants, a fact
which numismatists and economic historians are almost equally
prone to forget.

Coins are primary evidence in all periods of history, but as we
approach modern times this role becomes less and less important,
since they can tell us little or nothing that we do not know far
better from other sources. This does not mean that the study of
modern coinage is useless. Human attitudes towards coinage have
changed surprisingly little over the centuries, and the observation
and study of numismatic phenomena in a modern context, where
written evidence and the comments of contemporaries are available, can sometimes suggest explanations for similar phenomena
in the past. Charlemagne's difficulties over persuading his subjects
east of the Rhine to accept the use of coin have many parallels in
modern colonial experience. Further, even though the evidential
value of coins may decline, their illustrative value persists, though
this is something that varies greatly from one period to another.
French gold coinage of the fourteenth century brings vividly
before us the glories of Gothic art and the pride and luxury of the
French royal court; Roman and Renaissance coin portraits are
splendid artistic achievements which at the same time tell us much
about the Roman idea of Empire and the Renaissance concept of
virtù; the heraldic intricacies of German coin types in the seventeenth and eighteenth centuries are convincing testimony to both
the complex structure of the Empire and the family pride of
German princelings in an age before French armies simplified the
political geography of Europe. But it frequently happens that the
art of coinage is strangely divorced from that of its time. The

artistic pre-eminence of Athens in the fifth century B.C. and of
Florence in the fifteenth century A.D. could not be deduced from
the coins of the two cities, for commercial considerations and
republican sentiment combined in both cases to maintain their
coin designs at a traditional and indeed somewhat archaic level.
It is hard to believe that Suger and the rebuilding of Saint-Denis
were contemporary with the unimaginative plainness of French
royal deniers of the mid-twelfth century, or the glories of the
Kariye Camii with the shoddy coinage of fourteenth-century
Byzantium. But if a low level of numismatic achievement does not
necessarily imply a low level in other branches of art, a high level
cannot be achieved without excellence elsewhere. Coins in the
most favourable circumstances are beautiful objects, worth looking at because they are admirable products of their times.

They are also something more. It has been said that a sense of
the past is always made up of small things vividly perceived. Over
and above the evidential and illustrative value of coins, their
evocative quality should not be forgotten. 'Time, which antiquates
Antiquities, and hath an art to make dust of all things, hath yet
spared these *minor* Monuments.' Sir Thomas Browne was not
thinking of coins when he wrote these moving words, but they
aptly express the feelings of many numismatists when handling
their material. The story of individual coins, the names of those
who have owned them in the past and the objects they have been
used to purchase, are inevitably lost to us, though Addison's 'Life
and Adventures of a Shilling' (in No. 249 of the *Tatler*, 11 Nov.
1710), is skilfully evocative on this topic. The professional
historian, turning over crinkled parchments or yellowing pages
and seeing the very ink in which words were written, has often the
feeling that he is making personal contact with their authors; it is
something very different from seeing the words reproduced on the
printed page. A numismatist obtains the same feeling and the same
pleasure, less individualized but no less real, from touching and
handling coins.

The Origins of Money and Coinage

There can be few who have not at some time asked themselves how
coinage and money originated, and it is worth while suggesting
an answer to this question.

There are two separate problems involved, for although coins
and money are frequently confused in ordinary speech, in studying
their origin and evolution they have to be kept distinct. Coins are

objects used to give concrete expression to monetary values, but they share the field with cattle, rings, cowries, and other forms of 'primitive' money on the one hand and with paper money, bills of exchange, and so forth on the other. Since coinage is a practical device that has been invented at specific times and places and transmitted by imitation from one society to another, its study can be carried out by methods to which the historian is accustomed. Money has on the other hand existed from time immemorial in virtually all societies, and the hints provided by early language, literature, and law can only be interpreted with the aid of a knowledge of its working in modern 'primitive' societies. The study of its origins has therefore to be pursued by the anthropologist rather than by the historian. Only when the anthropologist and philologist have done their work can the historian take over, studying the spread of money and of coinage and seeing how far the latter has proved acceptable—often it has not, for coinage is far from being the universally convenient device that economists believe it to have been—and how it has been adapted to the 'monetary' systems which each society had already devised for itself.

The concept of 'money', of using some particular commodity (or commodities) as a standard for measuring values, and incidentally as a store of wealth and a means of exchange, seems to have originated independently in most communities, though in the choice of commodities there has subsequently been much borrowing by one from another. The account of its origins given in most textbooks of economics goes back to Aristotle's *Politics* (I, 1256b–1258a). Money, in Aristotle's opinion, originated through the requirements of exchange. First there was barter, such as still existed in his day amongst barbarous communities on the edge of the Greek world. Then, to facilitate exchange, men agreed on some commodity in general use, as for example iron or silver, and treated it as a standard. Later still, to avoid the trouble of having to weigh or otherwise measure them on every occasion, pieces of metal were made of uniform weight and marked in some fashion so that they could easily be recognized. 'Money' was in this way embodied in 'coin'. Elsewhere, in a difficult passage in the *Nicomachean Ethics* (V, 1133a–b) whose meaning has been much discussed, Aristotle gives money a more abstruse origin as being connected with the search for reciprocal justice: it is the common mean between objects and services which cannot otherwise be satisfactorily evaluated against each other.

That a purely economic explanation of the origins of money is correct may well be doubted. In societies based on the extended family the need for exchange is much reduced: the family will be able to satisfy a high proportion of its needs within itself. Barter involves highly fluctuating values. Many commodities will vary in their relative desirability according to the season: at one moment they will be common and 'worth' little, at another they will be rare and 'worth' a great deal. Ability to 'pay' will also be very unequal: one person can afford to give more than another for the same commodity. Quality will affect transactions, and introduce a variable that is hard to allow for. In any case, barter accounts for only a small part of the transfer of commodities and services from one person to another in primitive society. Many payments are of a customary character, determined by political, religious, or social considerations, and have no precise idea of 'value' attached to them at all. The phenomenon known as gift-exchange is wide-spread, and its ethos is independent of, and almost antagonistic to, the notion of money. The reputation of a man depends on his giving more than he receives, partly because in that way he creates obligations on which he can draw in time of need, partly because generosity is in itself a satisfying sensation and reflects credit on the person displaying it. All in all, the relationships between goods, services, and needs in a pre-market economy must be adjudged too fluid and uncertain to have provided the elements of stability and predictability which are implicit in the idea of standards.

The practice of legal compensations, which in Anglo-Saxon times were known as wergelds, is in fact more likely to have brought about the concept of value, and of scales for measuring them, than purely economic considerations. The English word 'worth' is cognate with 'wergeld': if wergeld is the *geld* paid in compensation for the life of a man (*wer*), so is 'worth' (Gothic *wairþ*, from *wair* 'man') the abstract notion of the 'value' of a man, just as in Latin *virtus* is 'manliness', though in a metaphorical rather than a literal sense. Many codes of primitive law show how the initial wergeld paid for death was extended downwards to cover lesser injuries to a man's person or property and upwards where the victim was of a higher social status or there were aggravating circumstances present. Such a scale of values, once arrived at, would be easily transferred to services and goods by way of brideprice and by the buying and selling of slaves, both of which involve living beings and the compensation of the family for loss of service. It is no accident that in Ulfilas' translation of the Bible, our only surviving monument of the Gothic tongue, *wairþ* is only used in relation to the value of a slave, although in a metaphorical sense (I Corinthians 7:23), or that the thirty pieces of silver, the price of blood

(Matthew 27:6, 9), is a 'counter-worth' (*andawairþ*). Wergeld and money are institutions which in their origins are closely bound up with each other.

The objects used for primitive money are so varied in character that it is doubtful if their evolution can be comprehended under any single formula. But a few generalizations may be risked. Measurement, and particularly measurement of value, is a more sophisticated operation than mere counting, and it is likely that the earliest objects used to express value in most societies were natural products which could be counted and whose ownership conferred prestige as well as being useful. Cattle are consequently the most widespread of all forms of primitive money, and slaves have played the same role in many societies. It was an easy transition from these 'natural' units to what one may term 'made up' ones, such as axes, knives, cauldrons, gongs, and rings. The notion of 'utility', of the 'commodity' element in many types of primitive money, should not be stressed. More emphasis was always placed on the number of the cattle than on their quality, and the sole usefulness of many forms of primitive money—cowrie shells, the stone money of Yap—arose from the fact that other people desired them, though some it is true, like gold rings and bead necklaces, could be worn on the person and the prestige attached to ownership made doubly pleasurable in this fashion. A later stage was formed by objects that could be measured by length or area (strings of wampum, lengths of cloth), or by volume (grain, honey), or by weight (metal). These bridged the gap between objects of high value, used initially for compensations, and those intended for medium or low values once the transition from compensations to commerce had been made, though there was always a kind of no man's land where customary payments were involved and it is often far from clear whether the objects employed were invested with a monetary aura or not. Often, at the lowest level, we find the widespread use of 'natural' countable objects, with cowries the most widely used but fish, skins, or animal teeth as other possibilities, and then 'made-up' countable objects, of which the best-known is coin. The notion of making up units of metal to pieces of uniform weight, however, is one that occurred in only a few societies—in Asia Minor, in India, in China—and it is from these that coinage spread to become the generalized system that we know today.

2
Coinage: The Western Tradition

The Western tradition of coinage is a highly complex one. One is inclined to regard its early stages as partly Greek and partly Persian, but the coinage of the Persian Empire was in fact Lydian in derivation and confined to Asia Minor. In the late Hellenistic period Western coinage began to develop along divergent lines, one evolving as that of the Mediterranean world, where it fused with the partially independent traditions of Rome, and the other, by way of the Parthian and Sassanian coinages, providing the main element in Muslim coinage. In Christendom the monetary traditions of Byzantium and western Europe themselves parted company, that of Byzantium influencing the coinage of the Muslim world and that of medieval Europe undergoing repeated transformations until in the sixteenth century it evolved into the 'modern' system. In the age of colonization this was carried throughout the world and, in a somewhat degenerate form, with paper replacing gold and 'silver' reduced to a token status, it is that familiar to us today. The detailed history of these developments is so complex that no more than an outline of them can be given here.

Greek and Related Coinages

The area in which Western coinage originated is more certain than the date or circumstances. The earliest coins were struck in western Asia Minor, and are small globular pieces of electrum impressed with a design on only one face, the other bearing the mark of a punch. Electrum is a natural alloy of gold and silver found in the Pactolus and other rivers of the region, and was at first thought to be a separate metal. Large numbers of electrum coins, varying in weight from 4·73 g. to 0·13 g. and taken by scholars to represent fractions from a third to a ninety-sixth of a unit (stater) of about 14·2 g., were found in 1904/5, mixed with a few pieces not bearing any design, in the base deposit in the temple of Artemis at Ephesus. These are regarded by numismatists as the earliest type of coins known. In due course such coins came to be supplemented by ones of pure gold and of pure silver, whose introduction was attributed by Greek tradition to the Lydian king Croesus (561–546 B.C.). Greek tradition also related that when King Pheidon of Argos came to introduce silver coins, he consecrated a number of iron spits, the form of primitive money which they replaced, in the temple of Hera. Several bundles of such spits came to light during the excavation of the site in the 1890s. It was indeed the spit currency that provided two of the basic terms of later Greek money, drachma and obol, for drachma meant basically a 'handful' (δραχμή, from a word meaning 'to grasp') of spits (ὀβελίσκοι).

It has sometimes been supposed that the first coins were struck by merchants— this is suggested by the diversity of their designs, and by the fact that one very early type, of which three specimens are known, has the device of a deer accompanied by the phrase ΦΑΕΝΟΣ ΕΜΙ ΣΗΜΑ, 'I am the mark of Phanes'—but that the monopoly of issue was quickly assumed by the state. This is by no means clear; they may well have been started by local dynasts or officials, who would have found them obviously convenient for paying mercenaries or workmen, since they would be the easiest way of making up a pay packet and stamping it with the mark of its originator and its value. The date has been much discussed. Nineteenth-century scholars usually attributed the invention of coinage to the late eighth or early seventh century B.C., a date as early as this being necessary if Pheidon's traditional role was to be accepted, since it was probably in the second quarter of the seventh century that he ruled. A careful study of the coins from Ephesus, however, has induced recent scholars to advance the date to the third quarter of the seventh century B.C., and to regard Pheidon's role as an invention of patriotic local historians. Although most classical numismatists are now satisfied that the revised date is correct, with the origins of coinage to be placed soon after 650 B.C., the archaeological and stylistic considerations involved have not always convinced classical historians. The professional reluctance of the latter to discard the written evidence in favour of Pheidon cannot, however, be reconciled with the now accepted dating of the earliest Aeginetan coinage as not earlier than c. 550 and perhaps as late as 530 B.C.

From Asia Minor the use of coin spread mainly westwards. In Asia Minor itself the Persian satraps struck coins of Lydian

(a)   (b)

FIG. 1. Early coins of Asia Minor. (a) Stater of Phocaea, early 6th cent. B.C. El. 16·08g. The mint is identified by the punning device of a seal (φώκη) and the letter φ (imperfectly formed) beneath it. The two punch marks of the reverse appear in slightly altered positions in relation to each other on different specimens, thus showing that the punches were not themselves fixed together. (b) Daric of the time of Xerxes, 485–465 B.C. A/ 8·37 g. Dating depends on style and hoard evidence, since the coin is without specific attributions.

inspiration, their gold darics and silver shekels showing the King of Kings in the guise of a running archer, sometimes armed with spear as well as bow, but most of the Achaemenid Empire remained content with older forms of money and credit. In the west, coinage was taken up by the Greek city communities of the Aegean, of the Greek mainland, and ultimately of southern Italy (Magna Graecia), Sicily, and elsewhere in the western Mediterranean (e.g. Marseilles). Its spread can be dated only very approximately, with the help of independent evidence. Coinage must have reached South Italy well before 510 B.C., since there are coins of Sybaris, which we know to have been destroyed by Croton in that year, and must have reached Marseilles by c. 450, since some of its earliest coins were mixed with datable ones of Phocaea in a great hoard found at Auriol (Provence) in 1867. It was only very slowly that coinage was adopted by non-Greek peoples. The Carthaginians struck their first coins in Sicily in the late fifth century, but for the payment of mercenaries and not for trade, while Tyre, Sidon, and other Phoenician cities did not begin much earlier. Egypt, apart from some early fourth-century imitations of Athenian tetradrachms and an issue of gold pieces stamped with the hieroglyphs *nefer nub* ('fine gold') which were used for paying Greek mercenaries, did not adopt coinage till after the time of Alexander the Great, and Rome, despite its contacts with the Greek world, remained firmly wedded to primitive bronze lumps until the end of the fourth century B.C.

The earliest coins have an impression on only one face, the

device being that engraved on the surface of the lower die, while the other side is marked by one or more of the punch heads which were used to force the metal downwards against this. It was a natural transition, however, to furnishing the upper punch die with a design, and in this way the biface coins to which we are accustomed took shape. Most coinage struck before the mid-sixth century B.C. remained uniface, and the practice was retained for the electrum coinage preferred by Phocaea, Cyzicus, and some other cities of western Asia Minor down to the late fourth century. The evolution of biface coins was not as clear-cut as we are apt to think it, since two convex designs on a coin is not an obviously natural arrangement. Some cities (e.g. Athens, Gela) experimented with an intaglio design sunk in the traditional square of the upper

FIG. 2. Didrachm of Sybaris (S. Italy), *c.* 520 B.C. Æ 8·42 g. The mint is indicated by the ΣV(βαρις) above the bull. The reverse consists of the same type, incuse.

die, and a group of south Italian cities, notably Sybaris, Metapontum, Caulonia, and Poseidonia, tried using an upper die with the design in relief, corresponding to the same design incuse on the lower die, so that the resulting coin would have a design in relief on one face and incuse on the other. This device is on the surface more logical than that of two convex types, and it had the incidental advantage of better defacing the impressions of an earlier type if old coins were used as blanks. But it required great accuracy in the alignment of the upper and lower dies, and it was probably for technical reasons that it was abandoned by the few cities that had experimented with it.

Greek coins of the classical period, before *c.* 350 B.C., were predominantly of silver, a metal which was found in reasonably large quantities in the Hellenic world. The mines of Laureion, which supplied the needs of Athens in the three centuries following the Persian wars, are the most famous, but others, notably in Thrace and Macedon, were of comparable importance. Electrum coins were limited to a few localities in Asia Minor, and not till the time of Philip of Macedon was gold found in sufficient quantity for regular minting. Persian gold darics were fairly widely used in Greece itself, but the only Athenian gold issue of the period was prompted by the economic crisis near the end of the Peloponnesian War, when in 407 B.C. the gold that adorned the statues in the Parthenon was melted down for the purpose. Bronze was first used for coinage in the late fifth century in Sicily and Magna Graecia, where the metal in an unminted state was already the standard currency of the native population.

Greek silver coins are in general large and thick, only roughly circular, and have rounded edges, retaining very largely the appearance of the blobs of metal from which they were made. The general weight level was unusually high by later standards; the Athenian tetradrachm, a common denomination, weighed just over 17 g. The coins are extraordinarily diverse in design, with a head or symbol of a deity usually occupying the obverse and a local symbol, often religious in character, the reverse. Only a few cities attempted designs of any complexity, but racing chariots are

      (a)   (b)   (c)

FIG. 3. Silver coins of Selinunte, Gela, and Corinth. (a) Didrachm of Selinunte (Sicily), late 5th cent. B.C. 7.45 g. The type, a wild celery (σέλινον), which gave its name to the river on which the city was founded and was adopted as the city badge, identifies the mint. (b) Didrachm of Gela (Sicily), early 5th cent. B.C. 8.81 g. The mint is named on the reverse (ϹΕΛΑΣ), the type being the forepart of a swimming man-headed bull, the local river-god Gelas. (c) Stater of Corinth, late 4th cent. B.C. 8.71 g. The mint is indicated by the letter Q, i.e. *koppa*, the original initial of Corinth (Κόρινθος) which disappeared in classical Greek but was borrowed by the Romans as the letter Q. The privy mark by Athena's head is a chimera.

typical of the coins of Syracuse; the mining districts of Macedon favoured crude representations of oxen or of maidens carried off by satyrs; and some cities in Crete had a taste for mythological scenes. Designs were in high relief and in general of great beauty; we know the names of a few die-sinkers (Cimon, Euainetos) who were proud enough of their work to sign it, usually in minute letters carefully integrated with the design, at the truncation of the neck or on the headband of a goddess. The variety in design was largely a consequence of coinage being regarded as a symbol of sovereignty and independence, so that every city was anxious to possess its own; there are even a few localities, so unimportant that they entirely escape mention in our literary sources, which are known solely by their coins. Much of the coinage circulated only locally, but some types had an international reputation: the 'turtles' of Aegina, the 'owls' of Athens, with the head and symbol of Athena (see p. 85, Fig. 47a), the 'colts' of Corinth, with a Pegasus as their obverse type. The coinages of these important commercial centres remained extremely conservative and old-fashioned in their designs, much inferior artistically to the issues of many of the smaller states.

The conquests of Alexander the Great (336–323 B.C.) resulted in an immense extension of the area in which coined money was used, and changed its character in a number of respects. The hoarded treasures of the Achaemenids and the Pharaohs were now available for minting, and mines could be exploited over a much wider area. Coinage was now introduced on a large scale into Egypt and throughout the former Persian Empire as far as Bactria

FIG. 4. Tetradrachm of King Lysimachus of Thrace, 323–281 B.C., with head of the deified Alexander. Æ 16·98 g. The curly hair, ram's horn (symbol of Alexander's identification with Zeus Ammon), and upward gaze are typical of the posthumous Alexander portraits. The reverse gives the king's name ΒΑΣΙΛΕΩΣ ΛΥΣΙΜΑΧΟΥ ('of King Lysimachus'; see p. 77) and shows a seated Athena holding a Victory, with an eagle as privy mark.

and India. The typical tetradrachm of the Hellenistic period is a broader and thinner coin than the old tetradrachm of Athens had been, and the coinage of the monarchies is marked by the widespread use of personal portraiture. This had been unknown in classical Greece, though fine portrait coins had been struck by some Persian satraps in Asia Minor. Even Alexander had used on

FIG. 5. Tetradrachm of Antiochus I Soter, 280–261 B.C. Æ 17·02 g. The reverse reads ΒΑΣΙΛΕΩΣ ΑΝΤΙΟΧΟΥ ('of King Antiochus') and shows Apollo seated on the omphalos, the sacred conical stone at Delphi which was believed to mark the hub of the world.

his coins only the heads of Athena or Heracles. But Lysimachus (323–281 B.C.) placed on his coins the head of the deified Alexander, and thenceforward portraits of living rulers became common, so that we have splendid series of the Antigonids in Macedonia, the Seleucids in Syria, and some of the Ptolemies in Egypt, to say nothing of important individual personages like Philetaerus, the founder of the kingdom of Pergamum, and Mithridates VI of Pontus, the great but ill-fated enemy of Rome. It was in distant

FIG. 6. Tetradrachm of Demetrius I, king of Bactria, c. 200–185 B.C. Æ 16·78 g. The king wears an elephant's skin head-dress symbolizing his Indian conquests. The reverse shows Heracles, with club and lion's skin, in the act of crowning himself, thus marking the completion of his Labours.

Bactria (Afghanistan) that portraiture reached its height. The heads of Demetrius I, Euthydemus II, Antimachus, Eucratides, Menander, Amyntas, and other rulers, of some of whom we have no literary record at all, are regarded by many as forming the finest sustained artistic achievement in the whole history of coinage.

It was also during the Hellenistic period that coinage began to be widely accepted in the west Mediterranean area and in the Celtic world. Its use spread throughout Spain, the models being usually those of the Greek cities of the coast, and very widely among the Celts of the Danubian area and of Gaul, and even into

(a)   (b)

FIG. 7. Tetradrachm of Philip II of Macedon (359–336 B.C.) and Celtic imitation. (a) Original. Æ 14·46 g. (b) Celtic imitation from the Danubian area. Æ 12·88 g.

remote Britain. The models here were largely coins of Philip of Macedon, but the derivatives were often cast instead of being struck and the designs wonderfully deformed into surrealist patterns, with fantastic horses or wheels and horses' limbs detaching themselves as separate elements in the designs and Apollo's curls becoming an enormous cloud of hair sometimes attached to a tiny face, sometimes to none at all. The coins are often of poor quality metal, with electrum, silver, or even copper alloys replacing the gold of the original types. The use of bronze became everywhere more general in the Hellenistic period than it had been earlier. In Egypt the larger denominations were so thick and heavy that unlike earlier classical coins they could only be struck in low relief, and their flans were cast and then scraped clean of debris by a rotating tool whose positioning accounts for the small central depression often visible on each face.

Roman Coinage

It was in this Hellenistic world that Roman coinage came into existence. Copper is found in many parts of Italy, and the Romans were only one of many peoples of the peninsula to use bronze by weight as their standard of value. The practice is recalled by many words still in daily use. Such terms as pound, stipend, expense have as a common element *pendere*, to hang, 'suspend' (i.e. in a balance); the equivalents of 'pound' in the Romance languages (livre, lira, etc.) come from *libra*, implying to hang 'freely'; and 'estimate' comes from the combination of the Latin work for bronze (*aes*) with a Greek word τιμή implying worth. The earliest Roman 'coins' were huge pieces of bronze up to a pound in weight, cast instead of struck because of their size. They were marked with only relatively simple devices (heads of deities, a sea shell, a wheel, a Pegasus, a dog, etc.), but the practical Romans, unlike the Greeks, added marks of value, with upright strokes indicating units in pounds and globules those in ounces. Since these cast pieces of bronze (*aes grave*), replacing irregularly sized bronze lumps (*aes rude*), do not antedate 280 B.C., their creation was no doubt suggested by Greek coinage, but in metal and fabric they are so different that they are best regarded as representing an independent coinage tradition in their own right. Their history is a strange one of 'debasement', this being carried out by the simple process of repeatedly and drastically reducing their weight, till eventually, by the Lex Papiria of 91 B.C., they reached the semi-uncial level, at which a bronze coin weighing only half an ounce had the nominal value once attached to a full pound of metal. By that time the as, the unit, had the familiar design of a Janus head on the obverse and a ship's prow on the reverse. The late coins were struck, being no longer of such a size as to require casting.

The growing political importance of Rome made it difficult in the third century B.C. to manage satisfactorily with a clumsy monometallic coinage of bronze. Silver coins on the Greek model began to be struck, initially in the central and south Italian dependencies of the Republic: first what are commonly termed Romano-Campanian didrachms and then coins known from the chariot on their reverse as quadrigati; finally, shortly before 211 B.C., denarii having a value of 10 asses and victoriati having as reverse type a Victory crowning a trophy. The denarius was a

FIG. 8a. Roman Republican bronze. Libral as, *c.* 225 B.C. 251·4 g.

FIG. 8b. Roman Republican bronze. Sextantal as, *c.* 200 B.C. 26·3 g. A comparison with the preceding coin illustrates the rapid depreciation of the bronze in the course of some twenty-five years, during the Second Punic War (218–201 B.C.) and the First Macedonian War (215–205 B.C.). The obverses show a head of Janus, and the reverses a ship's prow, with mark of value above.

silver coin weighing *c.* 4 g., having on the obverse the head of Roma and on the reverse the Dioscuri, the Heavenly Twins, who had come to Rome's rescue at the battle of Lake Regillus. Like the bronze coins it bore a mark of value (X). Issued partly by the College of Moneyers (*tresviri monetales*) and partly by generals in the field, it set the pattern for Rome's coinage in the future. Being less traditional than the bronze its features could be altered, at first discreetly by the insertion of moneyers' initials or other privy marks and later more drastically, the head of Roma being replaced by that of another deity or person of note, the Dioscuri by some other device: military scenes, triumphal processions, public buildings, sacrificial implements, symbolic representations of all kinds. The magistrates who determined the designs used them to vaunt the persons and deeds of their ancestors, so that the sequence of Republican denarii, which can be fairly closely dated, becomes

FIG. 9. Early Roman silver. (a) 'Romano-Campanian' didrachm, 269 B.C. 6·90 g. The obverse shows a head of Hercules with a club beneath, the reverse a wolf and twins with the inscription ROMAN(orum?). The dating depends on a combination of literary and hoard evidence. (b) Early denarius, *c.* 211 B.C. 4·51 g.

Fig. 10. Late Republican denarius, *c.* 104 B.C. Æ 4·10 g. Struck by Q(uintus) (Minucius) THERM(us) M(arci) F(ilius). The reverse type, a Roman soldier protecting a fallen comrade from attack by a barbarian, presumably represents some well-known incident in the moneyer's family history. The obverse type is a helmeted head of Mars.

a kind of running commentary on the whole early history, both true and legendary, of the city. Denarii are artistically inferior to the coins of classical Greece, since the die-sinkers often tried to crowd too many details on the restricted surface of the coins, but with their hundreds of different, carefully designed types they are much more interesting than Roman bronze. Gold, as in the classical Greek world, was only rarely struck, for the most part in emergencies.

(a)   (b)

Fig. 11. Two denarii of Brutus. (a) Æ 4·08 g. Type struck *c.* 55 B.C. showing the head of Libertas, duly labelled, and on the reverse L. Junius Brutus, an ancestor of the moneyer, walking as consul between two lictors with rods, with a smaller attendant in front. (b) Æ 3·80 g. Type struck (in Greece?) in 43 B.C. by L. Plaetorius Cestianus on behalf of Brutus (BRVT IMP), having on the obverse the head of Brutus and on the reverse two daggers and a cap of liberty, with the inscription EID(ibus) MAR(tiis), a reference to the murder of Caesar. Both coins allude to Brutus' role as a champion of liberty, but it is done much more overtly on the second of the two.

Imperial Roman coinage was essentially a continuation of that of the Republic, but with the 'Roman' and 'Greek' elements integrated into a single system. Coinage was also now exploited on behalf of the emperor instead of by relatively unimportant magistrates, and the propagandist features of the denarius were transferred to coins of other metals. There was now an abundant coinage of gold and a double series of subsidiary coins, the sestertius and dupondius being of brass (*orichalcum*) and the as and its

FIG. 12. Sestertius of Nero, A.D. 54–68. Æ 25·02 g. This type, issued in A.D. 64 and showing the temple of Janus with closed doors, celebrates the peace 'by sea and land' concluded with Parthia late in A.D. 63.

half (semis) or quarter (quadrans) being of copper. The subsidiary coins were marked with the letters SC, indicating that their token character had been authorized by the Senate (*Senatus Consulto*), but in their themes they cannot be differentiated from the coinage of gold and silver. The portraiture of living persons, first allowed to Julius Caesar on the very eve of his assassination, was fully exploited thenceforward, the series of imperial portraits that resulted, realistic and sometimes ruthlessly unflattering, being of the highest quality. Obverse inscriptions vary greatly in content: thus Hadrian may prefer a succinct IMPCAESARTRAIAN-HADRIANVSAVG or HADRIANVSAVGCOSIIIPP, while Trajan sets out his achievements at length, as on a dupondius of A.D. 102 reading IMPCAESNERVATRAIANAVGGERDACPMTRPVII, i.e. *Imperator Caesar Nerva Traianus Augustus Germanicus Dacicus Pontifex Maximus Tribunicia Potestate VII*, the German and Dacian titles celebrating the emperor's victories in these two countries and the reference to the seventh repetition of the Tribunician power giving the date.

The reverses of Imperial Roman coins are extremely varied in type, often with inscriptions and allegorical persons or concepts announcing the inspiration or objects of imperial policy (*Pietas, Concordia, Pax*) or depicting its tangible results: the harbour of Ostia, the conclusion of peace with Parthia in A.D. 63, the Colosseum, Trajan's Forum and his bridge over the Danube, the vicissitudes of the imperial post, temporary remissions of taxes, the travels of Hadrian, the victories of Titus or Trajan. These designs are particularly effective because of the large size of the coins, the sestertius of the first and second centures A.D. having a diameter of 1·5 in. and weighing as much as 25 g. The silver denarii, as in Republican times and unlike the silver coins of classical Greece, remained typically small, but they were struck in enormous numbers and their economic role can scarcely have been inferior to that of the gold and the *aes*. In the eastern provinces of the Empire the local coinage, called by numismatists 'Greek

FIG. 13. Greek Imperial coin of Smyrna. Caracalla, A.D. 198–217. Æ 23·50 g. The reverse type shows three temples, with the goddess Roma seated in the central one. The inscription gives the honorary titles of Smyrna, ΠΡΩΤΩΝ (i.e. 'First', with 'city of Asia' understood) and .Γ.ΝΕΩΚΟΡΩΝ, i.e. 'Thrice Temple-Founder', with ΤΩΝ ϹΕΒΑϹΤΩΝ ('of the Emperors') above. Νεωκόρος was a title much coveted by Eastern cities.

Imperial' because issued by Greek cities under Roman tutelage, was still flourishing, the bulk of it being in bronze. Although most of it is artistically of poor quality, its use for advertising local interests and cults—of 'Diana of the Ephesians', of Aphrodite at Cnidus, of the god Sandan-Heracles at Tarsus, of the Severan temples at Smyrna, of Isis or Sarapis at Alexandria—makes it a historical source of great importance.

The Roman imperial system collapsed, through inflation of the silver coinage, in the third century A.D. Caracalla (A.D. 211–17) created a double denarius, apparently called the antoninianus, and its debasement in the second half of the century drove first the denarius and subsequently all denominations of brass and copper out of circulation. A new system was created by Diocletian and Constantine, different in appearance, denominations, and minting arrangements from the old. The whole of the new coinage was imperial, the 'senatorial' and local elements being eliminated, but since the coins were struck at a number of mints throughout the Empire, they had to be furnished with an elaborate series of mint and privy marks to ensure coherence and control. Portraiture and variety of design went out of fashion; the imperial effigies became purely conventional and eventually were shown facing instead of

(a)   (b)

FIG. 14. Solidi of Constantius II, A.D. 323–61. (a) Mint of Antioch, A.D. 348–50. *N* 4.46 g. The SM before the mint-mark AN stands for *Sacra Moneta*, and the Γ that follows it marks the third officina. (b) Mint of Constantinople, A.D. 353/4. *N* 4·44 g. The dates of the coins are indicated by the *Vota* legends held by the seated figures of Roma and Constantinopolis. The latter is distinguished by her mural crown and her foot on the prow of a ship, since the city was founded to celebrate Constantine's naval victory over Licinius at Chrysopolis in 324. Neither the profile nor the three-quarter facing imperial bust can be regarded as a portrait.

in profile, making a true likeness almost impossible to achieve. Gold and silver coins remained, but were lighter than before, while the 'bronze' coinage was in fact alloyed with small amounts of silver and its units were in consequence much lighter than their counterparts of the early Empire. The coins, however, were still classical in their general features, and were recognizably 'ancient', not medieval or modern in appearance.

Byzantine and Medieval Coinage

The reformed coinage of the fourth century lasted barely a hundred years. In the early fifth century it was transformed, in some measure as a result of the Germanic invasions. The middle elements in its pattern of values, the silver coinage and the larger multiples of bronze, ceased to be struck, leaving only three denominations of gold coinage, the solidus of 4·5 g. and its half (semissis) and third (tremissis), and the lowest denomination of bronze, a tiny, illstruck nummus half the size of one's little fingernail and weighing less than a gram. Thereafter the coinages of the eastern and mainly Greek-speaking provinces, which survived as the Byzantine Empire, and of the western and mainly Latin-speaking ones, which were conquered by various Germanic peoples, developed along quite different lines. In the East a coinage of heavy pieces of copper, the follis (of 40 nummi) and its fractions, was reintroduced (A.D. 498), and a silver coinage was added later, so that Byzantine coinage retained a link with antiquity in using the three traditional monetary metals and possessed a full hierarchy of coin values, as was desirable in a

FIG. 15. Follis of the Byzantine Emperor Romanus I, 921–44. Æ 5·39 g. Both obverse and reverse inscriptions give him the title of 'Emperor of the Romans'. Byzantine coinage is sharply differentiated from that of Latin Christendom in including one or more denominations in copper.

flourishing economy. Its coin designs were largely novel, with elaborately hieratic imperial representations and much use of Christian symbols, first the cross and later images of Christ and the saints. Western coinage failed to revive in the same way. First the copper nummus and then the gold solidus disappeared, and in the sixth century the Germanic kingdoms of the West found themselves left with only a single denomination, the small gold tremissis. It was this coin that formed the link in the West between antiquity and the Middle Ages.

The history of medieval coinage falls into three periods whose limiting dates vary from one country to another. The first period, that of the gold shilling, corresponded roughly to the sixth and seventh centuries. The tremissis of late imperial times weighed, in Roman terms, 8 carats, the equivalent of 1·5 g. The shilling of the Germanic world, which was not a coin but a weight of gold, corresponded to 20 grains (barleycorns), the equivalent of which was 1·3 g. Once the Franks and their neighbours were firmly

(a)   (b)

FIG. 16. Visigothic tremisses. (a) Mid-6th cent. N 1·41 g. A pseudo-imperial type, with blundered inscriptions and grotesquely rendered types (imperial bust and Victory holding a wreath). (b) Leovigild, 568–86. Mint of Toledo. N 1·49 g. This 'national' coinage dates from the last five years of the reign. Visigothic coins henceforward regularly bear the name of a king and a mint, in contrast to Frankish coins, where royal control appears to have been non-existent and most coins have the names of moneyer and mint instead.

established in the Empire, it would be natural to reduce the weight of the tremissis and make it correspond to the shilling. This was eventually done over most of the West, the change usually coinciding with the introduction of 'national' coin types to replace the earlier Germanic issues which had been copied, with steadily declining fidelity, from Roman prototypes.

The second period of medieval monetary history was that of silver monometallism, replacing the gold monometallism of the preceding era and roughly dating from the beginning of the eighth to the end of the twelfth century. The sole coin in use, over most of the West, was the silver penny (Lat. *denarius*, Fr. *denier*, It. *denaro*), though halfpennies and farthings were occasionally added. Its multiples, the shilling (*solidus, sou, soldo*) of 12 pence and the pound (*libra, livre, lira*) of 20 shillings, were no more than monies of account, sums reckoned in them having to be paid with 12 or 240 actual pennies. The latter were initially small, ill-struck

(a)   (b)

Fig. 17. Reformed pennies of Charlemagne and Offa. (a) Denier of Charlemagne, 768–814, of the mint of Melle (METVLLO) in Poitou. Æ 1·64 g. The monogram is that of KAROLVS, as it appears on the king's charters. (b) Penny of Offa of Mercia, 759–96, struck at Canterbury by the moneyer Eoba. Æ 1·26 g. (19½ gr.). The ℳ above Offa's name stands for *Merciorum*, followed by *rex* beneath.

coins of the same weight as the earlier gold shilling, but were transformed in the late eighth century, under Charlemagne on the Continent and Offa in England, into broader, thinner, and somewhat heavier coins, the standard weights of which were 32 Paris grains, i.e. wheatgrains (= 1·7 g.), amongst the Franks and 24 grains, in this case barleycorns (= 1·6 g.), in England. The area over which silver or billon pennies were used—billon is a technical term for silver less than 500/1000 fine—came in the end to be virtually conterminous with the frontiers of Latin Christendom, although peripheral regions in the west and north remained faithful to various types of primitive money.

The pennies of the feudal age are of an almost infinite variety of types, since in many countries the right of minting was widely diffused by grant or usurpation, and even where this was not the

FIG. 18. Eleventh-century French and English pennies. (a) Robert II of France, 996–1031. Paris denier. Æ 1·29 g. The parts of the letters are very clearly made with a number of separate punches (see p. 103). (b) William the Conqueror, 1066–87. Penny of Class VIII (c. 1083–6). Æ 1·40 g. (21.6 gr.). Struck at Dorchester by the moneyer Oter. The PAXS in the circles on the reverse gives the type the name by which it is generally known.

case some rulers adopted the practice of frequent changes of type as a fiscal device (*renovationes monetae*). The designs are usually very crude—a ruler's head, a cross or other symbol—and over large areas there was a sharp decline in weight and fineness, especially in the twelfth century. Flemish mailles and Venetian denari of *c.* 1200 weigh 0·4 g. or less, and the fineness of the Venetian coins was about 250/1000, so that their silver content was only about a twelfth of that of contemporary English sterlings. In places where the weight of the penny declined without there being any corresponding reduction in diameter the coins became so thin that the designs on one side were blurred and largely defaced by those of the other. It was to remedy this that in some parts of Germany, and in adjacent countries, there were introduced the

FIG. 19. German bracteates of the 12th cent. (a) Frederick I Barbarossa, 1152–90, mint of Altenburg in Thuringia. Æ 0·95 g. Altenburg is known from documentary sources to have been an imperial mint, and this type of coin is common in Thuringian hoards. (b) Otto I of Brandenburg, 1170–84. Æ 0·95 g. An armoured figure is common on bracteates of secular princes in this part of Germany, but the coin is unusual in giving the name of the prince and the place where the coin was struck.

thin pennies, struck on one face only, which are known to numismatists as bracteates (from *bractea*, a leaf). Such coins, despite their low weights (*c.* 0·5 g.), were sometimes between one and two inches in diameter, and the elaborate coin types which this made possible are amongst the minor masterpieces of numismatic art.

The third period of medieval coinage, extending from the beginning of the thirteenth to the middle of the fifteenth century, may be characterized as that of the groat and the florin. The small, debased pennies of the late twelfth century, with their low purchasing power, became more and more inconvenient as trade and town life began to play an increasingly important role in society. In 1202 the Venetians, faced with the task of paying large numbers of extra workmen taken on at the Arsenal to construct the fleet for the Fourth Crusade, introduced a coin of good silver, weighing just over 2 g. and representing two soldi (24*d.*) in money of account. It was called a ducat, since it was struck for the dogeship or duchy (*ducatus*) of Venice, but as the use of similar multiples spread through Italy in the first half of the thirteenth century, they

(a)   (b)

FIG. 20. Denaro and grosso of Enrico Dandolo, doge of Venice, 1192–1205. (a) Denaro. Billon. 0·32 g. Concave, presumably to underline the fact of its being of very base metal, since this was the way by which debasement was then indicated in Byzantine coinage. (b) Grosso. Æ 2·15 g. The seated Christ and the two standing figures are Byzantine in appearance, but the banner which St. Mark hands to the doge is a purely Western symbol.

were more generally termed grossi (denari) i.e. 'large' pennies, which became gros in French, groat in English, and groschen in Germany. The French gros tournois was introduced in 1266, the English groat in 1351, after a false start in 1278. In most countries halves, thirds, or quarters were also struck, and as the new coins were in time debased or changed their type the coinage pattern became one of great complexity. Since the penny did not drop out of use, Latin Christendom came to have at its disposal a wide range of denominations, reverting thus in some measure to the monetary pattern of antiquity. By Greek standards, however, the

FIG. 21. Gros tournois of Louis IX of France, 1227–70. Ꞃ 4·18 g. The type is that of a denier tournois, with borders added, the twelve cusps in the reverse border indicating the value of 12*d*. (one sou). The term *tournois* derives from the inscription TVRONVS CIVIS, deniers of this type having been originally minted by the abbots of St. Martin's of Tours.

coins remained very light; the English groat of four pence, one of the heaviest, weighed no more than 4·7 g.

In another respect also there was a return to ancient conditions. During the period of the silver penny no gold coinage had been regularly struck in western Europe outside the areas reconquered from the Muslims or strongly influenced by them, i.e. Spain, Sicily and a few towns of South Italy, and the Holy Land. Small quantities of Byzantine and Muslim gold coins could be obtained through trade for special purposes, for example, for use as alms or in supplying bullion for jewellery and works of art, but gold played no regular role in commerce. This position changed in the thirteenth century. The Emperor Frederick II, for political rather than economic reasons, issued in 1231 a gold coin of classical design known as an augustale for his south Italian kingdom, and in 1252 both Florence and Genoa introduced gold coins, known

FIG. 22. Augustale and gold florin. (a) Augustale of the Emperor Frederick II, 1198–1250, issued from 1231 onwards in his south Italian mints of Brindisi and Messina. ꞏ 5·25 g. Classical in style, and struck in higher relief than was normal on medieval coins. (b) Gold florin of uncertain date, between 1252 and 1303, showing St. John the Baptist and the lily that formed the badge of the city. ꞏ 3·50 g. The date is indicated by the symbol above the saint's right hand, which was changed every six months and marked one of the magistrates responsible for the coinage during that time. The surviving mint register listing magistrates and symbols starts only in 1303, and since the horseshoe symbol on this specimen belongs to the preceding period the coin cannot be dated precisely.

as a fiorino d'oro (florin) and genovino d'oro respectively, each weighing 3·5 g. Their example was in due course widely followed: Venice ordered the striking of a gold ducat in 1284; France had an extensive gold coinage by 1300; Hungary, which had its own gold mines, introduced a florin of its own in 1325; the Low Countries began to strike gold in the 1330s; and the English noble (p. 85, Fig. 47b) dates from 1344. Once again, as was the case with the groat, the coins were struck in great variety, and in some countries were eventually drastically debased.

FIG. 23. Masse d'or of Philip IV of France, 1285–1315. Aʹ 7·06 g. First struck in 1296. This coin, which had a value of 25s. and took its name from the sceptre (*masse*, our 'mace') held by the king, is typical of the showy feudal coinage of the later Middle Ages. The reverse inscription, 'Christ conquers, Christ rules, Christ reigns', made part of the coronation acclamations and was used on French gold coins from the time of St. Louis to the Revolution.

Modern Coinage

The coinage of the *ancien régime* and the nineteenth century differed from that of the Middle Ages in a number of respects. The coins were much heavier; they belonged to a different artistic tradition; they involved a subsidiary coinage of copper; and they were machine-made and not hammer-struck. Nor were they the sole form of 'money' in use, for they were largely supplemented by bills or banknotes. The first three of these features were established in the course of the century 1450–1550. The fourth began in the mid-sixteenth century, and the fifth rather over a hundred years later.

The transition to a heavy silver coinage in western Europe was surprisingly anticipated by nearly a hundred years in the East. Grossi heavier than 4 g. were rarely struck in Latin Christendom, and although the Byzantine silver hexagram had weighed 6·8 g. it had existed only in the seventh century, while the miliaresion that succeeded it had rarely exceeded even 3 g. In the mid-fourteenth century, however, Byzantium had ceased to mint gold coins, presumably owing to a shortage of the precious metal. Their absence was a serious inconvenience, and the usurper Andronicus IV (1376–9) introduced a heavy silver coin, modelled in its appearance on the grossi of the West but much heavier (*c.* 8·8 g.), so that it was worth half the now disused gold coin. It was continued down to the reign of John VIII (1425–48), under whom it became slightly lighter in weight (*c.* 7 g.), and although there was a gap of some twenty-five years between its disappearance and the introduction of a heavy silver coin in Venice, it is possible that one may have suggested the other. Venice, as the delay in the creation of the gold ducat had shown, was sometimes slow to innovate where coinage was concerned.

The earliest heavy coins in the West were made possible through the exploitation of newly discovered mines at Schwaz in the Tyrol, which prompted several states first to strike silver coins representing the pound in local money of account, and, subsequently, still heavier ones corresponding in value to those of the gold coins of the day. The immediate impulse was a local shortage of gold, since Portuguese expeditions down the west coast of Africa were diverting to the Iberian peninsula the gold of Guinea that had previously reached Italy by way of the Sahara and North Africa. The first heavy coin was the lira tron, created by the doge Nicolò Tron at Venice in 1472 and weighing 6·5 g. Two years later Galeazzo Maria Sforza introduced a still heavier silver lira at Milan weighing 9·6 g. In 1484 the Archduke Sigismund of the Tyrol struck a silver coin worth a half gulden and in 1486 one equivalent to a full gulden and weighing an ounce (31·9 g.). Since the new coin was of silver, like the traditional groschen, it was known as a guldengroschen or guldiner, or sometimes from its weight as an unzialis. Similar coins were struck from 1500 onwards at various mints in Saxony, where large silver deposits were found in the 1490s at Neustadt (Annaberg), Schneeberg and Buchholz on the northern slopes of the Erzgebirge. In 1519 the Counts of Schlick, in Bohemia, began to strike guldengroschen at their new and enormously productive mines in St. Joachimstal.

These coins between them provided the models for new issues which in the sixteenth century spread throughout Europe and transformed the whole appearance of the currency. The lower denominations, of *c.* 8 g., were generally called testoons (Fr. *testons*, It. *testoni*) from the duke's head (*testa*) that characterized the Milanese series, though in South Germany their thickness

FIG. 24. Testone and guldengroschen. (a) Testone (lira) of Galeazzo Maria Sforza, duke of Milan, 1466–76, first struck in 1474. Æ 9·55 g. The globule behind the head shows that the coin had the value of one lira in money of account. (b) Guldiner of Sigismund of the Tyrol, dated 1486. Æ 31·57 g. The shields are those of his many feudal estates. (c) St. Joachimstaler of Stephen and his brothers, counts of Schlick and Bassano, struck between 1519 and 1526. Æ 28·82 g. The types are St. Joachim and the double-tailed Bohemian lion. The reverse bears the name of King Louis of Bohemia-Hungary, who was killed at the battle of Mohacs in 1526.

caused them to be termed dicken. The larger ones of *c.* 25–*c.* 30 g.
bear a great variety of names, of which the most widespread was
taler (shortened from St. Joachimstaler), i.e. our 'dollar', though
the English 'dollar' has traditionally been known as a crown
because the earliest issue, struck by Edward VI in 1551, was the
equivalent of the gold five-shilling piece of this name. The Spanish
version is most familiar to us as a 'piece of eight' (*reale de a ocho*),
since it had the value of eight reales, but was also known as a duro
or piastre. European silver-mines fell into the background after
the discovery of the immense riches of the New World in the
second half of the sixteenth century, and it was largely through the
output of the mints of America, where those of Mexico City and
Potosí were opened in 1535 and 1574 respectively, that coinage in
the European tradition came to dominate the world. Although
American discoveries of gold cannot be neglected, and those of
Portuguese Brazil made their contribution to the financing of the
Industrial Revolution, the coinage of the modern world, prior to
the nineteenth century, was essentially one of silver and not, as
many people suppose, one of the more precious metal.

The second novel feature of modern coinage, the replacement
of the conventional effigies of medieval coins by genuine portraits
accompanied by Roman instead of Gothic lettering, was a consequence of the revival of naturalistic art and of the interest in the
individual as a person that characterized the Italian Renaissance.
It was also strongly influenced by Pisanello's invention of a new
art form, the medal, in 1438 (see p. 175) and by the study of
classical antiquity, since this included the collecting of Roman
coins. The earliest coin portraits were those of Francesco I Sforza,
duke of Milan, and Ferdinand I of Naples, both dating from the
1450s, and within the next few decades the example of these
princes was followed by other rulers in the peninsula, in particular
by Duke Ercole d'Este at Ferrara and Modena. There are few
examples outside Italy prior to 1500, but in the course of the next
century portraiture became fairly general, though it was avoided
by purely republican states (Venice, Genoa, Florence before 1530)
and even, for reasons not altogether clear, by some monarchies.
All portrait coins of Philip II of Spain were struck in Italy or in the
Low Countries, not in the Spanish peninsula.

Another element in the ancient minting pattern which was
revived in the early modern period was the use of copper. The
billon pennies of the fourteenth and fifteenth centuries had only a
minute purchasing power, since their silver content was minimal:
indeed most forms of late medieval 'black money', as it was

collectively called, look as if they are nothing but copper. They had the disadvantage of being much subject to counterfeiting, since their value theoretically depended on their silver content and this could not possibly be verified. England, the sole country to retain the use of pure silver for its fractional coinage, was no better off than its neighbours, for its halfpennies and farthings were so tiny that they were too easily lost, besides being inconvenient and expensive to strike. The remedy, from the modern point of view, would have been to create a purely token coinage, with its value depending simply on convertibility, but this was alien to the ideas of the time. The alternative solution was to abandon silver altogether and strike copper coins whose metallic value would be equal to that of the silver or billon ones they replaced. This was first formally done by Venice and Naples in 1472, and their example was soon widely followed in Italy, but copper money was not introduced into the Low Countries till 1543 or into France till 1572. Some countries, however, preferred to leave the provision of small change to private enterprise. In England the making of copper farthings under licence was first permitted in 1613, and by 1672 the Government had brought itself to the point of making copper halfpennies. But even as late as 1797 it was left to Matthew Boulton to make twopenny and penny pieces of copper for circulation, and it was not until the 1820s that copper coins were issued on a vast scale by the Royal Mint to drive private tokens out of circulation. Even so, the notion that the monetary value of the coins should approximate to their face value persisted, and it was not until 1860, with the replacement of the copper pennies by much lighter bronze ones, that the fully token nature of subsidiary coinage was accepted.

The fourth innovation, the use of mechanical striking, resulting in coins with fully circular flans protected by a milled or lettered edge, was without any ancient precedents, and the gap between the invention of the main processes and their general adoption was often a long one. The techniques involved and their history are described in Chapter 5.

A further phase in the evolution of the monetary pattern of the West came with the introduction of paper money in the late seventeenth century. Bills of exchange, promises to pay, and similar legal instruments had been employed by merchants and bankers from the earliest times, and leather, parchment, or paper had occasionally been used for obsidional money (see p. 169), but an essential feature of true paper money is that the bills or notes shall represent round sums and be of general acceptability. As was

the case with token money, such paper units were originally
private in character and in many countries, at least in form, have
remained so. The first issues of banknotes, those of the Bank of
Sweden between 1661 and 1664, were the product of local circumstance. The Swedish government, anxious to find a use for the
rich copper deposits at Falun in the north of the country, had
introduced what is known as plate-money (*plattmynt*), and since
the copper equivalent of a silver daler formed a rough plate five
inches square, a tenth of an inch thick, and weighing $1\frac{1}{2}$ lb., and
multiples of up to 50 dalers were struck, the desirability of a more
convenient form of currency was acutely felt. The Swedish notes,
however, were of a local and temporary character and had a very
limited circulation. State issues of paper began in England during
the late 1670s ('Orders of the Exchequer') and there were extensive

FIG. 25. Swedish plate-money. Æ One-daler piece dated 1768, with crowned initials
of Adolphus Frederick (*Adolphus Fridericus rex Sueciae*). Slightly reduced in size.

FIG. 26. Swedish five-daler banknote, dated 1662. Slightly reduced in size.

issues during the great recoinage of 1696, but the Bank of England began the issue of notes in 1694 and in Great Britain the future lay with banknotes, not government bills. The reverse was the case in France, where the use of paper money began as an administrative expedient during the war of the League of Augsburg (1688–97), the Government having changed the value of the coins in circulation and called them into the Mint to be countermarked. Since this could not be done immediately, the receipts given for the sums deposited began to circulate among the merchant class, who expected to be repaid in coin with only a brief delay, and in 1701 the receipts were formally made legal tender. The Government was not slow to realize the possibility of issuing such 'receipts' against non-existent deposits, and in 1704 began to print notes on a vast scale. The concept of paper money spread surprisingly quickly, and in the course of the eighteenth century most of the states or banks of western Europe were issuing notes of their own. In the colonies, which suffered from a chronic shortage of

FIG. 27. Pennsylvania 15s. note, printed by Benjamin Franklin and D. Hall in 1759. Slightly reduced in size. Franklin published a pamphlet entitled *A Modest Enquiry into the Nature and Necessity of a Paper Currency* in 1729, and his firm was subsequently active in printing paper money for Pennsylvania, New Jersey, and Delaware.

coin, the device was often used for quite small sums. The earliest paper issued on the American continent was a total of £7,000 in units of between 5s. and £5 issued by the Massachusetts Bay Colony to pay the soldiers on an expedition against Canada in 1690, and later there were repeated issues of paper or parchment bills from 1d. upwards. In early days, notes were sometimes at a premium over actual coins, since they did not lose value through wear. But the possibility of their misuse was apparent from the first, and few governments resisted the temptation to exploit this from time to time.

Between the seventeenth and nineteenth centuries the coinage pattern elaborated in western Europe came gradually to dominate the world. Its rise was first apparent in the sphere of international trade. From late medieval times the Venetian ducat had competed successfully with Muslim gold coins all over the Near and Middle East. The invasion of the Far East by the Spanish-American dollar had begun before the end of the sixteenth century. Later the Maria Theresa dollar established a minor sphere of influence in the Levant and the countries surrounding the Red Sea, and in due course the pound sterling became the most widely accepted currency of all. The displacement of domestic currencies took place more slowly, and was a result partly of fashion and partly of convenience. Western coins were not more obviously attractive than those of the Muslim world or of India, but they were the coinages of countries whose political and economic achievements, even if in some cases unwelcome, were undeniable, so that when for practical reasons hammer-striking was abandoned in favour of machine-striking there was a tendency for local types to be replaced by ones of European inspiration. As for the primitive money of many African communities and the age-old system of copper cash used by China and its neighbours, these were wholly unsuited to the economic requirements of the modern world.

The history of colonial currencies is a topic in itself. Overseas minting in the precious metals on a significant scale was under the *ancien régime* practically limited to the Spanish-American colonies and Brazil, where immensely rich mines of silver and gold had been found in the sixteenth and the late seventeenth centuries respectively. The French and English colonies were in contrast starved of coin by their home governments. The ways in which the colonists satisfied their needs, whether with coins either struck locally or adapted by cutting or countermarking those of neighbouring lands, or with paper, or by the widespread use of primitive currencies (tobacco, cony skins) evaluated in monetary terms, form one of the most instructive chapters in the history of coinage, for they often suggest how other communities in earlier and less adequately documented periods may have coped with their monetary problems.

The pattern of Western coinage changed substantially in the nineteenth century. Heavy silver coins of dollar size, which had been struck in enormous quantities over the preceding two hundred years, went out of fashion, in part because of an increasing use of gold, of which the greatest discoveries in world history took place in the space of half a century (California in the 1840s, New South Wales and Victoria in the 1850s, the Transvaal in the 1880s, Alaska and Western Australia in the 1890s), and in part because of the use of paper. At the bottom end of the scale, available supplies of copper, despite fresh mining, were inadequate to the needs of a vastly increased population with all kinds of new requirements, and, despite the extensive use of new metals (nickel alloys and, much later, aluminium), all subsidiary coins became no more than tokens. The same fate in due course overtook silver, reduced to a token status by the adoption of a gold standard, while gold itself did not survive the shock of the First World War. Coins today, in the apt phrase of a modern economist, are essentially banknotes printed on metal: their face value is conferred on them

by governments and is quite unrelated to that of their metallic
content, while their actual purchasing power is something that not
even governments can control. Money, in the classic definition of
economists, is supposed to provide a standard of value, a means of
exchange, and a store of wealth. Though contemporary coinage,
despite the absence of gold, may not appear very different from
what it has always been, only the first function, and that to a
decreasing degree, still remains. Coins and tokens have become
interchangeable terms, and coins tend more and more to be
produced for the needs of vending machines and collectors.

3
Coinage: Eastern Traditions

Western numismatists are accustomed to regard the history of European coinage, from its Greek origins to its worldwide acceptance at the present day, as forming a self-contained subject quite distinct from the coinages of the non-European world. They are in this no different from their opposite numbers elsewhere. Both China and Japan have a centuries-old tradition of coin-collecting and numismatic study, and the interests of scholars in these countries always stopped short at the frontiers of the world of copper cash. A Japanese dealer's coin list in the author's library, printed at Osaka in 1793, includes amongst the hundreds of coins and amulets which are illustrated only a single coin actually from Europe—though there are several of European type from South-East Asia—and nothing from India or the Muslim world. The distinction between European and non-European coins, so far as the West is concerned, is basically linguistic, for the legends on non-European coins are couched in languages and inscribed in characters which most Western scholars and collectors, unless they are specialists, are unable to read. Historically, however, the distinction is one that is largely false, for only the Chinese mone-tary tradition owed nothing to Greece. Western and Muslim coinages share a common origin, and Indian coinage, though distinct in origin, has throughout its history been profoundly influenced, either directly or indirectly, by that of the West.

Muslim Coinage

Until quite recent times the most widespread and uniform system of coinage in existence has been that of the Muslim world, not that of Europe. The area over which it has at one time or another extended is enormous, stretching from Spain and Morocco to the

Malay Archipelago and from Kazan to Zanzibar. Its uniformity
results from the fact that almost the whole of it is epigraphic and
employs the Arabic script, contrasting both with the pictorial coin
types that have dominated the Western tradition and with the
Greek or Latin lettering that has accompanied them. But despite
their external differences the two coinages go back to the same
source and have influenced each other more than once in the course
of their history. The traditional Muslim denominations are the
dinar, the dirhem, and the fels, of gold, silver, and copper respectively. The dinar is a derivative of the gold solidus of the late
Roman Empire—its name came through Syriac from *denarius
aureus*, i.e. 'gold coin'—the dirhem was the drachma of antiquity,
and the fels was the follis of early Byzantine times. Even at a much
later date the ghurush, the basic silver coin of the Ottoman Empire,
took its name from the groschen of its Austrian neighbour.

Muslim coinage derived ultimately from that of the Parthian
Empire, which was founded in the third century B.C. and at its
greatest extent included the whole area between the Euphrates and
Afghanistan. Parthian coins, which are normally of silver, were
basically Hellenistic, the coins having on one side the head of a
ruler and on the other either the seated figure of the founder of
the dynasty or a Greek deity surrounded by a long inscription
arranged as a square. The later issues, however, are far removed
from their Greek models, the royal effigies having become more
and more markedly oriental and the reverse types crude in style
and design. The distinction became more obvious under the
Sassanians (A.D. 227–642), whose coins (dirhems) are again predominantly of silver, but with very large and thin flans and having
as their regular reverse type the fire-altar and two attendants
appropriate to the Zoroastrian faith. The inscriptions, which are
in Pehlevi, record the mint and the date by the king's regnal year.
Although the portraits are heavily stylized, the rulers are distinguished from each other by variations in the design of their
elaborate crowns and in the details of their beards and the huge
bun of hair worn at the nape of the neck.

The Arabs, during the first half-century of their career of
conquest, made few changes in the coinage of the occupied provinces. In the Persian regions they took over the broad, thin silver
dirhem, doing little more than add a pious formula and sometimes
a governor's name in the margin. In Syria and Egypt they used the
solidi they found in circulation or managed to import from the
Empire, but they issued an extensive local coinage in copper,
which in Syria and Palestine was modified from Byzantine types

FIG. 28. Arab-Sassanian dirhem. Kahtan (name of governor?). Struck at Herat in A.H. 67 (= A.D. 686/7). 4·09 g. The types (bust of the last Sassanian ruler Yezdigird III, who was killed in 651, and Zoroastrian fire-altar and attendants) are purely Sassanian, but the Arab governor's name is inscribed in the obverse margin and the mint and date are in Pehlevi characters on the reverse. There is a countermark of uncertain significance, imposed during the decade preceding the great coinage reform of A.H. 77, in the upper right border of the obverse.

mainly by the addition of the mint name in Arabic and sometimes by the elimination of Christian symbols. Not until the late 690s was a major monetary reform carried out by the fifth Umayyad caliph 'Abd al-Malik and his great minister al-Hajjaj, governor of Iraq. The weights of the coins were modified, the dinar being reduced from 4·5 g. to 4·25 g. and the dirhem from *c.* 4 g. to 2·9 g., and the whole of the Arab-Byzantine and Arab-Sassanian coinage was called in and reminted. The earliest of the new types showed on the gold and copper the figure of the standing caliph and on the silver a *mihrab* (prayer niche) or similar design. The representation of a living person on the gold and copper caused an outcry amongst the orthodox, for although representational art is not formally forbidden in the Koran, a strong tradition hostile to it had grown up. These transitional coins were therefore almost at once replaced by new designs, of which the essential elements are an inscription round the edge and in several lines in the 'area'—what in Western numismatics is termed the 'field'—on either side. These inscriptions are at first limited to the Muslim profession of faith, having as its basic elements 'There is no God but God, who has no associate', 'Muhammad is the messenger of God', and 'God is one, God is eternal; he begetteth not, nor is begotten', together with the date (reckoned from the Hijra in A.D. 622) and, on the dirhems, the name of the mint. On later coins this impersonal inscription was generally expanded by the name, patronymic, and title of the ruler and sometimes by further religious formulas, more especially under some Shi'ah rulers who made a heretical addition, 'Ali is the friend of God', to the profession of faith.

Fig. 29. Arab dinar and dirhem. (a) Dinar of A.H. 77 (= A.D. 696/7). N 4·25 g.
(b) Dirhem of A.H. 81 (= A.D. 700/1), struck at Basra. Æ 2·86 g.

This pattern has dominated the whole of Muslim coinage down
to almost the present day. Variations have of course occurred:
inscriptions arranged in several concentric circles instead of across
the field; ornaments and frames around the inscriptions; great
variations in the script, from the square monumental Cufic of the
early coins to the more elaborate Nashki script of the later Middle
Ages and the wonderfully elaborate Nastaliq of the Safavid period
in Persia. Ottoman coins are characterized by the *tughra* or
signature of the sovereign, a marvellously elaborate monogram
incorporating the name and patronymic of the ruler and varying
from one sultan to his successor. Only occasionally has the
epigraphic tradition been abandoned. In Syria and parts of
Mesopotamia in the twelfth and thirteenth centuries the local
dynasts (*atabegs*) issued large copper coins intended to serve as
dirhems which had designs copied sometimes from ancient Greek,
Hellenistic, or Byzantine coins but often original and astrological
in character. One of the most attractive of these was the sun and
lion of the silver coins of the Seljuks of Rum (Asia Minor), which
was reputedly a consolation offered by Kai Khusrau II to his

FIG. 30. Copper dirhem of Mosul, A.H. 556 (=AD 1161). Maudud, 1149–69. Æ
10·40 g. The obverse derives from the head of Arethusa on Greek coins of Syracuse.
This type had been copied in antiquity by several dynasts in Asia Minor, which
explains how it could serve as a model for die-sinkers in twelfth-century Syria.

beautiful Circassian wife, since, not being able to place her features upon the coinage, he put on this her horoscope instead. Much later the Mogul emperor Jahangir issued a whole series of zodiacal mohurs, and even scandalized the faithful by showing a seated figure of himself with a wine cup in his hand.

Despite the contrast between the epigraphic character and religious content of Muslim coinage and the pictorial and Christian aspects of that of the West, the two have frequently interacted. Imitations of Muslim coins were issued by the Latin conquerors of Spain and Sicily between the eleventh and thirteenth centuries, and even in the Holy Land the crusading princes did not scruple to issue money which proclaimed, in however corrupt a form, that Muhammad was the prophet of God. Later inscriptions were often in good Arabic, so that those subjects of Alphonso VIII of Castile who were able to read might learn from their coins that these were struck by Alphonso ben Sancho, and that he was the Emir of the Christians and the Pope their Imam. In twelfth- and thirteenth-century Europe, with its silver monometallism, Muslim gold coins filled a role corresponding to that of Persian darics in classical Greece, providing an internationally recognized standard of payment and sometimes serving as a means of exchange. The late-twelfth-century *Liber Censuum*, a register of payments due to the Papacy from religious houses in every country in Europe, reckoned them largely in terms of morabitini, mazmudini, melechini, and other Muslim coins. Venetian ducats were widely used all over the Near and Middle East from the fourteenth century onwards, and when Muhammad the Conqueror struck the first Ottoman gold coins after the fall of Constantinople he used the ducat as the standard of weight and fineness for his altun (1477). Exactly the same was done by the Safavid rulers of Persia for their ashrafi.

Modern Muslim coinage does not differ in any essential respect from that of Europe. That it uses the Arabic script and language, and is dated by the Hijra—or sometimes jointly by the Hijra and the Common (i.e. Christian) Era—is only to be expected. The assimilation began in the eighteenth century, when the Ottoman sultan Suleiman II (1687–91) introduced a large silver dollar, of the weight and fineness of the Dutch rixdaler, which in Turkish was called a ghurush and was known to eighteenth-century travellers as a piastre. Portraiture was accepted in Persia, which never fully shared the common Muslim prejudice against representational art, in the nineteenth century, but elsewhere it was not introduced until after the First World War, when Egypt and Iraq became independent. The two extremes are now represented on the one hand by Turkey, which abandoned Arabic script and Hijra date alike in 1933 and whose higher denominations have shown in succession the heads of its presidents, Kemal Atatürk and Ismet Inönü, and on the other by the rigidly orthodox Hedjaz (Saudi Arabia), which still avoids any form of pictorial representation. Other states come in between, the now general absence of portraiture being due more to republican sentiment than to religious scruples, although Afghanistan, while still a monarchy, used as its coin types a *tughra* on the Ottoman model and a hall of audience with throne, or subsequently a mosque with *mihrab* and *minbar* (pulpit). The future development of Muslim coinage will no doubt run parallel to that of the Western world, but it is to be hoped that it will retain its artistic independence and the use of the Arabic script whose beauty has been one of its greatest claims to distinction in the past.

Indian Coinage

The coins of India, using the word here in its geographical sense, together with those of much of South-East Asia, form a distinct branch of numismatics, for despite their diversity in detail the vast majority differ markedly in appearance from those of Europe and China. This is true even of the coins issued by Muslim rulers, for the style of their Arabic script is bolder and often more crudely flamboyant than was customary in Syria or Iraq. Indian coins, like Western coins, are of gold, silver, and copper, but they tend to be thicker and heavier, and usually less perfectly rounded. A number, indeed, are square. This shape was much used in the Indo-Bactrian series, especially for copper coins, and it recurs quite frequently later, for example in the Muslim kingdoms of Malwa and Kashmir in the later Middle Ages and for some handsome gold and silver issues of Akbar and Jahangir of the late sixteenth and early seventeenth centuries. Although it is a shape that has sometimes been used for coins in other parts of the world, for example for the silver millarès of some Muslim dynasties of Spain and North Africa between the thirteenth and fifteenth centuries A.D., it is common only in India and must be regarded as a characteristic feature of the native coinage. A high proportion of Indian coins, not merely those of the Muslim states, are epigraphic, with inscriptions couched in an extraordinary diversity of foreign and native scripts.

The importance of Indian coins as a historical source cannot be overemphasized. They are particularly valuable for the period preceding the Muslim invasions, since, while the profusion of sutras, law books, and religious writings dating from these centuries provide much information about society, they contain virtually no political narrative. This has to be pieced together from the records of outside observers, Greek or Chinese, where these are available, and from the evidence of inscriptions and coins, which fortunately exist in abundance. The decipherment of the Kharoshthi script used for some of the edicts of Asoka and other early Sanskrit and Prakrit inscriptions was only made possible by the existence of the bilingual coins of the later Indo-Bactrian rulers; coin finds have often been the key to the identification of otherwise anonymous archaeological sites; and the history of the later Indo-Bactrians, the Sakas, the Kushans, the Andhras, the Guptas, and many minor dynasties has been built up mainly on numismatic evidence, especially after coins began to be dated according to various eras in the second century A.D. Even in later times numismatics often makes substantial contributions to our knowledge, for example in reconstructing the history of the Pathan kings of Delhi and the administrative and economic reforms of Akbar.

Different as Indian coinage is from that of its neighbours, it has repeatedly been strongly influenced by them. This is not true of the extreme south, where the coinage has for the most part developed in isolation. But the north and centre of the subcontinent, as far down as the Kistna, have been exposed to a succession of invaders from across the Hindu Kush. A few of these, like Tamerlane and Nadir Shah, did little more than destroy on the most horrifying scale, and others, like the Greeks, influenced little beyond the Punjab and Sind. The tendency of all the early invaders to base their power on the extreme north-west, with Taxila and Peshawar as their centres, indeed explains why this region plays so prominent a role in the story of Indian numismatics. But even when most of northern and central India passed under the dominion of outsiders, from the Kushans to the Moguls, a substantial portion of the coinage remained Indian in character, and one type of coin cannot be studied to the exclusion of others.

The background to Indian coinage was a great variety of primitive currencies ranging from cattle to cowries. Gold in the Vedic period passed by weight, the unit being the *rati*, the scarlet and black seed of the Indian liquorice or weather-plant (*Abrus precatorius*) which was eventually standardized as the equivalent of 0.12 g. and so was rather lighter than its Greco-Roman equivalent, the carat. The earliest actual coins, however, were of silver, not gold. They consist of small, thin, roughly squared pieces of metal, struck to an original standard of *c.* 3·5 g. and bearing up

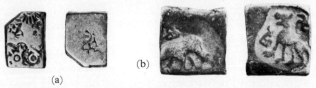

(b)

(a)

FIG. 31. Early Indian coins. (a) Punch-marked silver (Allan Class 2, IIa). 3·32 g. There are five symbols on the obverse, one on the reverse. (b) Copper coin from Taxila (Allan Class IIa). 8·89 g. The obverse shows an elephant and a 'mountain' symbol, the reverse a lion with the same symbol and a swastika. The punch-marked coins are customarily classed according to the system devised by John Allan in his catalogue of the coins of ancient India in the British Museum (1936).

to five symbols (flowers, geometrical patterns, etc.) impressed by separate punches. Over 300 such symbols are known. Their meaning has given rise to much conjecture, and in detail they are unexplained, though it is generally supposed that the earliest of them were due to silversmiths or bankers, not to any state. Punch-marked coins certainly antedated Alexander's invasion (327/6 B.C.) and may go back to the sixth or seventh century, though the early ones have not been found in firmly datable archaeological contexts and attempts to establish their chronology by statistical estimates of their rate of wear do not carry conviction. Their later use over-lapped that of 'Western' types of coin; a Taxila hoard of 160 punch-marked coins included a silver piece of Diodotos (*c.* 245 B.C.), and in South India they circulated later still, for a hoard from Coimbatore district included a denarius of Augustus. The technique of building up coin designs by separate punches remained sporadically in use for centuries, for example on gold coins of the Calukya kings who ruled in the Deccan as late as the eleventh century A.D., though conversely there exist copper punch-marked coins of the second century B.C. on which all the designs have been impressed by a single punch.

The earliest coins struck between two dies of Western type are the splendid silver drachms of Sophytes (Saubhuti), a local ruler who entertained Alexander in India after the defeat of Porus. They show his helmeted portrait copied from an early coin of Seleucus I, and have on the reverse a cock and his name in Greek. But they exist in isolation, designed and struck by some Greek artist in the king's service, and for a hundred years the use of coin in India

FIG. 32. Stater of Sophytes, *c.* 300 B.C. Æ 3·78 g. The obverse is copied from the helmeted head on a coin of Seleucus Nicator, itself derived from that of coins of the Persian satraps in Asia Minor.

made little progress. Although Greek or Seleucid coins were occasionally imitated or countermarked, there is nothing that can be specifically ascribed to Chandragupta, Asoka, or other kings of the great Maurya dynasty (*c.* 320–*c.* 185 B.C.). But it is probably to this period that one should ascribe the square copper coins from Taxila and Mathura, a holy city on the Jumna between Delhi and Agra, having purely Indian types (e.g. elephant and lion), though they may be earlier in date and in that case represent an independent invention of the device of striking coins between two dies. In any case, it was these coins that despite their rarity established the fashion of the square shape.

As the Mauryan Empire fell into decline, Demetrius I of Bactria (*c.* 200–*c.* 185 B.C.) became master of the Punjab. There he began to strike square copper coins of Indian type and Indian weight standard with Greek and Kharoshthi inscriptions, and from then onwards, particularly after the Greeks had been eliminated from Bactria as a result of the double pressure of the Parthians and the nomad Sakas, there exists an abundant Indo-Greek coinage, often with bilingual inscriptions and types that are partly Greek, partly Indian (portraits; deities such as Zeus, Heracles, and Athena; elephant or humped bull). The kings are known almost exclusively from their coins, though the greatest of them, Menander (*c.* 165–

FIG. 33. Indo-Greek tetradrachm of Hippostratus, 1st cent. B.C. Æ 9·56 g. The obverse has the king's bust accompanied by his name and title, with the epithet 'Saviour', in Greek (ΒΑΣΙΛΕΩΣ ΣΩΤΗΡΟΣ ΙΠΠΟΣΤΡΑΤΟΥ), and the reverse shows the king on horseback with the same inscription in Kharoshthi. The coin is struck to the Indian and not the Attic weight standard.

c. 130 B.C.) figures prominently as 'Milinda' in a famous Buddhist text recording his discussions with the sage Nagasena and his consequent conversion. There were some twenty-five of them in all, the last being Hermaios (*ob. c.* A.D. 20), whose coinage passes directly into that of the Kushan king Kujula Kadphises. Parallel to the purely Indo-Greek series are those of the Sakas themselves, who entered India *c.* 126 B.C. after developing a taste for Greek art in Bactria, and of their relations the Pahlavas. Many of these coins are remarkable for a profusion of privy marks that should eventually permit a much closer dating and localization than is at present possible. The unlovely coins of the so-called Western Satraps (Kshatrapa), who made themselves masters of the north-west Indian coastline and whose coins still retain Greek features, are chiefly important because on them first appears dating by the Saka era (from A.D. 78) which thenceforward provides a much firmer basis for Indian chronology.

FIG. 34. Stater of Vasudeva, *c.* A.D. 185–*c.* 220. A´ 8·06 g. The obverse inscription gives the king's name (*Bazodeo*) and titles, and the type shows him standing, wearing armour, and sacrificing on a small altar. The reverse shows Shiva standing with trident in front of bull.

The most remarkable coin series of the early centuries A.D. are those of the Kushans and the Guptas. The Kushans, whose 'eras' remain uncertain but who ruled between the first century B.C. and the third century A.D., represent a further wave of intruders from outside. Their greatest ruler Kanishka (late first or early second century A.D.), whose capital was Peshawar, extended his sovereignty from Kabul and Benares as far south as the Vindhyas. The Kushans struck an abundant gold coinage—their predecessors had minted almost exclusively in silver and copper—some of it concave in form, with a great variety of deities (Indian, Greek, Persian) as types, although in Tibetan tradition Kanishka was a Buddhist and indeed played a prominent role in the consolidation of the doctrines of Mahayana Buddhism. The weights of these coins correspond closely to that of the Roman aureus, and it is generally believed that the gold for them was largely supplied by melting down Roman coins, since both Pliny and the *Periplus of the Erythraean Sea* provide plentiful evidence for the export of Roman bullion to India at this period. The Kushans likewise struck copper, in such quantities, indeed, that specimens could still occasionally be found amongst the small change used in the bazaars into the late nineteenth century. The Guptas, for their part, were the first native dynasty to unite northern India since the downfall of the Mauryas. The two centuries of their rule (*c.* A.D. 320–*c.* 535) were ones of great cultural achievement, and have always been looked back to as the golden age of Indian art and literature. Their gold coinage is abundant and, although by now purely Hindu, extremely varied in type, besides being of high artistic quality. The king is shown in an infinity of roles—standing

FIG. 35. Stater of Skandagupta, A.D. 455–*c.* 480, of archer type. *N* 9·30 g. The obverse gives the king's name and titles, and the type shows him standing l., holding bow and drawing arrow from quiver, with *Garuda*-headed standard (symbol of Vishnu) to l. The reverse shows the goddess Lakshmi seated on a lotus.

beside a standard, holding a bow, on horseback, slaying a lion— and Hindu deities appear as a matter of course. Long after the dynasty had ended, imitations or derivatives of its coin types continued to be struck by the princes of north and central India, and the Gupta era was used for dating down to the thirteenth century.

The great variety of dynastic coins issued during the four centuries between the downfall of the Gupta Empire and the Ghaznavid invasion in the late tenth century require no special comment. The pseudo-Sassanian coinage of the White Huns, though usually treated as Indian, belongs rather to the coinage of Central Asia, and the only native innovation of note was the creation of the bull-and-horseman type by the Rajput kings in the ninth century. A great change came with the introduction of Muslim coinage. This goes back formally to the annexation of the Punjab by Mahmud of Ghazni in 1021, but the coinage of the eleventh and twelfth centuries consists mainly of billon and copper, and effective Muslim rule over northern India really dates from the conquests of the Ghurid Mu'izz ud-Din Muhammad, 'martyred' by an Indian fanatic in 1206. It was in the thirteenth

century—there is an obvious parallel in Europe—that coinage in
the three traditional metals began to revive under the first of the
six slave dynasties of Delhi who ruled between 1206 and 1526.
Their coins are usually finely designed, with admirable calli-
graphy, the Profession of Faith being expanded by the names of
the Four Orthodox Caliphs and the sultans excelling themselves
in the invention of grandiose titles: 'The second Alexander, the
right hand of the Caliph', 'The Supreme Head of Islam, the Caliph
of the Lord of Heaven and Earth'. The mint names on the coins
are an important source for the political geography of the period.
The most interesting coins are those of Muhammad ibn Tughlaq
(1324–51), an unquiet reformer who rarely carried any of his
projects through to a successful conclusion and whose uncertain
temper is bluntly summarized by the great Arab traveller Ibn
Battutah, who had both served and feared him: 'This king is of all
men the fondest of making gifts and of shedding blood.' He tried
a long series of monetary experiments, not the least remarkable of
which was the attempt to substitute brass and copper tokens for
the silver coinage, a project which, as a contemporary historian
comments, 'turned the house of every Hindu into a mint'. It is to
the sultan's credit that he recognized the utopian character of such
a scheme under the conditions of medieval India, and redeemed
the tokens, genuine and counterfeit alike, at his own cost.

The battle of Panipat (1526) inaugurated Mogul rule in India,
but the coins of Babur (*ob.* 1530) and the first reign of Humayun
(1530–40) are essentially Central Asiatic (Timurid) in character.
It was the usurper Sher Shah (1540–5) and Humayun's son, the
great Akbar (1556–1606), who between them inaugurated what
was to be the final phase of hammer-struck coinage in India.
Babur introduced in 1542 the silver rupee (from Sanskrit *rupya*,
'wrought silver'), a new and heavy coin weighing originally 11·5 g.,
and the copper dam of 21·4 g., which were to become the standard
coins of the country, and increased the number of mints to over
twenty. Akbar introduced the gold mohur, slightly lighter than
the rupee (11·0–11·35 g.). The coins of Akbar and of his son
Jahangir (1606–27) are of quite bewildering richness and variety,
both sovereigns using them for display purposes on a scale
hitherto unknown in Indian numismatics. The most famous single
series is that of the zodiacal mohurs of Jahangir, already alluded
to (p. 43), but others of both rulers are not inferior to them in
interest: mohurs with a facing portrait of Akbar issued by his son,
mohurs with animal figures (hawk or duck), half-mohurs with the
figures of Sita and Rama, rupees dated by their month of issue and

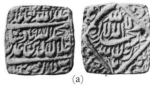

(a)   (b)

FIG. 36. Mohurs of Akbar and Jahangir. (a) Square mohur of Akbar, dated A.H. 987
(= A.D. 1579/80) and struck at Fathpur, the new capital constructed by Akbar which
did not survive his death. *N* 12·12 g. (b) Zodiacal mohur of Jahangir, struck at
Agra and dated A.H. 1030 (= A.D. 1620/1) and regnal year 16. *N* 10·89 g. The type
shows the Ram (Aries) skipping, with sun above.

sometimes alternately square or round according to the month,
coins with an elaborate variety of verse couplets, huge multiples
in gold and silver, of which the largest, a multiple of 200 mohurs
or nearly 5 pounds avoirdupois, is known only from a cast in the
British Museum. After the death of Aurungzeb in 1707 the
system began to disintegrate, partly through the introduction of
the practice of farming out the mints, but down to the mid-
nineteenth century the many virtually independent states of the
subcontinent continued to use the Great Mogul's name on their
coins. Although the later issues are much inferior artistically to
those of the late sixteenth and early seventeenth centuries, the
high standard and purity of the basic gold and silver coins were
maintained for over three hundred years.

Side by side with the coinage of north and central India there
was also that of the Deccan and the coastlands of the south. Its
early history is very obscure, since coin inscriptions tend to be
either brief or altogether absent and written sources for the history
of the country are inadequate. The bulk of the coinage is of gold—
there are important deposits at Kolar in Mysore—and copper,
with silver struck in only a few localities. The gold and rare silver
coins have the peculiarity of being sometimes extremely small in
size: a silver tare struck at Calicut in the sixteenth century weighs
between one and two grains and ranks with the 1/48th drachma
(*hemitetartemorion*) of classical Athens as one of the tiniest coins
ever made. South Indian coinage could be omitted here if it were
not for the fact that the great inland state of Vijanayanagar was at
the height of its power when the Portuguese reached India in the
sixteenth century, and its coins, and those of the coastal kingdoms,
made a noteworthy contribution to the circulating medium, and
in particular to the monetary vocabulary, of all states trading
round the Bay of Bengal. The chief gold coins were what the
Portuguese termed the pagoda (*c.* 3·5 g.) and its tenth the fanam,

the first name being apparently a corruption of one of those
(*bhagavata*) used for the hun and the other of panam, the names
of the coins in Tamil. The fanam was also struck in silver. The
half-pagoda was known as a kashu (from Sanskrit *karsha*), but this
term was more frequently applied to a copper coin of the same
weight, which became in Portuguese caixa, in English cash, and
was subsequently applied to the copper coinage of all South-East
Asia and eventually to that of China.

The transition in India to 'modern' coinage was a complicated
process, since there were two largely distinct elements involved.
One was the minting of coins of European type by the various
powers, Portuguese, Dutch, Danish, French, and English, who
had contrived to settle in India; the other was the introduction of
mechanical methods of striking both for some of these and for
coins minted by the British East India Company in the name of
the Great Mogul. The Portuguese struck gold coins at Goa from
the earliest days, those of John III (1521–57) having as their type
the standing or seated figure of St. Thomas, the reputed Apostle
of India. The other powers minted in their various settlements in
the seventeenth and eighteenth centuries a strange mixture of
European and native denominations and types. Machinery was,
not surprisingly, first introduced in the mints of the East India

FIG. 37. East India Company rupee in name of Shah 'Alam II. Æ 11·66 g. The
obverse gives the name and titles of the Great Mogul and the date A.H. 1202 (= A.D.
1787/8); the reverse gives the mint of Murshidabad, the regnal year 19, and the
Company's mark, a cinquefoil. The coin has oblique milling on the edge and was
in fact struck at Calcutta between 1793 and 1818.

Company, which like other vassals of the Moguls had from the
early eighteenth century been striking coins in the name of the
reigning emperor. The dating, however, is difficult to establish
in specific cases, partly because the mints sometimes took as their
models the coins of places like Farrukhabad or Murshidabad
which were certainly not in British hands, and there was much

immobilizing of dates to circumvent the money-changers' habit of charging a commission (*batta*), ostensibly to compensate for wear, on all rupees that were not *sikka*, i.e. fresh from mint. A major change occurred in 1835, when the Company issued rupees from all its mints with portraits of William IV—they are actually dated 1834—and also struck them to a uniform weight of 180 grains (11·66 g.) instead of to the slightly varying weights used previously in accordance with local custom. Down to the end of British rule (1947) the sovereigns of a few of the major native states (Gwalior, Hyderabad, etc.) preserved their rights of coinage intact, and their coins often display an interesting blending of Western and Indian motifs.

The influence of Indian coinage naturally extended beyond the confines of the subcontinent, but mainly to the north and east, although Persian coinage underwent a brief 'Indian' phase after the expedition of Nadir Shah in the eighteenth century. In two cases the countries involved, Tibet and Burma, are surprising. Tibet was formally a part of the Chinese Empire, but its inhabitants had no use for heavy cash of a purely token character, and in early times, in so far as they used coinage at all, they made do with that of Nepal. In the late eighteenth century, when they began to issue coins themselves, they took that of this country as their model, and when the Chinese set up an official mint at Lhasa in 1793 they accommodated themselves to local needs, issuing coins of the accustomed Nepalese type but with era and year in Chinese characters. As for Burma, the earliest coins, of uncertain date, are purely Hindu in type, with a humped bull, what appears to be Shiva's trident, and an inscription in Nagari characters. When a native coinage was revived in the late sixteenth century the models again came from India but were now Muslim in character, with epigraphic silver coins copied from those of Bengal and having inscriptions at first in a number of alphabets, Burmese, Arabic, or Nagari, but ultimately in Burmese only. There was, however, no unified monetary system, each region according to its needs and possibilities using coin or metal by weight, and foreign merchants preferring imported Spanish dollars or south Indian pagodas and fanams. The first coins of Western type to be struck were beautiful dollars and half-dollars, having as their type the peacock of the royal seal, which were introduced by Mindon Min in 1853, the year of his accession.

Further afield, the 'bullet' coinage of Siam is generally regarded as *sui generis*, but although its form is unique it is in part Indian in derivation. The coins, almost globular in shape, were made by

FIG. 38. Siamese four-bat piece (*tam lung*). King Mongkut, 1851–68. Æ 61 g. The marks are the *chakra*, the serrated wheel which was a symbol of the Hindu god Vishnu, and the *mongkut* or Siamese crown which was the king's personal mark.

bending short lengths of silver in two, so that the ends came together, and impressing on them one or more usually two small punch marks. They are often treated as a kind of primitive money because of their curious form, but are true coins, for they are uniform in weight, corresponding to the bat or tical of *c.* 15 g. and its multiples or fractions, are stamped, and are issued by a public authority. Their Thai name *p'ot duang*, i.e. 'curled-up worm', describes them very well but does not help in explaining their origin, the most likely suggestion being that they were intended to represent the shape of cowrie shells. The symbols punched on them (geometrical patterns, flowers, an elephant, etc.) are in any case Hindu, and despite the apparent gap in date it seems likely that the idea of marking them in this way came from India, for the derivative punch-marked coins of the Calukyas referred to above (p. 46) have been found east of the Bay of Bengal, for example on the island of Cheduba, off the Arakan coast. The dating of the first 'bullet' coins is uncertain, as is the interpretation of the earliest symbols, but it seems likely that they go back to the thirteenth century and that the signs indicate rulers or eras, as the modern ones certainly do. They ceased to be struck, except for presentation purposes, in 1860, when a coinage of Western pattern was introduced by King Mongkut.

Beyond Burma and Siam lie the countries which the classical world, in so far as it was aware of their existence, thought of as the spice-yielding regions of Further India (*India Ulterior*), and whose Indian affiliations we ourselves recognize by the term Indonesia. Their monetary history is extremely complex, and only known with any exactness for the very modern period. Against a background involving the long-continued use of a great variety of primitive currencies one discerns a disjointed pattern of foreign influences—Hindu, Muslim, Chinese, European—and a number of strange coinage forms, the best-known of these being the early-

FIG. 39. 'Tin-hat' coin of Pahang. Tin. 3 kg. The characters on the top read Yu Li Ssu, 'Have profit company', and the pseudo-Arabic inscriptions on the sides give the date A.H. 1281 (= A.D. 1864).

nineteenth-century 'tin-hat' money of Pahang (Malaysia), with three denominations of coins having the shape of flattened square top-hats with inscriptions on the tops and brims. Hindu influence is strongest on the early coinage, where such exists; later, after much of the population had adopted Islam, there is a mixture of Hindu and Muslim elements, with extensive copying of pagodas and fanams and some invention of novel types. European influence is represented mainly by Holland, with the ubiquitous VOC of the United East India Company (Vereenigde Oost-Indische Compagnie). There is also some 'cash' of Chinese inspiration, but the coins tend to be of tin rather than of bronze or brass and the central holes are often circular or hexagonal instead of square.

Chinese Coinage

The Chinese monetary tradition contrasts in almost every respect with those of the West, of Islam, and of India. Chinese coins were cast and not struck; they bore inscriptions only, not designs; and they all had a central hole, a device not adopted in the West until

the nineteenth century and then for only a few coinages and for
quite different reasons. The coins were nearly always of a single
denomination, instead of forming a hierarchy of values, and
remained in circulation almost indefinitely, so that a nineteenth-
century scholar could comment on the incongruity of still finding,
in every thousand coins he examined, ten or twelve of the Sung
period (twelfth century A.D.) and even two or three of the early
T'ang (seventh century A.D.). There were no gold coins at all in
historic times, and whereas in the West the state has in most
periods used silver for its main coinage and often delegated the
issue of copper to subordinate institutions or private individuals,
in China it was the state that issued the copper coinage, while the
striking of stamped silver ingots was left to merchants. Paper
money only became common in the West in the eighteenth century; in China it was sporadically in use between the eleventh and
fourteenth centuries and was invented several hundred years
earlier still. Cowries, grain, and cloth were employed as currency
well into historic times, while cowries had never been used in
Europe or the Near East and the currency grain of China was rice
instead of wheat or barley and the cloth was silk, not wool or linen.

Cowrie shells and utensil currency form the background to
Chinese money. Cowries have been found in the treasure pits of
the Shang-yin kings at An-yang, in Honan province north of the
Yellow River, which date from somewhere between 1500 and 1000
B.C., and the character for cowrie (*pei*) is an element in many of
the terms used for money and exchange. They remained in use
for over two millennia in backward regions of the Empire, for they
were known to Marco Polo, and the records speak of 1,133,119
strings of cowries being received by the Treasury in taxes as late
as 1329. It was no doubt the custom of stringing them together
that gave rise to the same practice for metal coins. The two utensil
currencies were bronze knives (*tao*), used originally in the Shantung peninsula and neighbouring areas corresponding to the state
of Ch'i, and spades (*pu*), initially used in the remaining states of
China north of the Yellow River but later mingling with knife
money in what are now the provinces of Shan-si and Chih-li. The
actual utensils presumably formed the highest units, while fractions were provided by making stylized and non-functional
miniatures of these, a few inches long, often marked with their
places of minting and their values, the latter depending on their
weights. They were used in the late Chou period, roughly between
the seventh and third centuries B.C., and can be broken down
typologically and stylistically into separate classes (Prototype

(b)

(a)   (c)

FIG. 40. Early Chinese currencies. (a) Late Knife coin (*tao*) with legend *Ming*, referring to the town in Shan-si where it was made. Æ 15·0 g. The reverse (not shown) has the legend *tai*. (b) Spade coin (*pu*) from Wei, 403–225 B.C. Æ 25·4 g. The reverse is blank. (c) *Pan-liang* of Shih Huang-ti, 221–210 B.C. Æ 26·1 g. The inscription gives the value. The reverse is blank. All three are original size.

spades, Hollow-Handle spades, etc.), but despite the finding of numerous hoards their history is still imperfectly known. As with early Roman bronze coinage, their weights were repeatedly reduced, and metrological interpretation is complicated by the probability that surviving specimens are sometimes only funerary money which never served as currency, like the imitation paper money burned at modern Chinese funerals. Inscribed bronze coins having a round or square hole in their centres, so that they could be strung together, were added to the picture in about the sixth century B.C. In the 'barbarian' hill country of south China, athwart the Yangtse, which was better furnished with precious metals than the alluvial plains of the north, there was some use of small slabs of gold, bearing one or more square stamps reading 'yuan of Ying' of 'yuan of Ch'en', yuan being both a unit of weight and a monetary denomination and Ying and Ch'en successively capitals of the southern state of Ch'u.

A demonetization of the utensil currencies and a sole reliance on round coins with a square central hole was decreed by Shih Huang-ti (221–210 B.C.), the 'First Emperor', who united China and built the Great Wall. His *pan-liang* ('half-ounce' or 12 chu) coins vary in diameter from about 3 in. to 2 in. and in weight from *c.* 10 g. to *c.* 6 g., and have the value indicated by two characters to the right and left of the central hole. This type of coinage was continued under the Western and Eastern Han dynasties (202 B.C.–A.D. 220), despite attempts at reaction; the usurper Wang Mang (A.D. 7–23), who at one time 'nationalized' all the gold of his subjects in return for copper 'cash', reintroduced both cowrie and knife currencies as part of an attempt to establish a hierarchy of denominations. From 118 B.C. onwards the value of the round coins was altered to 5 chu and the weight of even these was repeatedly reduced. The use of coin spread slowly and irregularly, with salaries and tax assessments sometimes reckoned in cash, sometimes in grain, and payments being usually effected in a mixture of both. It was indeed only in 112 B.C. that the issue of coin was finally restricted to state agencies or mints instead of being allowed to local authorities, as had frequently been the case earlier. The four centuries of political confusion that followed the end of the Han period saw a large-scale reversion to cloth and grain currencies, and indeed to simple barter, though the use of coin never completely disappeared.

A new era opened with T'ai-Tsung (A.D. 627–49), second ruler of the T'ang dynasty, and it was his coins that established the pattern that lasted for over twelve hundred years. The typical

Chinese 'cash' are of brass or bronze, usually about an inch in diameter, weigh between 3 and 5 g., have a broad raised edge to guard them from clipping, and bear four characters. Those above and below normally indicate the era periods, which at first were changed at irregular intervals of several years, when some propitious event justified a sovereign in proclaiming a new one, but which since the accession of the Ming dynasty in 1368 were allowed to run on so that they corresponded to each emperor's reign. The right and left characters read 'current treasure' or something similar, so that the whole inscription is to be understood as 'current treasure (of the) such-and-such period', thus providing a rough date for the coin. The inscription is sometimes extended to the reverse, often with the name of the mint, and Chinese characters were varied with Mongol ones under the Yuan dynasty (1280–1367) and Manchu ones under that of the Ch'ing (1644–1912).

The quality of Chinese cash varied greatly over the centuries, those of the Ming and of the middle Ch'ing period (late eighteenth century) being the most esteemed for the purity of their metal and excellence in striking, but they were sometimes heavily alloyed with lead or even totally replaced by iron coins of inferior value. The quantities struck by the many mints of the Empire almost surpass belief: as early as the ninth century we hear of an annual output of 135 million, and in the 1660s the output for a period of four years exceeded 2,000 million a year. Multiples, with their values inscribed on them, were sometimes issued, but they too easily lent themselves to 'debasement', i.e. to their being alloyed or made lighter than they should have been; they were con-

(a) (b)

FIG. 41. Chinese cash. (a) Kao-tsu (T'ang dynasty), 618–27. The characters read K'ai-yuan t'ung pao, i.e. 'Current treasure of the K'ai-yuan era'. The reverse is blank. Brass. 4·45 g. (b) K'ang-hsi (Ch'ing dynasty), 1662–1732. The characters read K'ang-hsi t'ung pao, and on the reverse the word 'East', i.e. the mint of Tsinan (Shantung), is inscribed in Manchu and Chinese characters. Brass. 4·46 g. The two coins show how little change had taken place in the space of a thousand years.

sequently always unpopular and never lasted for long. The unit
coins themselves were known as li but to Europeans as cash, from
the Portuguese word originally applied to the copper coins of
South India (see p. 52). Since their purchasing power was low,
they commonly circulated in strings of ten or a hundred, though
the multiple of a hundred would normally consist of 95–97 coins,
the deduction being nominally made to pay for the stringing. It
was partly this practice of stringing that explains the longevity of
the coins in circulation, since it greatly reduced the factor of wear.
The hole in the centre was square for technical reasons. The
process of casting resulted in each coin having at its edge a small
projecting piece, where the molten metal had entered the mould,
and the simplest way to render it perfectly circular was to fit coins
on to a bar of square section and turn the resulting cylinder of
metal against a chisel or file to remove all irregularities.

One would have expected that the inconvenience of having to
handle and transport huge masses of low-value coins would have
resulted in the introduction of gold and silver multiples, as was the
case with ancient Rome. The precious metals did in fact play a
quasi-monetary role from early times, though the traditional value
ratios between them, 1:10 for gold–silver and 1:100 for silver–
copper, often bore little relationship to how they were exchanged
in practice. Gold was probably never available in sufficient
quantities for a large-scale coinage, despite the yuan coinage of
Ch'u and the occasional use of gold ingots weighing one *chin*
(244 g.) in the period of the Western Han (202 B.C.–A.D. 8). A brief
issue of silver coins was made in the late twelfth century, but it was
abandoned after three years, and even after the metal became more
abundant in the fifteenth century, when Yunnan and the moun-
tainous regions of the south-west were permanently annexed to
the Empire, the use of silver coin was not revived. Ingots stamped
by merchants, on the contrary, circulated from very early times.
They are known as sycee silver, supposedly from the Cantonese
pronunciation of a word meaning 'spun silk' and perhaps originally
representing some value equivalent. The ingots normally take the
form of small, thick, slightly oval oblongs resembling a Chinese
shoe with both ends raised, a feature due to their being rocked to
and fro as they cooled, and having a maker's mark, or that of an
assayer or government bureau, impressed or sometimes written
in black ink on their upper surface. The weight system was based
on the *liang*, known to Europeans as the tael—the word was once
again a Portuguese corruption of a south Indian weight unit (*tola*)
by way of Malay *tahil*—and roughly corresponding to the Euro-

FIG. 42. Sycee silver ingot, of one tael. 36 g. Three stamps can be seen in the interior.

pean ounce but rather heavier (*c.* 35 g.), though varying considerably from place to place. Ingots of one tael are the commonest, but they are found in varying multiples up to fifty, and nineteenth-century accounts of life in the Treaty Ports describe the carrying of trays of fifty-tael ingots backwards and forwards across the cities as banking accounts were settled at the close of the day. Existing specimens are almost all modern, but the traditional shape is illustrated on paper money of the twelfth century and specimens found in excavations have been dated back to the Han period.

The invention of paper money was an even more remarkable consequence of the inconvenience of copper cash. The stimulus was similar to that of the plate-money in seventeenth-century Sweden, but China had precedence in the invention of both printing and paper, and Chinese government issues antedated those of the Bank of Sweden by at least 800 years. No notes prior to the twelfth century have survived, but Chinese historical works include illustrations of earlier specimens, those of the mid-seventh century being generally regarded as fanciful and only those of the early ninth century as reliable. In the later Middle Ages their novelty greatly impressed Marco Polo, who gives a detailed account of their manufacture. Specimens are now very rare, apart from a few of the first Ming emperor T'ai-tsu which came to light as part of a foundation deposit discovered during the sack of the Summer Palace in 1900. These have the form of large rectangles of coarse bluish-grey paper, about 13 in. high and 9 in. wide, which have on one side a design in black ink having a border of stylized dragons and arabesques and showing the value pictorially—ten strings of

FIG. 43. Chinese paper currency. Note worth one kuan, of the Hung-wu era (1368–98). Much reduced in size. The note is worn, and the vermilion imperial stamps, though visible, are not legible. The note has on the other side (not shown) a smaller printed design giving the value, corresponding to the upper part of what is shown here, and another imperial stamp.

cash—with the name of the note ('Circulating Government Note of the Ming Empire') and denomination ('One Kuan') together with details of authorization, including penalties for counterfeiting, and the date. The final authorization took the form of a large square seal stamped twice in vermilion ink on the upper and lower parts of the note. Only the earliest notes had behind them specific cash deposits, as banknotes were required to have in the West, and they suffered in consequence from depreciation through over-issue. It was this that caused their abandonment in the early fifteenth century. No specimens seem to have been printed later than the Yung-lo era (1403–25), and eighteenth-century visitors from Europe knew of them only as curiosities occasionally preserved in private houses. When the use of paper money was revived in the mid-nineteenth century the form was indeed Chinese, but the stimulus was European and the object that of supplying a hard-pressed Treasury with ready cash during the T'ai-p'ing rebellion.

It was towards the end of the same century that the traditional coinage of China succumbed to Western influence. Mexican and other Spanish-American silver dollars had been reaching China in increasing quantities since 1557, when the Portuguese were permitted to settle at Macao. At first they were melted down and turned into ingots, but in Canton and other ports they had come by the late eighteenth century to be accepted as normal currency. Specimens are often covered by the tiny chop-marks impressed by merchants and bankers who had satisfied themselves regarding their weight and fineness. The striking of equivalent Chinese coins

FIG. 44. Formosan dollar, c. 1837. Æ 29 g. The obverse type is the God of Longevity, the reverse a sacrificial vase. The inscriptions are in Chinese on the obverse, in Manchu on the reverse. There are seven chop-marks on the reverse.

began in 1837, when the Provincial Treasurer of Fukien issued in Taiwan dollars bearing the image of the God of Longevity and the inscription 'silver cake of standard purity'. In the 1860s silver dollars and corresponding small change were struck by both the T'ai-p'ing and the generals attempting to suppress their rebellion. These early coins were primarily intended as military pay, but in 1887 the Governor of Kwangtung petitioned the emperor for authority to strike silver dollars as regular currency. Permission was duly granted, and striking began at Canton in 1889. Other provincial mints followed suit, but their products were variable in weight and fineness and only accepted at a discount outside the provinces where they originated. In the late 1890s the Peking mint accepted the inevitable and itself started striking dollars and appropriate fractions, together with very small numbers of gold coins. Although the design was basically Eastern—the type was the imperial dragon—the form was Western and the inscriptions were normally in English as well as Chinese. The minting of the old type of cash was abandoned at about the same time—they were replaced, for example, at Canton in 1900, by copper cents, imitated from those of Hong Kong, worth ten cash and struck instead of being cast. Eventually, with the establishment of the Republic in 1912, the square-holed coins which had endured for over two millennia were formally demonetized, although it may be suspected that their final disappearance was brought about more by the debasement of the cent and the operation of Gresham's Law than by government decree.

Derivatives of Chinese Coinage

Chinese influence determined the basic character of three other coinages of the Far East, those of Korea, Japan, and Annam. This was in part a natural result of the superior wealth, power, and culture of the Middle Kingdom, in part a consequence of the fact that while these neighbours of China spoke different languages they used what was essentially the same script, so that the characters on Chinese coins are intelligible beyond China's frontiers, just as arabic numerals are understood throughout the West despite being vocalized differently in each national language. Almost everywhere in the Far East coinage started from the same basis, a circulating medium consisting of copper coins with a square hole in the centre, but the details of its history vary from one country to another.

Korea, the closest of China's neighbours and by no means

always forming a single political unit, was the most completely under Chinese influence. It was the only one, in very early times, to make use of a utensil (knife) currency, and in the early fourteenth century its rulers attempted, though unsuccessfully, to introduce the use of paper. The earliest locally minted coins were iron and copper cash struck in A.D. 996, the 15th year of Songjong, the sixth king of the Koryo dynasty. They are purely Chinese in type, having on one side four characters meaning 'Lasting, original, heavy treasure' and on the other two characters reading *Tong Guk*, i.e. 'Eastern Country', a Chinese name for Korea. These were succeeded (998–1009) by very similar coins with the inscription 'Beginning original treasure'. In each case the first two words of the inscriptions had been used much earlier for era-names by T'ang emperors of China, but it is not clear that they are actual imitations of the coins of these eras, though they are commonly so described. A century later there was another brief period of minting (1097–1105), but coinage played only a marginal role in the economy and for several hundred years coins introduced from China were more important than local issues.

Not until the seventeenth century does the continuous sequence of Korean coins begin. The first issue, that of 1625–33, with the inscription 'Choson (i.e. Korean) currency', was succeeded by a long-lived and immensely abundant coinage known as the *Sang p'ong t'ong bo*, i.e. 'Always even currency', which lasted from 1633 to 1891. The coins, known colloquially as *yopchon*, i.e. 'leaf coins', had usually the values of one, two, or five mun, the Korean term for the Chinese character usually rendered 'cash', and form a series much favoured by collectors, since they were issued by a great variety of government agencies and from 1732 onwards usually bear furnace and series numbers on the reverse. In 1883 there was even a brief issue of silver coins of the same type to the value of one, two, or three chon, the chon being a tenth of a Korean tael. Patterns for a series of gold, silver, and copper denominations on the European model, the designs being basically similar to those of the contemporary coins of Japan, were prepared in 1883, essentially as a sequel to the treaties of 1882–4 which 'opened up' Korea to the Great Powers, but the first actually to go into circulation were those dated 1886 or 1892.

The early history of Japanese coinage is not unlike that of Korean. Coins of the Chinese pattern, bearing characters meaning 'Wado-Initial Treasure', were first officially issued in A.D. 708 in a flush of enthusiasm following the opening of copper-mines in the province of Musashi which were so productive that the name of

the era was changed to Wado ('soft copper'). Between that date
and 958 there were twelve issues of what are traditionally known
as the *Honcho* (or *Kocho*) *Juni Sen* ('Twelve Japanese Imperial [or
Antique] Coins'). Like their Chinese prototypes they were basically of bronze, but a few silver coins were included in the first two
issues (708, 720) and even some gold in the second, though until
recently only a single specimen of the latter, found during repairs
to a temple at Nara in 1794 and now in the imperial collection, was
known to exist. The last issues were half the weight of the earlier
ones, and much inferior in style and fabric. Minting ceased after
the twelfth issue, and for the next six centuries such coins as Japan
needed were imported from China, though in fact the chief forms
of currency were rice and cloth. Copper was at first, quite simply,
in short supply, since the influx from newly discovered mines was
offset by its constant withdrawal from circulation for domestic and
religious uses, especially with the spread of Buddhism. The giant
statue of Buddha erected at Nara in 1195 required over 900,000 lb.
of copper, and 330,000 coins were melted down for the making of
the great bell at Kamakura in 1235. Not till the late thirteenth
century was there a turn for the better, for the output of domestic
copper-mines was high and the use of paper in China freed much
copper coin for export. Japanese temple records of this period
show a marked tendency for Chinese cash to be substituted for
payments in kind. Even under the Ming emperors Chinese coins
could on occasion be imported on a huge scale, ostensibly as 'gifts'
to the Shoguns but actually in payment for Japanese swords, which
were highly appreciated in China. A mission in 1434 returned
with a 'gift' of 30 million cash, another in 1451 with 60 million, and
yet another in 1480, after a special plea of need, with 101 million.
The situation was indeed paradoxical, for Japan was at that time
exporting copper to China on a large scale, but the Japanese
population persisted in preferring imported coin to their own
occasional and chaotic local issues. For large payments gold and
silver ingots were used, together with gold dust made up in brocade
bags of regular size.

A new and more effective coinage was introduced in the late
sixteenth century. The period over which it continued corresponds
roughly to that of the Tokugawa Shogunate (1603–1868), but it
took its origins in the Azuchi-Momoyama period of national
unification that preceded this (1568–1600). The causes were in
part political, in part economic. The economic causes were a
sudden and unprecedented expansion of copper and silver production in the period after 1526, partly as a result of the discovery

of new mines and partly through improved methods of smelting which allowed the recovery of silver from argentiferous copper ores. The increase in gold output came a little later, mainly after 1575. On the political side were the careers of the three great soldier-statesmen, Oda Nobunaga (*ob.* 1582), Toyotomi Hideyoshi (*ob.* 1598), and Tokugawa Ieyasu (*ob.* 1616), who between them created the Japanese state as it was to last till the nineteenth century by breaking the power of rival feudal lords and of the great Buddhist monasteries. After 1600, the Tokugawa shoguns ruled the country from their own centre of power at Edo (Tokyo). All three were very conscious of the economic element in the maintenance of political power and of the need to control the new sources of wealth; indeed, the correspondence of many of the great feudatories of the period is unexpectedly full of details regarding the discovery of new mines and the profits to be drawn from them. A detailed account of Hideyoshi's income at the time of his death in 1598 shows it to have included no less than 19,000 troy oz. of newly mined gold and over 400,000 oz. of silver. It was consequently natural that all three rulers should have exerted themselves to further the use of coin. In 1569 Nobunaga prohibited the continued use of rice as a medium of exchange in his own dominions, ordering the employment of gold or silver for all transactions above a certain level and copper for those below it, and attempting to fix a standard exchange rate between them.

The main gold coins of the new era took the form of large, oval plates (*ban*) of cast metal, stamped near the edges with the crest of the *kiri* flower and sometimes other symbols, and inscribed in black ink with the mark of value and the name of the mint superintendant or other issuing authority. They were normally of two denominations, the oban ('large plate') and the koban ('small plate'), an oban being about 17 cm. long and 10 cm. broad and weighing some 160 g. The koban was the equivalent of the ryo, the standard unit of value in gold, and one oban was worth ten kobans. The earliest known dated oban is of the 14th year of the Tensho era, i.e. 1586. But the records of the Tamon In temple at Nara show there were gold coins already in circulation by 1572, and when Tokugawa Ieyasu gained control of the gold-producing province of Kai in 1582 it was reported that its previous master Takeda had minted over a quarter of a million gold pieces, some specimens of which, stamped with his mark, are known. Oban and koban pieces continued to be minted down to 1863, though the quality of their gold is often poor and their weights very variable. Fractions were struck from time to time, mainly in the eighteenth

FIG. 45. Tensho oban, 1573–92. N 165 g. About half-size. The four crests at the edge represent the *kiri* flower. The inscription in black ink includes a statement of the value (10 ryo, i.e. nominally 40,000 mon or copper coins) and the signature of a member of the Goto family, superintendant of the mint. Since the inscription could be rewritten only on payment of a fee, the coins were usually wrapped in cotton wool or other soft material to prevent it being erased. The reverse (not shown) has usually one or two stamps.

and nineteenth centuries, the most familiar ones having the form
of small rectangular pieces of metal with types usually involving
one or more *kiri* flowers, an era mark, and a statement of value.
The usual denominations are one or two bu (ichi-bu, ni-bu;
bu = 'part'), but there are still smaller pieces of one or two shu
(is-shu, ni-shu; *shu* = 'fraction', i.e. 1/16th of a ryo). In addition
to the imperial issues there was a considerable amount of provincial gold, much of it of great historical interest.

Fig. 46. Japanese silver coins. (a) Go-momme gin, dated Meiwa Year 2, i.e. 1765.
18·16 g. (b) Is-shu gin, dated to the Ansei era, *c.* 1854. 8·48 g. The value (1 shu) is
indicated on the reverse. Momme is the name of a unit of weight (*c.* 3·75 g.).

The earliest silver coins are contemporary with the earliest gold,
but most of them are known only from contemporary records and
were presumably issued by local lords in silver-producing areas.
Very rare silver coins of the same type as the copper were issued in
1587 and 1593, but they did not prove popular, and the main silver
issues assumed quite different forms. The higher denomination
(*cho-gin*), issued from 1601 onwards into the nineteenth century,
takes the form of large oval pieces of slovenly fabric, with era dates
and other identification stamps. They have often been heavily
chop-marked in circulation. The smaller denominations, which all
date from the eighteenth and nineteenth centuries, are rectangular,
like the lower denominations of gold, and apart from the five-
momme piece (*go-momme gin*) of 1765 are named as are the gold,
but with the addition of *gin* ('silver') after the term of value
(ichi-bu gin, etc.).

Finally, side by side with the coins of precious metals there were
huge issues of subsidiary cast coins of the traditional type, made
almost indifferently in copper, bronze, brass, or iron. Much

unofficial minting of bronze had always taken place, to judge by
constant legislation against counterfeiting, so that there was no
lack of available skill. The issues of Hideyoshi (1587, 1592) seem
to have been of little importance, but the Keicho-Tsuho coinage
of 1606 was of sufficient consequence to justify legislation pros-
cribing the use of Chinese cash (1608). In 1636, during the
Kan'ei period which had opened in 1624, there began the series
known from its inscription as the Kan'ei-Tsuho, 'Current Treasure
of Permanent Liberality', which continued from 1636 to 1859
with many variations in size, metal, design, and style, according
to the mint and period at which it was produced. Some idea of the
number of these subsidiary coins in circulation can be gauged from
the fact that nearly 485 million pieces of the variant known as the
Tenho-Tsuho were issued in the sixth and following years of the
Tenho period (1835 ff.). An interesting variation in design was the
use of wave patterns on the reverses of some eighteenth- and
nineteenth-century issues. Some early-nineteenth-century local
issues are large and oval in shape and have characters only above
and beneath the central hole, instead of to its right and left as well.

The adoption of Western patterns of coinage was a natural
consequence of the fall of the Tokugawa Shogunate in 1868, since
one of the main objects of the Meiji reforms was to bring about the
modernization of the country. Modern minting machinery was
installed in the Tokyo mint under British supervision in 1869, and
in 1870 the new types of silver coin went into circulation, the unit
being the yen of 100 sen, corresponding to the dollar, and fractions
of 5, 10, 20, and 50 sen being struck. The types bore on the obverse
a dragon pattern surrounded by a circular inscription giving the
country, date (3 Meiji), and value, and on the reverse a sun, the
national emblem of Japan, in a wreath with a chrysanthemum
above. Gold and copper coins were added in 1872 and 1873/4
respectively, but the process of adjustment was difficult, since the
old gold–silver ratio in Japan had been markedly different from
that obtaining in the rest of the world and the weights of the silver
coins had to be drastically reduced in 1873. Although some of the
most recent types are pictorial in character, with a view of Mount
Fuji or the Phoenix Hall of one of the great temples near Kyoto,
it is still felt inappropriate to place the reigning emperor's head
on the coins of his country.

The final coinage which was profoundly under Chinese influence was that of Annam. This state was formally part of China
until the tenth century A.D., making use in consequence of the
imperial coinage, as indeed it was often to do in the future.

Indigenous Annamese coinage began in the late tenth century and lasted without substantial change for over 900 years. It consisted of cash on the Chinese model, with inscriptions giving an era date, and is chiefly remarkable for the variety of base metals used in its fabrication, the latest issues consisting almost exclusively of zinc and being very fragile to handle. The coins were known locally as *dong*, i.e. 'current money', and were customarily made up in strings of 600 known as *kwan*, but they were called *sapèques* by the French from their name in Malay (*sa-pek*). A limited gold and silver coinage was introduced during the reign of Nguyen Phuc-Anh (1801–20), an able ruler who brought to an end several decades of civil war and assumed the era name of Gia-Long. The coins of both metals issued by him and his successors were rectangular in form, geared in weight to the luong of *c.* 38 g., the Annamese equivalent of the tael, and furnished with inscriptions giving their date and value. The Minh-Mang emperor in the 1830s added to these some very rare struck piastres and half-piastres, the earliest local 'dollars' to be struck by any ruler in the Far East, having as their types an imperial dragon accompanied by an era-numeral and a sun surrounded by four characters meaning 'Current money—Minh-Mang'. Tuʻ-Duʻc (1848–83) issued heavy specimens of the ordinary cash type weighing between 20 g. and 30 g. and forming multiples of from 20 to 60 of the smaller dong, but they are easily confused with very similar medals or charms which were made in enormous numbers at about the same period. A full series of coins of Western type came in with the French occupation (1882), but the local preference for the old copper cash was so strong that this continued to be officially minted, with its square central hole, up to the end of the Second World War, thus long outlasting its existence in its original home.

4
Types and Inscriptions

The primary function of type and inscription is that of making clear to users the identity of coins. This is not the same thing as identifying coins in a manner intelligible to the modern numismatist. The user would know without further assistance whether the *Willelmus rex* on a coin was a king of England, or of Scotland, or of Sicily; a later scholar would not. The amount of information required by users would depend upon circumstances. On coins likely to circulate only locally, all that was necessary would be a design different from those of earlier issues and of neighbouring mints. On coins likely to circulate widely the identification would tend to be more detailed and specific, though some types would have become in their day so well known that simple identification would suffice. Three further considerations in the study of coin types have to be taken into account. One is the fact that coins can serve as instruments of propaganda, so that the complexity of their designs and inscriptions normally exceeds the minimum required for simple identification. Another is the fact that not all the details are intended to instruct the public: indications of mint or issue are usually more or less private marks placed on the coins for the benefit of the administration or intended to facilitate the working of the mint. A third is the existence of imitative coinages, where the issuer does his best to avoid differentiating his own products from those of his model since he hopes to benefit by having one confused with the other. The designs of such coins cannot therefore be interpreted solely in the context of the mint responsible for them, and create problems of mint attribution that are discussed in Chapter 6.

It is customary to classify the elements of coin design under the three headings of *type*, *inscription* or *legend*, and *accessory symbols*. The first, which comes from a Greek word meaning something struck or impressed, is the technical term applied to the main designs on both faces of the coin. The second explains itself, and the third covers such minor features as date, mint-marks, and issue marks. All three are not necessarily present. Most Muslim coins have no type, and a high proportion of coins have no mint or privy mark. The central part of the coin, which is occupied by the type, is known as the *field*. When the type is placed on a line, like the seated Britannia on a 50p piece, the space between the line and the edge of the coin is known as the *exergue*, from two Greek words implying 'outside the work', i.e. outside what is really important, in the same sense as the French *hors d'œuvre*. It is customarily abbreviated in coin descriptions to *ex*. The type is sometimes separated from the inscription by a linear or beaded border, which on medieval coins is often very elaborate and known as the *tressure*. It is usually cusped and can be described as a tressure of, for example, eight lobes or arches; when there are only three or four lobes it is more simply designated a trefoil or quatrefoil. Accessory symbols are for the most part functional in character, but type and inscription are usually in part non-functional, going far beyond the need for mere coin identification.

Types

It is impossible to comprise the great variety of coin types under any single formula, or even to categorize them in any satisfactory fashion. The division into principal and secondary types seems an obvious one, but while in many cases such a distinction can be easily made, it cannot in all. The figure of a pagan deity on an ancient Greek coin, of Christ or the Virgin on Byzantine coins, of a patron saint on some city coinages of the Middle Ages, was each in a very real sense thought to take precedence over the city badge or imperial figure on the other face of the coin, yet it was un-questionably the city authorities, or the emperors in the case of Byzantium, who were responsible for the issue of the coin. Nor can types be divided into the two categories of functional and non-functional, since while there are a few that are distinctly one or other—the mark of value on a sixth-century Byzantine follis is solely functional, the elaborate cross fleury on the reverse of a late medieval écu is purely decorative—the vast majority are to some degree both. The best that can be done is to note and comment on some of the main categories that are found.

A representation of the issuing authority, either general or

particular, is the most common of all coin types. General representations cover such things as the emblem of the state—Athena's
owl on the coins of Athens, the fleur-de-lis on coins of medieval
Florence, the figure of Britannia on many modern British coins—
whilst specific representations may be the head of a sovereign or
his personal badge or coat of arms. Where both general and
specific representations occur it is normally the specific one that is
effectively if not logically the more significant. The queen's head
is more important than either Britannia or the royal coat of arms,
St. John than the fleur-de-lis of Florence. Symbolic representations do not vary greatly save in minor details, else they will cease
to be recognizable, but personal ones can vary almost indefinitely.
French gold coins of the fourteenth century may show the king
seated on a low throne, or on several varieties of throne with
elaborately decorated back and sides, or standing beneath a
canopy, or on horseback. When characterized portraiture is in
vogue a number of different portraits will be used in the course of
the reign. There are times when monograms are in fashion, as
under the Carolingians, when portraiture was rare and the king's
monogram was envisaged as authorizing the coins in the same
manner as it did the charters that he issued.

The second most important group of coin types consists of
religious representations, which have been used from the earliest
times down to the present. Figures of deities abound on the coins
of classical antiquity; the Zorostrian fire-altar with attendants is
a mark of Sassanian coinage; crosses in endless variety are
characteristic of European coinage. Many issuing authorities have
patron deities or saints: the head of Athena on coins of ancient
Athens and Corinth, the standing figure of Poseidon with a
thunderbolt on those of Paestum (Poseidonia), St. Ambrose with
his whip scourging the Arians on those of medieval Milan, St.
Stephen and his stones on bracteates of Halberstadt. Sometimes
the symbols of such persons are substituted for the individual: the
stag or bee, sacred to Artemis, on coins of ancient Ephesus, the
lion of St. Mark on coins of Venice, the crossed keys of St. Peter
on some coins of Rome. Such symbols in course of time tend to
become traditional, and cannot necessarily be taken as reliable
guides to the religious beliefs of the societies in which they are
used. Certainly they were often misunderstood by their users. A
contemporary writer tells us that the seated Constantinopolis on
solidi of the Byzantine emperor Justin II was thought by some to
represent Venus, and one can reasonably wonder whether the
elaborate paraphernalia of gestures and attributes associated with

religious types under the Roman Empire was intelligible outside a very limited circle of users.

The third major group of coin types consists of those which may be described as pictorial in character. Their incidence is very variable. The most conspicuous and elaborate series is that of Roman coins of the late Republic and the Empire, a few of which have been described in Chapter 2 (pp. 19–21). These were for the most part commemorative in character, in the sense that they were intended to be relevant to the particular occasions when the coins were issued. A different form of pictorial type is found on those medieval coin series where regular coin renewals (*renovationes* or *mutationes monetae*) were practised, since the withdrawal and replacement of issues at very short intervals made necessary a huge repertory of different designs on which to draw. These might often be variations on a single theme—St. Maurice shown in different guises on Magdeburg bracteates, the horseman types on coins of Thuringia, the different forms of lion and lion monument on those of medieval Brunswick—but they are sometimes purely fanciful, with an endless variety of animal and floral decorations which do no more than separate one issue from another and would not, without evidence of date and localization from coin finds, help us at all in deciding when or by whom such coins were struck. Pictorial types also include the variety of natural objects which in some ancient and modern coin series have been used to call attention to the sources of a state's wealth, from the grapes on coins of classical Soli and the silphium plant on those of Cyrene to the salmon and farm animals which form the reverse types of the coins of modern Eire.

There are, finally, purely functional types consisting of marks of value, often occupying the whole reverse of the coin. They are characteristic of the copper coinage of Byzantium for a period of three and a half centuries, from their introduction by Anastasius I in 498 to their replacement by inscriptions across the field under the Emperor Theophilus in the 830s. They came again to be widely used in Europe in the nineteenth century, though in modern times the value in figures tends to be supplemented by the name of the denomination in words. Differing reverse types are perhaps a commoner way of distinguishing between denominations, but they have the disadvantage of not making plain the precise values of the coins or the relationships between them.

In any study of the meaning of coin types there are two possible complications that have to be kept in mind. One, the fact that types sometimes make no allusion to state or ruler and have purely

differentiating functions, has already been alluded to. The other
is the amount of borrowing, in the form of direct copying, that
frequently takes place. The best-known groups of imitative
coinages are those of barbarian peoples, who may be in either
commercial or political contact with more civilized states or in
actual occupation of parts of these. Examples of the first are the
Celtic imitations of Macedonian philippoi (above, p. 16, Fig. 7)
and South Arabian imitations of Athenian owls; examples of the
second are the Germanic imitations of late Roman gold coins and
the early Arab imitations of Byzantine folles. In their early stages
these imitations may be virtually indistinguishable from the
originals, which can result in serious errors of attribution. Imitations also occur in more sophisticated societies, when they involve
the adoption of coin types quite foreign to the usual issues of the
state in question. The standing figure of St. John and the fleur-
de-lis were originally proper to the gold florin of Florence, for the
city was dedicated to the Baptist and the flower was a pun (*flos*)
on the city's name. This did not prevent the coin type being
borrowed by over a hundred mints in other parts of Europe during
the fourteenth century, despite the fact that neither the Baptist
nor the lily were in any way related to the regular armorial devices
of, say, Flanders or Lübeck. There may also be direct copying
with no intention to deceive, simply because a die-sinker has seen
a type that pleased him. One may instance the moneyers of Edward
the Confessor reproducing on a silver penny the seated Constantinopolis from a solidus of the sixth-century Emperor Justin
II, or twelfth-century Norman kings of Sicily reproducing the
lion's mask of ancient coins of Messina and the date-palm of those
of Carthage.

Inscriptions

Coin inscriptions cannot be separated from types, since they are
alike in their purposes and in many features of their evolution. It
is just as difficult to divide them up into clear-cut categories,
though the decorative element is in general smaller and the
tendency to use them as vehicles for political propaganda rather
greater, since words are usually more explicit than designs. In
many cases, indeed, they are there to amplify and interpret the
types themselves, which users of the coins would have found it
difficult to do without such help.

The most obviously functional inscriptions are those which

assist or even replace the type in identifying and authenticating coins. They do this primarily by recording the name of the authorities under which they were issued: ΑΘΕ on coins of ancient Athens, Q (a dialect form of K) on those of ancient Corinth, *Florentia* on those of medieval Florence, *Ludovicus Dei Gra(tia) Francorum rex* on coins of Louis XII of France. Originally the coin—or sometimes the device on it—was thought of as being 'of' the people referred to, so that the inscription was notionally in the genitive plural: thus ΑΘΕ should be expanded into 'of the Athenians'. We know this from the fact that the word was sometimes inscribed in full, for example, ΚΑΤΑΝΙΩΝ, 'of the Catanians', on a coin of Catania in Sicily. This usage persisted into Hellenistic times, when personal names are normally placed on the reverses, separate from the royal portraits on the obverses, and are also in the genitive: ΑΛΕΞΑΝΔΡΟΥ, 'of Alexander', ΒΑΣΙΛΕΩΣ ΔΗΜΗΤΡΙΟΥ, 'of King Demetrius' . But the transition to a purely identificatory nominative was made quite early in many states, and at Rome the practice to which we are accustomed, that of labelling the head of the ruler with his name and titles in the nominative case, became fully established under Augustus. Variations have always been possible—sometimes the inscription has been thought of as an acclamation and put in the vocative or dative case—and laudatory or descriptive epithets have often been popular. The titles on Parthian coins, though couched in Greek, have a typically oriental flavour—Great King, the Just, the Well-Doer, the Saviour, the Philhellene—while the details of those affected by some Roman emperors provide the main clue to the dating of their coins (see p. 21). The incorporation of titles and epithets normally makes much abbreviation necessary, so that the inscriptions on Roman imperial coins have often to be interpreted with the aid of information provided by the study of classical epigraphy. This resort to abbreviation is found at its most grotesque on the coinage of seventeenth- and eighteenth-century Germany, when princes sometimes abbreviated their numerous titles so drastically that they become a kind of puzzle which only reference books can solve. Those of Duke Frederick of Württemberg (1593–1608) are reduced on some of his coins to v.g.g.f.h.z.w.v.t.g.z.m., i.e. Von Gottes Gnaden Friedrich, Herzog zu Württemberg und Teck, Graf zu Mömpelgard.

Similar to state and royal inscriptions are those which record the names of magistrates or moneyers. Generally the names of such individuals take the form of initials, monograms, or personal devices, and so appear less conspicuously as accessory symbols, but there are a few coin series in which they are used in the inscriptions themselves: the New Style coinage of Athens, the coinage of the Merovingian Franks, English pennies from the time of Offa to that of Henry III, a few Low Country deniers of the twelfth and thirteenth centuries. Another functional use of coin inscriptions is to record the denomination. It is rare in antiquity and the early Middle Ages, but on Muslim coins the name of the denomination has usually been incorporated into the date-and-mint formula, and it has been common in the West since the creation of multiples of the penny in the thirteenth century. In the fourteenth century we begin to find such inscriptions as GROSSI PRAGENSES—the plural is unexplained—on Prager groschen and BURGENSIS FORTIS on the bourgeois fort of Philip IV of France, and from then onwards there has been a slow and irregular evolution to the normal modern use of the name of the denomination as part or the whole of the reverse inscription. Since such identifications are meant to be generally understood, they are almost always in the vernacular, even though the obverse inscription, with the name and title of the ruler, may follow tradition and still be in Latin.

Mint names forming part of the inscription are unusual, though they do occur in some coinages, either in full, as on the coinage of Visigothic Spain, or abbreviated, as on English coins between the tenth and thirteenth centuries. A still rarer type of inscription involving a place-name is one specifying the source of metal. Isolated examples occur in antiquity and the Middle Ages, and there are elaborate mining inscriptions on the long series of silver talers—they are known as *Ausbeutemünzen*, literally 'Exploitation-coins'—of Brunswick-Lüneburg and other German states of the seventeenth and eighteenth centuries, and the *Flüssmünzen*, gulden made from the gold-washings in the Rhine (EX AVRO RHENI) and other rivers, which are mainly of the nineteenth century. A different source of metal is sometimes alluded to on siege (obsidional) coins, as in the inscription AVS DEN GEFAESEN DER KIRCHE VND BVRGER ('From the plate of the Church and the citizens') on ducats and talers of Frankfurt am Main struck during the French invasion of 1796.

Allusions to the type are sometimes rather infantile in character, as when on medieval coins inscriptions may occasionally name some quite ordinary object (BACVLVS beside a bishop's crozier, LEO beneath a lion), but they would be welcome on many Greek coins, where the identity of deities is often far from clear. They are common on Roman imperial coins, with their wealth of personifications as reverse types, and are most valuable when they explain or amplify a type instead of merely identifying it. Two of the most famous examples are the inscription EID(ibus) MAR(tiis), accompanying the daggers and the Cap of Liberty on the coins struck by Brutus in Greece after the murder of Caesar (p. 20, Fig. 11b), and IVDAEA CAPTA on coins of Vespasian commemorating the successful ending of the Jewish War, but these are only two amongst many hundreds in a series where, without their aid, we would often be quite unable to understand the type. Interpretative inscriptions recur from time to time in the Middle Ages and enjoyed a certain vogue at the Renaissance. In the latter period, however, the passion for *imprese* (personal devices) and *emblemata* overreached itself, and some coin types remain as obscure, even with the help of inscriptions, as they would have been without them.

Other inscriptions contain in varying proportions what can best be characterized as supplicatory, propagandist, and talismanic elements. Purely supplicatory inscriptions are uncommon, though there are examples: 'The Redemption of Zion' on Jewish coins, EN TOVTO NIKA ('In this sign conquer') on folles of the Byzantine emperor Constans II, DOMINVS MIHI ADIVTOR ET EGO DESPICIAM INIMICOS MEOS (Ps. 117:7) on coins of a number of Spanish, Portuguese, and Neapolitan monarchs in the fifteenth century. The phrase IN GOD WE TRUST, added by Secretary Salmon P. Chase to American coins during the Civil War and still on them, is a modern example. Religious propaganda has been most consistently used in the inscriptions of Muslim coins, which since the end of the seventh century have proclaimed to those capable of reading them the main articles of the faith, but in the West the element of 'propaganda', in the religious devices that came to form traditional reverse inscriptions from Carolingian times onwards, has usually been only implicit in their sources. Moral injunctions have been occasionally used on coins of the modern period. The three-shilling piece of Münster of 1602 contained an invitation to charity couched in biblical if highly materialistic terms, *Qui dat pauperi non indigebat* (Prov. 27:7), and the Geneva coinage of 1794 shows a curious mingling of Calvinism with the principles of the Physiocrats in such inscriptions as *Travaille et économise* and *L'oisiveté est un vol*. Proudhon would not have disagreed, though he expressed himself more pungently.

It is probably true to say that the vast majority of Western coin inscriptions are religious in content but talismanic in intention. The inscriptions themselves range from such simple phrases as *Signum Dei Vivi* (Rev. 7:2) on feudal coins of Maine or *A et O*, *principium et finis* (Rev. 1:8) on those of Siena to lengthy biblical verses (e.g. *Honor regis iudicium diligit* (Ps. 98:4) on Neapolitan gigliati) or liturgical phrases, like the great acclamation *Christus vincit, Christus regnat, Christus imperat* from the Coronation *Laudes*, which formed the reverse inscription of French gold coins from St. Louis to the Revolution (cf. p. 29, Fig. 23). This kind of inscription, indeed, is not necessarily religious in character: *Parcere subiectis et debellare superbos* from Virgil's *Aeneid* (vi. 853) occurs on the £20 piece of James VI of Scotland, and, more disconcertingly, *Roma Caput Mundi* on common Aachen pennies of Frederick Barbarossa. The precise reason for the choice usually escapes us, but sometimes it derives from the circumstances of the ruler concerned or some magical quality attributed to the verse itself. The inscription on the noble (below, p. 84), with its allusion to Jesus' mysterious escape from his enemies (Luke 4:30), was regarded in the fourteenth century as likely to be efficacious in warding off the attentions of highway robbers. *Decus et tutamen* ('An ornament and a protection'), the highly appropriate edge inscription of the higher denominations of English gold from the reign of Charles II onwards, was suggested to the Mint authorities by John Evelyn, who had seen it used as a device on the book-plate of Cardinal Richelieu.

Accessory Symbols

While the type of a coin, with or without the name of the state or ruler responsible for making it legal tender, is its guarantee so far as the general public is concerned, the administration may wish to keep a closer eye on the circumstances of its issue. It often does this with the help of accessory symbols supplementary to the type or inscription. These are usually intended as a protection against fraud on the part of mint officials, but sometimes their object is to identify a particular issue, often because it is debased, and a few, like engravers' marks, are completely non-functional from the government's point of view. The terminology is very imprecise, such expressions as 'mint-mark' being used where no mint identification is in question and 'privy mark' (Fr. *point secret*) when their details are plain to any attentive user, although their precise meaning may be concealed. They may be roughly classified as follows:

Mint-marks. These, in the strict sense of the word, indicate at what mint a coin has been struck. Usually when a state has only one mint, no mint-mark is employed. When several mints exist they may be distinguished from each other in various ways. The most usual is by a letter or combination of letters. This was the regular method in antiquity, and in modern times since the sixteenth century. Normally the letters are the initials or first letters of the mint in question, like TES on Byzantine coins to indicate Thessalonica or CC on American coins to indicate the short-lived mint of Carson City. Occasionally they are quite arbitrary, like A on eighteenth- and nineteenth-century Prussian coins to indicate Berlin or F on French coins between 1540 and 1738 to indicate Angers. Sometimes local badges are preferred to letters, such as the severed hand on Low Country coins struck at Antwerp or the ship on late medieval French coins of Bordeaux. In France, between 1380 and 1540, there existed an elaborate system by which the mints were indicated by a pellet or annulet placed beneath a particular letter in the legend. One under the first letter would mean Crémieu, one under the second letter would mean Romans, and so on. These *points secrets* were abolished in 1540 and replaced by a system of letters in the field, A for Paris, B for Rouen, etc.

Officina marks. In a large mint organized into a number of 'shops' (Lat. *officinae*), it has sometimes been considered worth while to put on each coin a mark to show in which of the workshops it was struck. The practice was very characteristic of Roman imperial mints between the fourth and seventh centuries A.D., the *officinae* being numbered and usually indicated by Greek numerals Α, Β, Γ, etc.) at the end of the inscription or following the mint-mark (p. 23, Fig. 14a) or in the field.

Magistrate's, moneyer's, and mint-master's marks. These three series, between which it is not possible to differentiate very clearly, have in common the object of identifying the person legally responsible for a particular issue. His name may be written in full, as were those of Athenian magistrates on the later New Style tetradrachms of the second and first centuries B.C., but more often initials or badges are used, as on Venetian, Genoese, and Florentine coinage in the later Middle Ages. At an earlier stage there may simply be small objects placed in the field, like the wedges, pellets, or annulets placed beside the leg or elbow of the seated figure of Christ on the reverses of Venetian grossi of the thirteenth and fourteenth centuries.

Issue or emission marks. These served the purpose of distinguishing
one issue of otherwise similar coins from another, either for the
purpose of financial control, as in late medieval England, or
because of debasement, when the metallic content of coins was
altered while their general appearance was left unchanged and the
attempt was made to keep them at their customary value. Since
mint and exchequer officials would need to distinguish between
the coins of varying alloy it was usual to make some scarcely
noticeable alteration in the design, such as changing the punctuation marks or the shapes of individual letters. Sooner or later the
merchant community would discover what had taken place, and
merchants' books of the fifteenth and sixteenth centuries contain
long and not always very accurate lists of such privy marks and
the supposed finenesses of the coins that bore them.

Dates. These may be regarded as a special form of emission mark,
since they indicate when a coin was struck, though they do not
necessarily imply any change in fineness or value. Ancient coins,
when they are dated, are usually so only incidentally. The
magistrates' names on Athenian coins were intended as measures
of control, and such dating as can be extracted from Roman
imperial coins is usually no more than a deduction from lists of
imperial honours in coin inscriptions (below, p. 141). But certain
Syrian series are dated, for reasons of general policy rather than
mint control, either by the Seleucid era (from 312 B.C.) or by a
local city calendar or by the regnal year of a particular ruler, and
the tradition of dating remained strong in the Near East. It appears
on the coinage of the Sassanians, on the coinage of Alexandria
under Roman rule from Augustus to Diocletian, and on Byzantine
coinage from 539 to the early eighth century. In each of these cases
the dating is by the regnal years of the sovereign. Almost all Islamic
coins, which continued in the same tradition, are dated, but in the
Christian West the practice appeared only very late, and was slow
to spread. Dating by the Christian era, apart from an isolated
thirteenth-century example from Denmark, started at the mint of
Aachen in 1373 and up to the end of the sixteenth century remained practically confined to Germany and the Low Countries.
The first English dated coin is of 1547, the first French regal one
of 1549, and in neither country was dating systematically applied
to the whole of the coinage till the nineteenth century. Obsidional
coins are occasionally dated by the month of issue, the most
conspicuous example being the Irish gun-money of James II.

Die marks. The particular dies used in striking coins have rarely been considered worth marking as such, though they can be recognized and their characteristics listed by the modern scholar where he finds it necessary to do it. Occasionally it has been done by the mint. In England, from 1864 to 1878 inclusive, the dies used for the gold and for all the silver denominations except the half-crown and the threepence were numbered, a fresh series being begun each year. The numbers, in tiny figures, are usually placed below the tie of the wreath on the reverse.

Mining marks. It is only very rarely that coins record the source of the metal from which they were made. This may be written out in full in the inscription, but is more usually indicated by a symbol or an inscription in small characters. Two examples are the elephant or elephant and castle beneath the bust on gold coins of Charles II and the word VIGO beneath that of Queen Anne on English gold of 1702 and 1703. In the first case the metal came from the Guinea coast, the elephant and castle being the crest of the Guinea Company, while in the second it came from the Spanish galleons captured at Vigo Bay on 12 October 1702. In both cases there was a strong element of advertisement in putting the information in question on the coins.

Engravers' marks. These are rare, as they were of no importance from the point of view of the mint, and their insertion implies a degree of self-consciousness and self-assertion on the part of coin designers which has not usually been allowed free play by public authorities. In classical times, a whole series of artists' signatures occur on the coins of Syracuse of the fifth and fourth centuries B.C., usually in minute letters on some part of the design or in the field, but the practice was virtually confined to Sicily. In modern times a good deal of work is signed, or at least initialled. Usually the signature is inconspicuous, like the *W.W.* or *W.Wyon* on the truncation of the beautiful 'young portrait' of Victoria. Unfortunately the practice of signing coin dies, unlike that of signing medal dies, does not go back as far as the Renaissance, so that almost all the magnificent Italian coin portraiture of the fifteenth and sixteenth centuries is anonymous and only in a few series is there documentary evidence allowing us to determine with certainty the names of the artists who worked in the mints.

It goes without saying that the study of symbols, mint-marks, and monograms is a difficult one, and often only prolonged research will show to which specific group any particular series belongs. They have often misled numismatists in the past. Tetradrachms of Alexander the Great have on their obverse a large number of symbols, which Ludwig Müller, an eminent nineteenth-century scholar who was keeper of the Royal Collection at Copenhagen, attributed on various grounds to different cities of the Empire: the prow to Magnesia, the thunderbolt to Pella, the amphora to Lamia, the cantharus to Mende, the helmet to Scione, and so on. These attributions, although doubted by many because of their conjectural character, were still widely accepted until E. T. Newell, most distinguished of American numismatists, showed in a modestly entitled monograph ('Reattribution of Certain Tetradrachms of Alexander') published at New York in 1912 that the coins of Müller's Class I, attributed to many mints in Thrace, Macedon, and northern Greece, were intimately linked with one another through their reverse dies: the prow with the thunderbolt, the amphora with the cantharus or helmet, the helmet with an ivy-leaf, and so on for 35 different symbols. The symbols are in fact magistrates' marks, selected at random, and all the coins of this class were struck at the one mint of Amphipolis.

Coin Descriptions

How coins are described by numismatists can best be shown from examples (Fig. 47). The first illustration is an Athenian tetradrachm of the fifth century B.C., of the type issued subsequent to either the battle of Marathon (490) or that of Salamis (480), it is not certain which, when Athena's helmet was first crowned with an olive wreath. The second is a noble of Edward III of England (1327–77), issued during the period 1351–61, between the reduction in the weight of the coin that took place in 1351 and Edward's abandonment of the title of king of France as a consequence of the treaty of Bretigny (1360). The third is a penny of George V of the year 1926.

1. *Obv.* Head of Athena r., wearing ear-ring and crested helmet adorned with olive leaves and floral ornament.
   Rev. ΑΘΕ vertically down on r. Owl r., head facing; behind, crescent and olive spray. All in incuse square.
   Tetradrachm. Æ Diam. 25 mm. Wt. 16·85 g. ↑ →

2. *Obv.* Ε DWARD⁖ DEI · GRA · REX · ANGL⁖ Ζ · FRANC⁖ D⁖ hYB' between two circles of pellets. Half-figure of king in armour, crowned, holding sword and shield bearing the arms of France and England quarterly, standing in a ship.

Rev. IҺꙃ · ꙦVTꙒꙏ · TRꙦИꙆIꙄИS · Ᵽ · ꙏꙄꙆIVꙏ · IꙆꙆORVꙏ · IBꙦT between two circles of pellets. Elaborate cross fleury, with in centre and a crowned leopard in each angle, in a double tressure of 8 lobes.
Noble Aᴠ Diam. 34 mm. Wt. 7·78 g.

3. *Obv.* GEORGIVS V DEI GRA : BRITT : OMN : REX FID : DEF : IND : IMP : Head of king, bare-headed, l. On truncation of neck, in minute letters, B.M. (for Bertram Mackennal). Beaded border. Raised edge, plain.
Rev. ONE PENNY Britannia seated r., with trident and shield, against background of sea. In ex., 1926. Similar border and edge.
Penny. Æ Diam. 30 mm. Wt. 9·51 g. ↑↑

(a)   (b)   (c)

FIG. 47. (a) Athenian tetradrachm. (b) English noble. (c) British penny of George V.

These descriptions could be shorter or longer according to need. Often, in a list of coins, one requires to do no more than make it clear to what country, reign, and denomination an individual coin belongs, and in the appropriate context 'Helmeted head of Athena r.' or 'Half-figure of king in ship' might well be sufficient. For closer work it would be necessary to give more detail, to state the number of olive leaves and their position on Athena's helmet, to amplify the description of the ship by noting the presence of the leopards and lis along the gunwale and the number of ropes connecting the mast with the prow and the stern. Where types themselves are of an unusual character, like the lulab and ethrog on Jewish coins or the heraldic devices of many late medieval and early modern coins, it is necessary to borrow terms from other disciplines in order to describe them. Most of the terms used in the above descriptions need no amplification, but there are a few details that require comment.

Obverse and reverse. These correspond to what are popularly called the 'head' and 'tail' of a coin. They are normally abbreviated to 'obv.' and 'rev.' (or ℞), and 'obv.' is often taken for granted and omitted, though 'rev.' must be specified. 'Obverse' is normally used for the face that bears the principal type, but some numismatists apply the term to that bearing the principal inscription, since this defines the authority by which the coin is issued. Others again, particularly in the field of ancient coins, use it for the face which took the impression of the lower (anvil) die when the coin was struck. Sometimes the three elements coincide, as they do on the two English coins just described, but where they do not the scholar has to decide for himself which criterion is best.

Inscriptions. When inscriptions are reproduced in print, the forms of the letters are imitated as far as the type founts available allow. They are often important in determining the date of coins, besides having sometimes been employed by mint-masters to differentiate one issue from another. It may be essential, for example, to know whether the letter E is in square capitals (E) or founded, and in the latter case whether it is open or closed (ℰ). Such Gothic forms as ℰ, ℿ, ℳ, etc. are, for no very good reason, described by British numismatists as 'Lombardic'. Where variant letter founts are not available, Roman capitals have to be used and some attempt made to describe the peculiarities of the original. Punctuation marks, technically known as *stops*, must either be reproduced or described, as also must any ligatures between letters and any marks of abbreviation or contraction. Any breaks in the inscription must be reproduced, for example that between ℰ and DWARD in the second coin described above, even if they do not correspond to that between actual words. It is taken for granted, unless the contrary is stated, that inscriptions follow the circumference of the coin and run in a clockwise direction.

Type and accessory symbols. When accessory symbols or other ornaments occur in the field, their position may be described in relation to the type (e.g. 'behind', or 'above head'), but is usually given as 'in the field l.' or 'in the field r.', left and right being as seen by the spectator. If the figure depicted on a coin is holding anything, and the object is described, left and right are from its point of view, not from the spectator's. Thus the figure of Britannia on the penny could be described as 'seated r., holding trident in l. and shield in r.' When armorial devices are described, the usual heraldic convention, reversing the relationship of left (sinister) and right (dexter), is observed.

Border. This may be beaded, when it is sometimes described as a 'border of dots', or linear, or something fairly complicated, in which case it has to be either illustrated or described in detail. The *edge* on modern coins is usually raised, as on the penny, to allow for the coins being stacked together, but this is an innovation of the nineteenth century except in so far as it occurred earlier as an incidental result of graining. The description of the edge of the penny as 'plain' means that it is not grained, the technical term for what is popularly called milled, as are the edges of the modern 5p and 10p. The placing of graining or of inscriptions on the edges of coins was introduced only in the sixteenth century, as a result of technical improvements in minting that took place at that period. On almost all earlier coins, which were struck without a collar and consequently are not perfectly circular, nothing need be said in coin descriptions about the edge; it is always presumed to be plain. Almost the only exceptions are the curious classes of Seleucid copper coins and Roman Republican denarii known as *serrati*, in which the edge is so heavily toothed that the coin resembles a cog-wheel. It is generally supposed that this was done to reassure the public regarding the quality of the metal of which the coins were made, but such an explanation cannot cover its employment in the Seleucid series, or indeed in the Roman one either.

Denomination. This is identified where it is known, which is not always the case. There is nothing on the vast majority of coins to indicate what was their legal value, and it is often surprisingly difficult to identify coins mentioned in contemporary texts with the actual pieces which have survived. There is a further complication which is apparent in the very ambiguity of the word denomination, for it can mean either the name of the coin or its value. The two are not necessarily identical, for contemporaries often used blanket words like penny, denier, or gros, adding when necessary a phrase indicating the denomination ('penny of two pence', 'gros de quatre deniers').

In the earlier phases of the study of any coin series much has consequently to be left undetermined that will be clarified later. The standard nineteenth-century book on Roman imperial coins, Henry Cohen's *Description historique des monnaies frappées sous l'Empire romain*, did not distinguish between the various denominations of brass and copper coins, being content to group them under the headings of G.B., M.B., and P.B. (*grand, moyen,* and *petit bronze*) according to their module. Its twentieth-century successor, Harold Mattingly and E. A. Sydenham's *Roman Imperial Coinage*, classifies the same coins confidently as sestertii, dupondii, asses, and quadrantes. Our knowledge of the monetary system of the later Empire, however, has made less progress, and the author of Vol. IX of Mattingly–Sydenham still classifies the bronze coinage of the late fourth century according to size as Aes I–IV (First–Fourth Brass), practically as Cohen had done.

Metal. This is designated in general terms, the words either being written in full or more often abbreviated as AV, AR, and Æ, the initials of the Latin names of gold, silver, and copper *(aurum, argentum, aes)*. These abbreviations have by now been used by numismatists for several centuries and are universally understood. Electrum (base gold) and billon (base silver), if distinguished at all, are usually written in full, but can be abbreviated to El. and B. Base gold is sometimes described as pale gold, since up to quite recent times gold was more often alloyed with silver than with copper. Brass, bronze, and copper are indiscriminately rated as Æ. In Italian works on numismatics the abbreviations O, AR, R, and M *(oro, argento, rame, mistura)* are often employed for AV, AR, Æ, and billon.

Module. The diameter of a coin is technically known as its *module*. Where a coin is not quite circular, it is customary to give the largest diameter; where the shape is quite irregular, the over-all dimensions are necessary. The module is normally given in millimetres (mm.), but for English and American coins inches are also used, 2·54 cm. equalling 1 inch. Older books, particularly those dealing with ancient coins, sometimes use what is known as Mionnet's Scale, elaborated by a French numismatist early in the last century. On this scale, the unit is a circle of 9 mm. and the figure

19 a circle of 78 mm. diameter, other numbers being irregularly spaced between these.

Weight. This is normally given according to the metric system, which is international, but in Britain grains are still much used. For English coins this has considerable justification, since it is the measure that since medieval times has been employed by the state to prescribe their weights, but outside this field it is a source of confusion and should be avoided. The English grain weighs 0·065 g.; the gram is 15·43 gr. The French *grain*, which was some-times used by numismatists into the middle of the nineteenth century, weighed 0·053 g.

Die axis. This is the term used for the relationship between the positions of the types of the two faces of a coin. If the penny of George V illustrated above were held upright and allowed to rotate around its vertical axis it would be found that the king's head and the figure of Britannia are in the same plane as each other. Such a relationship is expressed as $\uparrow\uparrow$, or simply $\uparrow$, the single arrow in the latter case representing the reverse and it being understood that the obverse is $\uparrow$. The opposite relationship would be $\uparrow\downarrow$ or $\downarrow$, and any other relationship could be expressed by pointing the arrow in a different direction. Die axes are not given in numismatic publications prior to 1900 and in some series they are superfluous, either because there is no regularity at all or because the regularity is so complete that it can tell us nothing. But during certain periods its presence or absence, or a preference for $\uparrow$ over $\downarrow$ or vice versa, can be a valuable auxiliary aid in identifying the mints at which particular coins were struck and establishing the relative chronology of their products.

Die identifications. In the description of the three coins above, there was no identification of dies and no estimate of condition or rarity. Any or all of these may be desirable in particular cases.

Die identifications are only required in intensive studies of a coin series, when a number of specimens of the same coin are brought into relationship with each other. This usually only occurs when a scholar has collected something approaching a corpus of all known specimens, but it sometimes arises in describing a coin hoard, and in such cases die analysis may produce results of the utmost value. The dies are given an arbitrary series of letters or numbers, and any particular die combination can be expressed by bringing the appropriate symbols of the obverse and reverse dies together. A series like O^1, O^2, O^3, etc. for obverse dies and R^1, R^2,

R³, etc. for reverse ones is the most convenient, but scholars who wish to avoid the uncertainty over which side of the coin is best regarded as the obverse and which the reverse sometimes use A¹, A², etc. for that struck by the lower (anvil) dies and P¹, P², etc. for that struck by the upper (punch) ones.

Condition. The condition of coins is often of great importance from the scientific point of view. This is true whether one is dealing with coins individually or in quantity. Only if a coin is in good condition can we be sure that it has given up all its secrets. On a poorly preserved piece there may be mint-marks or punctuation marks which we cannot identify for certain or even see at all. Its die characteristics cannot be properly studied and its weight will be no reliable guide to the theoretical weight to which the coin was struck. In hoard descriptions some analysis of condition is essential, for the relative wear of the coins may be important both for their dating and for the dating of the hoard as a whole.

Condition is sometimes expressed in the form C¹–C⁴, C¹ implying extremely fine and C⁴ poor, but in England it is more usual to express it by abbreviated descriptive epithets, the grades being FDC (*à fleur de coin*, i.e. fresh from the dies), EF (extremely fine), VF (very fine), F (fine), Fair, M (mediocre), and P (poor). The latter grades, however, are scarcely used, a coin in such condition only rarely having any commercial value. Where, as often happens, the condition of the two faces is not the same, this can be expressed by, for example, EF/VF. Unfortunately estimates of condition are highly subjective, and the word itself is ambiguous. How does one classify a penny which a child has put on a railway line for a train to run over? From the collector's point of view it is ruined, but its weight is unimpaired.

Faults of striking which affect the condition of coins are described in various ways, but often imprecisely. Three terms are usually employed: *double-striking*, *overstriking*, and *restriking*.

1. *Double-striking* is used for the blurring of the detail of the type or inscription—the doubling of the contour of a face or the outline of a group of letters—as a consequence of the upper die having slipped or the position of the partly struck blank on the lower die having altered between one blow and the next.

2. *Overstriking* is the use of an old coin instead of a freshly prepared flan as a blank. The old impression may be completely effaced by the new one, in which case there will be nothing to reveal to us that overstriking has taken place. But very frequently some traces of the earlier impression are still visible.

3. *Restriking*, in the strict sense, is a word that can be applied only to modern coinage, for it implies the re-use of original dies, usually for the benefit of the collector but sometimes to make mementos or commemoration pieces after the coins for which the dies were intended have gone out of use. Restrikes of this kind, which were made on payment of an appropriate fee by many European mints in the nineteenth century, were usually marked in some way, though not always very effectively, to distinguish them from genuine coins.

The correct use of these terms is unfortunately rare, and 'restriking' is made to do duty for all three. A sale catalogue may use a phrase like 'detail slightly blurred through restriking', where double-striking is meant, and the British Museum catalogue of Byzantine coins regularly describes overstruck bronze coins as 'restruck'.

If a coin has been damaged by agencies other than those of time, this must be stated separately. 'Cracked' implies damage done in the actual striking. 'Pierced' is used rather loosely for any sort of hole in a coin, though it should properly be confined to holes made without loss of weight, leaving 'drilled' or 'holed' for use where metal has been removed. 'Plugged' implies that such a hole has been filled with metal to make the coin more saleable. 'Scratched' and 'polished' (or 'buffed') are terms that explain themselves. 'Tooled' implies that the coin has been carefully worked over by a skilled engraver to bring up details erased by wear or corrosion. It is practically confined to Roman and Renaissance coins, and is often difficult to detect. 'Mounted' means that a coin is or at some time has been mounted as an ornament: such a mount inevitably leaves traces on the edge of the coin when it is cut away. 'Gilded' means what it says. Silver coins have often been gilt as ornaments, and coins of base gold have sometimes been gilt to give them a better colour.

Rarity. Indications of the degree of rarity of a coin are more characteristic of dealers' lists than of scientific monographs, but they have a place in the latter. A scholar using a museum catalogue may well find in it nearly as many specimens of a rare coin as of a common one, for museums are traditionally as anxious to acquire rarities as they have been reluctant to overload their trays with duplicates. The number of pieces available in such collections consequently bears no relation whatever to either the number known or the numbers likely to have existed in the past. A collector, knowing the market value of the coins, will be aware of this fact, and so will any scholar who has worked with hoards, but failure to allow for it may lead others into trouble. The point seems an elementary one, but it is often overlooked. Estimates of rarity are therefore desirable. They may be expressed either in words (extremely rare, very rare, rare, etc.) or in symbols. In the latter case the author must provide a key to whatever system he adopts, for there is none that is generally accepted. The one most commonly used is a gradation from C (common) through R^1 to R^8, the latter implying that only two or three specimens are known, but many variants are possible. It must always be remembered that, except in a series on which much research has been done, so that one has a fairly accurate idea of how many pieces are known, estimates of rarity are highly subjective.

Catalogue Arrangement

When large numbers of coins have to be catalogued or otherwise arranged in print, their descriptions are cut to a minimum and the various elements as far as possible tabulated and arranged in a series of columns across the page. A typical arrangement would be to have six columns containing a serial number, the denomination (abbreviated), metal, weight, and die position, the obverse inscription and type, the reverse inscription and type, the degree of rarity, and a reference, the last stating where the coin is published or in what collection it is to be found. Such a plan admits of all kinds of variations according to circumstances. If the catalogue is one of types only, such details as weight and die position will not be required; if it is of a single collection, there will be no need to state where the coin is to be found; if the coins are all of silver, there is no need to have an entry indicating the metal. What is essential is to set out the material as clearly and concisely as possible.

The real problem is that of arriving at a satisfactory order for the coins. Here the older reference works sometimes present features disconcerting to the modern reader. Cohen arranged his Roman coins under each emperor in alphabetical order of reverse inscription, the total for a single ruler often running to many hundreds of entries. This arrangement was a practical one, since reverse inscriptions are more variable than obverse ones, but it took no account of chronological order of issue or of metal, mint, or denomination, so that the scholar using it found it quite impossible to get a clear picture of the coinage of any reign. Theoretically the ideal arrangement is by issues, but these are often difficult to establish and themselves may cut across arrangements by mints or denominations that may be desirable on other grounds. In dealing with modern coins it is customary to give denominations priority over year of issue. No general rule can be formulated; the ideal arrangement is to present coinage as it was issued, but how the details are best dealt with will vary from one series to another.

5
The Making of Coin

The making of coin involves three processes, authorization, manufacture, and issue, which are respectively, legal, technical, and economic—or economic and political—in character. Except in the modern period most of what we know has to be deduced from the coins themselves, since mint records have only survived in any quantity from the thirteenth century onwards.

Authorization involves two separate kinds of activity, one private and the other public. Private are the instructions given to a mint by the government or other issuing authority. These will in varying degrees prescribe the weight and fineness of the coins, determine their design, assign to them a name and legal value, fix the prices at which bullion is to be bought and the profits and pay of the moneyers, and determine the amount of coin to be issued. They may in part be based on legal prescriptions of a public character, but in detail they will be determined by administrative practice and mint experience, and most of them never become public knowledge at all. The public aspect of minting is concerned with endowing pieces of appropriately marked metal with the quality of money, so that they become legal tender.

The conversion of bullion into coin by imposing a mark on it can be effected by either casting or striking. Casting was used for the earliest bronze coins of the Roman Republic, which were too large to be easily struck, for many Celtic coins, and for the manufacture of Chinese cash and its derivatives, but the Western tradition has in general been that of striking. The reason is mainly that struck coins are more difficult to counterfeit, for cast and struck coins are fairly easily distinguishable from each other and the occurrence of a cast coin amongst ones that are normally struck labels it at once as false. Struck coins are known as 'hammered' when they are struck by hand, as 'mill' or 'milled' when they are made by some machine. A mill in the original sense of the word implied machinery used for grinding or crushing, such as grain mills or powder mills, but by the sixteenth century it had come to mean any kind of machinery. As used by numismatists the term originally referred to the fact that the machines installed at the Paris mint in the sixteenth century for flattening the blanks were operated by a water-mill, but it was subsequently transferred to the 'milling'—more correctly 'marking' or 'graining'—round the edges of most modern coins.

Minting and the State

The right of minting has in almost all political communities been reserved to the state, but, either for its own convenience or because it is unable to resist doing so, the state may delegate to others the function of coining and sometimes even the right to coin. Though in practice these terms merge into each other, they are theoretically distinct. A feudal ruler might exercise the right to coin either *ex concessione principis*, by formal grant of the prince, or *centenaria praescriptione*, by immemorial custom, which in effect meant a successful usurpation in a more or less distant past, but in theory he did so in virtue of an authority delegated to him. A local moneyer in the reign of William I, on the other hand, exercised only the function of coining, not the right to coin; he did so on terms laid down by the king and he might be deprived of his function if he failed to fulfil these conditions or when the time of his appointment ran out. A position somewhere between a feudal prince and an eleventh-century English moneyer would have been occupied by a Greek city of Asia Minor striking bronze coinage in the second century A.D.; its privilege of minting had presumably to be approved by the Roman government, but how it was exercised was left to its own discretion. The last case is a good example of the way in which states are often prepared to leave the provision of subsidiary coinage either entirely or in large measure to local authorities, while reserving for themselves the striking of coins in one or both of the precious metals.

Even where states have been reluctant to delegate the right of minting, they have often been willing to delegate the function of coining. We are accustomed to thinking of the mint as a government department, subordinate in Great Britain to the Treasury, its staff having the status of employees and being paid directly by the government. The mints of the Roman Empire, and perhaps those of the Greek city-states, were not essentially dissimilar to this, save that the staff would have consisted largely of slaves. In medieval times the function of minting was usually contracted out to private persons, who undertook to strike coin on specified terms and pay the government on some agreed basis in return for the privilege. There might be no 'royal mint' at all, only moneyers who worked in their own homes or in houses provided by a municipality or other authority. Even where there was a royal mint, like that of the English kings in the Tower of London, the contract for coining would be put up to auction for a term of years. Not all minting is carried out by governments even today. Many countries find it inconvenient to have mints of their own, since coinage presses are uneconomic to operate unless they can be used all the time. In such cases coins are obtained under contract from other national mints or from private ones, of which there are a number in existence. A small H (for Heaton) or KN (for King's Norton) occasionally found in the exergue of pennies of George V of 1918 and 1919 reminds us that even the Royal Mint has to resort to outside help from time to time. Coin blanks are frequently purchased from private firms.

The essential element in mint instructions consists of the provisions regarding weight and fineness. Weights are normally expressed indirectly: it is not said that each coin shall weigh so many grains but that a specified number of coins shall be cut to the mark, or pound, or other weight unit. There is usually a provision for what in the Middle Ages was called a remedy or tolerance: not more than a specified proportion of coins shall be more than 1 grain, or 2 grains, or some other figure above or below the average weight, and even these must lie within a definite limit on either side. The size of the remedy depends on the value of the coin and the metal of which it is made. For gold coins the remedy will be very small, while for bronze coins it may be either wide or none may be specified at all. Fineness has traditionally been expressed directly, in terms of carats and grains for gold and of ounces or pence and grains for silver. These curious formulas were a consequence of the difficulty found by our ancestors in dealing with complicated fractions. They found it easier to work by analogy with larger units. Carats meant twenty-fourth parts because the Roman gold solidus had originally weighed 24 carats, and ounces or pence both meant twelfths, because there were twelve ounces to the pound and twelve pence to the shilling.

The designs and inscriptions on coins are usually expressed in mint contracts in only the most general terms, if at all, but mint and privy marks, where present, are set out in detail, since unlike the design itself they have financial and administrative implications. The names and values of coins are sometimes specifically prescribed, though not always; they may only be announced to the public when the coins are put into circulation. In actual practice coin names tend to be decided by the community and are sometimes no more than parodies of those which the coins officially bear, while values will usually find their own level quite independently of the scale theoretically laid down for them.

Medieval and early modern mint contracts usually specified the seigniorage, i.e. the profit due to the ruler, on each lot of coins struck, and also in some detail the price to be paid for bullion, the wages of the moneyers, and the sum due to the master. The latter was not normally left to buy bullion at the lowest price he could, thus enlarging his profit on the striking of each coin; the profit on each of these would be fixed and the master could only become richer by minting them in greater numbers. The custom of fixing the mint price of bullion was intended to ensure the public against too great a discrepancy between the nominal value of a coin and that of its metallic content, but it had the disadvantage of being too inflexible. When the commercial price of bullion rose above that offered by the mint none would be available for coining, which might in consequence be brought to an end for several years at a time.

It is only in modern times that governments have concerned themselves about the actual quantity of money that is coined and attempted to prescribe this in advance. In earlier times the most that was done was to lay down the proportions between the coins of different denominations that were to be struck. A Brabantine mint ordinance of 1466, for example, specified that for every mark of gold there should be coined 100 marks of silver and that for every 200 marks coined into pieces of 2 gros there should be 20 marks of 4 gros, 4 of single gros, 2 of half-gros, and 1 of quarter-gros. The reason for such prescriptions was that the cost of making higher denominations was much less than that of making lower ones to the same value—12 times as much labour was involved in making 12 pennies as in making 1 shilling—and moneyers consequently preferred to make heavy coins despite frequent shortages of small change and strong public demands for more.

Mints and Moneyers

The making of coin requires a staff and equipment. At their simplest these imply the services of a person accustomed to working in precious metals, capable of preparing alloys of specified quality and of striking the coins with dies prepared either by himself or, if he is not skilled enough, acquired from outside. They also require equipment similar to that likely to be available to a jeweller—furnaces, working benches, tools, balances—though usually on a larger scale.

We are fortunate in having several detailed descriptions of mints created under very primitive conditions in the present century, and with variations the picture must hold good of many mints in the past. An article in the *Numismatic Chronicle* for 1939 describes how a mint was set up by 'Ali Dinar, sultan of Darfur in the Western Sudan, in 1908. His country had previously relied for its coinage on irregular and very unsatisfactory imports from Egypt, and it was the finding of dies for making forged piastres in the house of the chief silversmith Hamid Muhammad that suggested to the sultan the possibility of striking coins of his own. Dies were made in the sultan's name by Hamid Muhammad, the other silversmiths having declared their inability to carry out so difficult a task. The striking was carried out in the palace yard. Five silversmiths arrived each morning from the town and were given one rial of silver and four of copper; these were melted together, cast into bars, hammered flat, and cut up with a circular punch into seventy blanks. One of the silversmiths struck these with a pair of dies, working under the supervision of a guard, and when they were finished their number and workmanship was checked and they were handed over to the head of the royal *worsha* (workshop). Five dies, kept under lock and key by this official, were used at various times, two of them having been made by Hamid Muhammad and three others, poor imitations of them, by the chief armourer. Hamid also did a certain amount of re-engraving of the dies as they wore out. At first the minting was done in the palace courtyard under strict supervision, but the noise eventually became intolerable and the whole operation of coining was moved to the *worsha* some distance away, with the result that the quality of the coins rapidly declined. At first, blanched by immersion in a solution of *ardeib* juice, they presented a relatively silvery appearance despite the quantity of copper they contained. Their acceptance was imposed very simply, for specimens were taken down to the market-place by two goldsmiths and displayed in company with the sultan's sword, with the warning that anyone refusing to accept them would forfeit his head. Merchants and others could bring bullion to the mint to be coined, but mint charges were high. In every 70 piastres struck the owners only received 49, the remaining 21 being divided between the sultan and the silversmiths as seigniorage and wages respectively. The sultan's share was used as a fund for purchasing copper and silver for new minting when required.

The basis of minting at Darfur was therefore government institution and supply of bullion; the dies were made by a goldsmith and an armourer with some skill in metal-working, and the minting itself was carried out by five goldsmiths or their slaves. It is a far cry from this to the large and complex staff required by such mints as those of London or Paris in the modern period, or even the mint of Rome in the heyday of the Empire, which we know from fragments of five dedicatory inscriptions of A.D. 115 to have had a staff consisting of a director and his deputy, 16 clerks (*officinatores*), 17 die-sinkers (*signatores*), 11 *suppositores* or workmen who placed the blanks in position for striking, and 38 hammerers (*malliatores*), besides melters, furnace men, and so on whose names have only survived in part or not at all. Most mints must have come somewhere between these, larger than that of Darfur but smaller than that of Rome, though many Merovingian mints and some later medieval ones may have been even smaller than that of Darfur.

It is only in a well-organized state, with a reasonably good system of communications, that minting is likely to be concentrated in a single centre. Where states are small, the number of mints in a given area is usually high. This is the case whether the states are formally independent, like those of ancient Greece, or technically subject to a superior authority, as in many of the feudal states of medieval Europe. There were over 100 mints in twelfth-century France and over 250 in thirteenth-century Germany. Even eighteenth-century France had no fewer than 30 mints, with the result that the country was better supplied with small change than contemporary England, where there was only a single mint at London and merchants in the provinces complained endlessly of the difficulty of procuring petty cash. Mints have frequently been placed at or close to a frontier so as to facilitate the recoinage of imported bullion and currency, or in mining towns where ample supplies of gold and silver are available and it is desirable to turn this into coin as quickly as possible.

Coins are made by moneyers, but the class of persons covered by this term is difficult to define. Basically it meant the technicians, those who made the blanks and dies and carried out the actual work of striking, but it could be extended in one direction to cover the wealthy entrepreneurs who took in hand the operations of late medieval mints for a term of years but who might or might not have a knowledge of the technicalities of coinage, and in the other to embrace the unskilled workmen, the men who in the Middle Ages were often called *operarii* (i.e. 'ouvriers') as distinct from *monetarii*, who tended the furnaces and did the rough work about the mint. In the later Middle Ages the moneyers normally formed a privileged corporation, bound to work in the mint when summoned for the purpose but enjoying exemption from military service and the right to the jurisdiction of their own courts by way of compensation for any disadvantages this obligation might involve. The very irregular character of their service meant that moneyers would either pursue other professions, such as that of goldsmith or banker, or would be compelled to move from one country to another in search of work. To some extent, indeed, they formed an international corporation, like freemasons, and for much the same reasons.

In modern times, though the titles borne by individuals amongst them are sometimes traditional, the staff of a mint is directly employed by the state. In earlier centuries these titles often reflected distinct roles, on the one hand private contractors and on the other the officials appointed by the king to supervise their activities. Thus there was in the English mint the duality of Master and Warden, of refiner and assayer, one group representing the technicians who did the work and made their profit, the other the representatives of the government who ensured that they did their work well and that the profit was not too large.

Hammered Coinage

Western, Muslim, and Indian coins, throughout most of their history, have been made in one simple fashion: a blank has been placed between two dies and the upper die struck with a hammer, so that the two between them leave their impressions on both faces of the resulting coin. The earliest coins, however, were struck upon one face only, and while theoretically this could be either the upper or the lower one of the original blank, it was in practice almost always the lower one. The design for the coin was cut in the hollow of an anvil and the metal blank forced into it by a punch, or more often a group of four punches clamped tightly together, hammered from above. There was no design on the heads of these punches; they simply made a deep indentation in the thick pellet of metal which served as a blank. A large part of the earliest coinage of Asia Minor and Greece to the end of the sixth century B.C. was struck in this way, and so was the whole of the gold and most of the silver coinage of Achaemenid Persia. The impression of the upper punch or punches is known as an incuse square, and often takes the form of some simple pattern (e.g. mill sail, like the four sails of a windmill) which serves to describe it.

The more usual practice is for both the upper and lower dies to have designs cut on them, so that when the blank is struck between the dies both leave their mark upon it. This is the traditional way in which hammered coining has been done throughout most of its history. It will be convenient to discuss it under four heads: (a) the making of dies, (b) the preparation of blanks, (c) the process of striking, and (d) verification. These operations did not necessarily take place under the same roof or in the same workshop. The making of dies was sometimes, as in Norman England, the work of a central organization which distributed them to moneyers in the provinces, while a modern mint may find it convenient to order from a commercial firm the blanks needed for the token currency. Numismatists are inclined to regard the making of dies as the most important aspect of minting, but this is a consequence of the design being the most obviously interesting element in a coin to the modern collector. Die-cutting was both easier and less important than is generally supposed; the most difficult operation was that of ensuring that the metal for the blanks, whether pure or of a prescribed alloy, was of the correct quality.

Die making. The dies used for hammered coinage were of hardened bronze or iron in antiquity, of iron or sometimes of steel in the Middle Ages. A number of medieval and early modern dies still survive. The typical upper die, known as the punch die (Med. Lat. *punzo*) or trussel (Fr. *trousseau*), was an iron bar varying in length from a few inches to nearly a foot and slightly larger in diameter than the coin which it was used to strike. The design was cut in its lower face, while the upper end, which received the blows of the hammer, became in time cracked and flattened, with its sides bent over outwards into what was known as a beard. The typical lower die, known as the staple or standard (Fr. *pile*) was likewise a bar several inches long, but was more complicated in shape. It ended below in a point and it was usually splayed outwards half way up, so that it could be forced into a block of wood and would stay in position without the hammer driving it further and further in. Sometimes the dies were square-headed, which allowed their alignment by eye in such a way that the designs of the two faces of the coin would bear a regular relationship to one another, or they

FIG. 48. English dies of the mid-fourteenth century now in the Public Record Office. They were used for Edward III's coinage of 1353–5 at the mint of York, the pair in the centre being for a penny and the other—the trussel and pile belong together —for a half-groat.

could have nicks put in their edges to show how they should be aligned.

Ancient dies had sometimes the same form as medieval ones, but there were many other varieties in use. Roman imperial dies, when they were made of hardened iron, were typically small and conical in shape; they were fitted tightly into a block of iron, which took the actual hammering and could easily be replaced. One of the major difficulties in studying ancient monetary techniques is that of knowing which surviving dies are official in character and which belonged to counterfeiters. It seems likely that there was a good deal of variation from place to place, especially in the classical Greek period, and that improved processes and methods might be devised in one place and only spread very slowly outside it.

The die face, which bears in intaglio a mirror image of the design which will ultimately be seen on one of the two surfaces of the coin, is made with the help of two kinds of tools, graving tools (burins) and punches. A graving tool with either a broad or narrow head—normally both types would be used—serves for gouging pieces of metal from the die face, while a punch—here many shapes are possible—is hammered directly into the die face, the metal pressed up on either side of the resulting cavity being removed with a graving tool or file. The first operation should technically be known as die-cutting, the second as die-sinking, but in

Fig. 49. Retouching a die in the Paris mint. Various punches and other tools can be seen on the bench. Direct work of this kind on the die face is now practically limited to medals.

practice the two words are used indifferently. Ancient dies, which were in high relief, were for the most part made with graving tools, while in the Middle Ages much greater use was made of punches. The letters would be broken down into their simplest components and rendered with the help of only two or three punches, while the design of a cross or a bust could be built up by the use of only a few more. In the later Middle Ages more elaborate punches were used for larger elements in the design—complete letters, a crown, in the sixteenth century even a complete bust. Their use can be detected by the exact identity of these features from one coin to another and sometimes by errors in their placing.

The actual methods used in the making of a die can only be reconstructed in outline. The dies for ancient coins seem usually to have been cut freehand, and working by eye alone has always been generally practised. Where regularity of outline is important, as with late medieval coins which have normally a circle of inscription surrounding the type, a pair of compasses would be used to mark the main outline. On fourteenth-century gold coins one can often see a central pellet marking the depression made on the die by one compass point and a faint circular line around the type and again near the edge of the coin showing the traces left by the other. The preliminary lines made by the compass could be deepened by graving tools or accentuated by beading, the latter often very irregular, for the punch head with two studs which ensured beading at regular intervals was only invented in the sixteenth century.

The time required for the making of a die must have varied greatly. A complicated pattern in high relief, like that on many Greek and Roman coins, would involve many hours of work. Benvenuto Cellini boasted of making the pair of dies for a medal of Pope Clement VII in two or three days, which was evidently regarded as an extraordinary achievement. The nineteenth-century counterfeiter Becker, who was an exceptionally skilful die-sinker, noted in his diary that it took eighteen hours to make the obverse die for a decadrachm of Akragas, though it is possible that if he had been working freehand and not attempting to copy a model closely he would have done it more quickly. The elaborate Gothic gold coins of the later Middle Ages must also have involved several hours of work, since although they are in very low relief the designs are extremely complicated. On the other hand, a medieval penny die of the eleventh or twelfth century could be made very quickly. Experiments by a modern scholar have shown that a passable reproduction of the upper die for an Anglo-Saxon coin, with a simple cross-pattern and a moneyer's name, could be made in fifteen minutes, while the obverse die, with the more elaborate bust and the name of the sovereign, required no more than half an hour. A medieval die-sinker would not necessarily have taken longer, since skill arising from long practice would compensate for the inferior quality of his tools.

It is probable that most dies used for hammered coinage were made directly, so that each one differed slightly from its fellows, but hubbed dies and cast dies were sometimes made. In the case of a hubbed die a master die is made in relief, not in intaglio, so that it in effect serves as an enormously elaborate punch; it is used for making the dies in intaglio which in their turn will be used for actually striking the coins. Cast dies appear to have been used in the medieval Islamic world, and perhaps also in antiquity, but even after subsequent sharpening of the details with a graving tool their surface was poor and it was difficult to make the metal hard enough for prolonged use. The nature of the metal was always a problem in die making. A punch-made die would probably last longer than an engraved one, since the metal in it would be compressed by the hammering, but it would be more likely to crack or develop other flaws through being heated and cooled several times to anneal it in the course of being made.

In a large mint die-sinking would be entrusted to one or more experts, who would do nothing else, and in some countries and periods dies have been made at a central office and distributed at need to provincial mints. Dies once made can be repaired and altered. The type and inscription on a worn die can be recut, the outlines of the design and of letters being sharpened by the use of a graving tool; a cracked die can be strengthened and in part repaired. Privy marks can be altered when a die is still in use and it is worth doing, and even fairly complicated inscriptions and designs can be recut if necessary. It is only occasionally that one notices the traces these have left on the coins, but it is probable that dies were altered more frequently than one supposes.

Since an upper die wears out more quickly than a lower one it has often been customary to supply them in sets rather than in pairs, two or more upper dies being associated with each lower one. Writs for the delivery of dies to Bury St. Edmunds in the fourteenth century usually specify *unum cuneum novum, videlicet unum stapellum et duos punzones*, and others of the reign of Edward III ordering the dispatch of lower and upper dies to Dublin or York do so in proportions of 1:3 or even 1:4. When dies wore out or when one coin type was replaced by another, the old dies would be formally defaced, as seals were defaced on the deaths of their owners. Central mints sometimes insisted on the recall of worn or obsolete dies from provincial mints in order to ensure that this was done, since an old die, if it remained undefaced, might be misused by dishonest moneyers or fall into the hands of counterfeiters. The ultimate fate of old dies, at least in the Middle Ages, was to be melted down, for up to the Industrial Revolution iron was a valuable commodity and there was a surprising amount of metal in a coin die.

The making of blanks. A necessary preliminary to the making of
coin blanks was the preparation of the alloy. If the metal involved
was to be used in a pure state, the bullion available had to be
assayed and if necessary purified. If an alloy of specified composition was called for, it had to be made either by melting the
metals together in the required proportions after they had been
refined or, less satisfactorily, by fusing together calculated proportions of alloys of known composition. Unfortunately, for every
mixture of two or three metals there is one proportion only, known
as a eutectic, where a uniform alloy emerges from such proceedings; for other proportions, as the molten metal cools, layers will
form in which one or other constituent is disproportionately
represented. Alloys of very base billon, with 5 per cent of silver in
them or even less, could never be produced with a composition
even approaching uniformity, so that many coins struck from such
alloys must have been without more than a trace of precious metal.
The preparation of the alloy was something on which moneyers
lavished enormous pains—we hear of the metal being sometimes
remelted no fewer than nine times—but it was a matter on which
it was difficult to get satisfactory results.

How the blanks were made would depend upon the ultimate
form of the coin. The blanks for large and heavy coins were usually
cast, at least in the ancient world. Those for Greek coins of the
classical period were normally cast in a globular form, which
explains the thickness and rounded edges of the coins, but the
later ones were cast in moulds of sand or terracotta, either individually or in groups. An alternative method was to cast the metal
in long strips and cut these up with a chisel into pieces of appropriate size, which were then grasped with tongs, reheated, and
worked by hammering into circular discs. In the sixteenth century
circular stamps were used for cutting the blanks from such strips,
but it is not clear that such methods were used in antiquity, though
they may sometimes have been employed for the thin coins of the
Middle Ages. The latter were normally made in a rather different
fashion, the strips or other cast ingots being hammered out flat
and very thin, till they could easily be cut up with shears. The two
operations are very clearly shown in the illustration of minting
operations in the Emperor Maximilian's *Weisskunig*, a fanciful
autobiography provided with elaborate woodcuts which are of
great interest for the costumes and manners of the early sixteenth
century.

The next stage was to treat the blanks with acid, which could
perform several functions. When the blanks were cast there would

FIG. 50. Operations in a mint of the early sixteenth century, from an engraving by Hans Burgkmair in the Emperor Maximilian's *Weisskunig*.

be fragments of ash, corrosion products, and the like adhering to the surface; these would now be removed. Where alloys of base silver were concerned, the 'blanching' was intended to remove a proportion of the copper close to the surface, leaving a spongy mass of silver which would be compressed when the coin was struck and give it a shining silver surface which, even if it soon wore off, served at least for a time to conceal the character of the coin. The acid used would depend on the function which the 'pickle' was intended to serve. In early times a mixture of salt and tartaric acid was very generally employed, while in later centuries this was sometimes replaced by dilute nitric acid.

After this was done the weights of individual pieces were adjusted to conform with the mint prescriptions, which in the case of gold and silver coins meant individual testing blank by blank. Those that were too light would have to be sent back for remelting; those that were too heavy would be reduced to the correct weight by filing the surface, the marks of the operation being removed by the subsequent striking. There was then usually another reheating, especially important for medieval blanks which had been hardened by the hammering of the sheets of metal, after which they would be dropped into water and dried in sawdust. Only then were they ready for striking.

Striking. This was the simplest operation of all, for it demanded little more than strength and practice. It used to be thought that the famous painting discovered in the House of the Vettii in Pompeii in 1895 showing jewellers at work was an illustration of minting, but in fact the Cupid wielding the sledge-hammer is only flattening a piece of hot metal on an anvil. Medieval coins, with their thin flans and low relief, could be struck by a single person holding the die in his left hand and wielding the hammer with his right. He could do this either seated or standing, the former being probably the more usual position. Several blows would often be required, particularly in the case of coins in high relief. In theory the first blow should cause the imprint of the dies to 'take' sufficiently to keep them in position for succeeding ones, but the blurring of designs on surviving coins (i.e. double-striking) shows that slipping was frequent. Good striking required skill as well as strength, for only practice could ensure that the blow came down vertically and the force behind it was evenly distributed over the surface. Practice likewise was necessary to ensure that the two dies were correctly aligned one above the other; coins are often found which are badly centred, part of one die or the other being off the flan at the moment of striking. There is always a tendency for the reverse of a coin to be more highly struck up than the obverse, since the hammer blow falls directly on the upper die while the pressure on the lower die has to be transmitted through the thickness of the coin. This could to some extent be avoided by skill in striking, but some workers might never master the knack. The blank might crack under the striking. This could not always be avoided, since some alloys would be more fragile than others, but its incidence could be reduced by experience in preparing the blanks, especially in the process of cooling them. Sometimes a coin would adhere to the upper die after being struck and escape notice, so that the next coin would be struck not with the upper die but with the obverse of an already struck coin. This would result in what is known as a brockage, in which a coin has an obverse impression in relief on one face and an incuse impression of the same design on the other.

Blanks might be struck hot or cold, and a study of the crystalline structure of coin surfaces shows that both methods were employed in the past. Each had its advantages and disadvantages. Cold blanks would be easier to handle but would require more force and several blows to bring up the design sufficiently. Hot blanks would be more awkward, especially for speedy working, and the heat transferred from them to the dies would soften the die faces and thus shorten their lives. It seems likely that hot striking was fairly general in antiquity, while in medieval and early modern times cold striking was the rule.

In recent years there has been much discussion regarding the number of coins a pair of dies would normally be used to strike. Any figures for ancient coins can be little more than guesswork. For medieval times we occasionally know the number of dies supplied to a mint in a given period of time and the value of the coinage struck, though the figures are rarely free from ambiguity. The evidence as a whole suggests that a pair of coin dies could normally be expected to strike about 10,000 coins, but that they were sometimes used to strike very much less—the Bruges mint in 1468–9 was only averaging 5,000 coins per pair of dies—and on occasion the figure could be pushed up to about 30,000. Much would depend upon circumstances. Where the mint made its own dies and could easily replace worn ones, these would be discarded more readily than where new dies had to be obtained from a central depot. A mint working under pressure would tend to keep its dies in use as long as possible. Mint officials would differ in their judgement of wear; one might be ready to discard a worn die while another would think it still fit for further use. Purely material factors—the height of the relief, the metal and module of the die, the metal of the coin—would all play their part. The determining factor must often have been the need for coin and the amount of bullion available for minting, not the number of coins a die could actually strike.

The length of time during which a die remained in use would vary according to the level of mint activity. When a mint was working under pressure a die might last only a few days. The mint of Bruges got through 2,000 dies in 18 months during 1468–9, and comparable rates of die consumption can be cited for other French and English mints of the same period. Where mint output was small, and in particular where high denominations only occasionally struck were involved, a die might last for years and be ultimately withdrawn because a new coin design was introduced, not because it was worn out. An obverse die for a dicken of Basel of 1499 was still in sufficiently good condition over twenty years later to be used with new reverses cut by Urs Graf, and on one coin in the Historical Museum at Basel such a die is linked with a reverse which bears the date 1535.

Verification. Once coins were struck, and before they were put into circulation, it was usual for them to be submitted to a final check. In part this was a simple inspection to ensure that they had been correctly struck, and must often have been quite perfunctory. More important was the verification of the alloy. This would in the main be a matter for the mint authorities themselves and would take place before striking, but a more public checking of the results by independent parties was often practised. The best known of such procedures is the English Trial of the Pyx, so called from the box or 'pyx' in which the coins selected for trial were kept. It is first heard of in the thirteenth century, having been probably introduced at the demand of xenophobic London businessmen who feared that the foreign experts who were being increasingly employed at the mint might take advantage of their position to cheat the public. The principle involved was the withdrawal of small samples from every batch of coins that were struck —1 gold coin in every 27 lb. by weight, 2 silver ones out of every 30 lb., or some such figure—and their assay by a jury of London citizens and goldsmiths either at stated intervals—three months, a year, whenever a new Master of the Mint was appointed—or before the coins went into circulation. Only the latter would have been any effective check on the quality of the coinage, and in practice the Trials of the Pyx were held under such varying conditions as to be little more than matters of form. Equivalent arrangements existed in many continental mints during the later Middle Ages and early modern period, the coins of a bishop or other ruler being tested by representatives of the town where they were struck.

The above description covers the making of ordinary flat coins struck on both sides. How aberrant forms of coin were struck we can as a rule only conjecture. The curious concave coins of the Byzantine Empire between the eleventh and the fourteenth centuries must have been struck between a concave lower die and a convex upper one, but this method made for bad workmanship;

much of the detail usually failed to register, double-striking was frequent, and the blanks often cracked in the striking. The early incuse coins of Croton, Sybaris, and other cities of Magna Graecia, which have the type in relief on one face and intaglio on the other, were struck between two dies, presumably hinged together, bearing designs which fitted into each other. With medieval bracteates and their successors, the thin uniface coins of sixteenth- and seventeenth-century Germany, the design was cut on the upper die only and the striking done against leather or some other soft material. This method had the advantage of making it possible to strike several coins simultaneously, a number of the paper-thin blanks being placed on top of one another, but the impression of the die would only come through sharply on the topmost blanks and the details on the lower ones would be blurred. True bracteates, struck with only one die, must be distinguished from what are called half-bracteates, which were struck by two dies but on such thin flans that only the reverse design comes out at all clearly, the obverse of the coin, and to a less extent the reverse, showing a mixture of obverse and reverse types. It was to avoid such unsatisfactory results that striking with only one die was introduced in twelfth-century Germany, though the bracteate technique was probably influenced by traditions of repoussé work as practised by goldsmiths from early Germanic times onwards.

Coins are sometimes found which have been overstruck on older ones. This bad practice saved the mint the cost and trouble of preparing the correct alloy and new blanks, but apart from aesthetic objections—the marks of the earlier striking could rarely be completely removed, and sometimes no serious attempt was made to do this—it had the disadvantage of involving a gradual reduction in the weight of the coins, since those used as blanks would be worn and consequently lighter than they had originally been when they left the mint. For this reason overstriking has usually been limited to token coins. The practice is one on which numismatists are apt to look with indulgence, since the sequence of overstrikes is sometimes, as in the Anonymous Folles of eleventh-century Byzantium, our best clue to the order and chronology of the issues involved.

Milled Coinage

Milled coinage has only existed during the past four centuries, and in some parts of Europe coinage continued to be 'hammered' until the end of the *ancien régime*. Mechanical methods of preparing the blanks and striking them can be regarded as an offshoot of the general progress in metallurgical knowledge in the sixteenth century, which saw the widespread adaptation of hydraulic power to the needs of mining and metal-working and the invention of such devices as the draw-bench, the trip-hammer, and the rolling mill.

The problems which the new minting methods were intended to solve were three in number. The first was that of securing flat and exactly circular blanks of even weight, the second that of marking their edges in such a way as to prevent their being tampered with, and the third that of securing a clearer 'strike' than could be effected by a hammer blow. These problems were not new, but they had all become more serious as a result of the introduction in the late fifteenth century of much heavier silver coins. Any unevenness in their thickness would seriously affect their weight; though they could not be easily clipped, substantial quantities of metal could be removed by filing their edges; and their area and thickness alike made them difficult to strike, since the force of the blow was spread over a much larger area and had to be transmitted through a greater thickness of metal if the lower die were to register at all.

The problem of securing circular blanks was that which mainly exercised would-be mint reformers in the first half of the sixteenth century. The two devices for effecting it were a rolling mill and a cutting press. The mill could be operated either by water power or by horse power, like that eventually set up in the Paris mint and known to us from a lively engraving in Diderot's *Encyclopédie* of the middle of the eighteenth century. In the first case the power would be transmitted directly to the horizontal rollers by a rotating water wheel, in the latter it was transmitted by an arrangement of gears from a rotating capstan. The metal would be cast in bars and then passed between the rollers several times till a strip or fillet of even thickness had been produced. Out of this the blanks would be struck by a cutting press, a machine whereby a broad circular punch was forced against the fillet opposite a slightly larger hole in an iron frame below, cutting a circular disc from the fillet as it did so. For fairly thin coins such a machine could be operated by a simple lever, but for thicker coins a screw press like that used for actually striking the coins had to be employed.

Marking the edge was a more difficult problem. If a coin is struck in a circular collar slightly larger than the blank, the latter will expand outwards at the moment of impact and the edges will receive the impression of any design the collar may bear. If this design is no more than a vertical 'graining', as on the 'milled' edge of a modern coin, the resulting struck blank can be extracted without difficulty, but if there is an inscription or an irregular graining, as was originally customary, this cannot be done.

Two alternative devices were used for getting over the difficulty, the segmented collar (*virole brisée*) and the marking machine. The first, invented in the late sixteenth century, was a collar usually made up of three sections which could come apart and allow the coin to be extracted from between them. It had the disadvantage of slowing down coining operations and requiring very great accuracy in striking. These disadvantages were shared by a variant in which the separate segments were replaced by a springy steel ribbon on which the required inscription or design could be engraved and which could be detached after the coin was struck. Collars were consequently very generally abandoned for coinage in the late seventeenth century in favour of a machine which marked the edge of the coin as a quite distinct operation. This machine consisted of two flat steel bars placed parallel to each other on a metal plate attached to a heavy table, the distance between them being just less than the diameter of the coin to be marked. One of the bars was fixed and the other could be moved backwards and forwards parallel to it by a lever and cog-wheel, so that a blank placed between them rotated when the lever was moved up and down. The edge inscriptions were cut on the inner sides of the two

Fig. 51. Machine for marking the edges of coins. From an engraving in Diderot's *Encyclopédie*.

bars, half on each bar, so that by making the blank perform a half revolution the whole of the inscription would be transferred to its edge. The striking of the marked blank would then follow as a separate operation. The marking machine was invented in London soon after the Restoration, but the Mint shrouded its affairs in such secrecy that John Evelyn, writing in 1697, was unable to discover who was responsible for it. An improved version, devised by a skilful mint engraver named Jean Castaing, was installed in the Paris mint in 1685, and since it was found to be highly satisfactory—it was estimated that it could mark 20,000 blanks a day— its use was extended to the provinces in the following year. A variety of this device, employed in Austria in the eighteenth century, had each of the bars slightly curved, since it was found that these gave a better impression than straight bars.

So far as striking was concerned, four alternative methods came into use. Two of them were mechanical devices for augmenting the strength of the traditional hammer blow, the others were developed out of the roller mechanism used for preparing the blanks.

FIG. 52. Plates for marking the edge of a Maria Theresa dollar (slightly reduced). The originals are in the museum of the Vienna mint.

FIG. 53. Screw press at work. From an engraving in Diderot's *Encyclopédie*.

One of the mechanical devices that could replace the hammer was the drop-press, working like a guillotine, where a heavy weight was hauled to the top of a tall narrow frame and allowed to fall on the upper die, but a much more important one was the screw press. This consisted of a strong metal frame having in the centre a vertical screw which could be rotated by the movement of a horizontal bar with a heavy metal ball at each end. Leather thongs or ropes, held by four men, were attached to the ends of the bars, and when the horizontal bar was swung round by the action of these men pulling with all their might the vertical screw came downwards with immense force and struck the upper die. The use of such a machine involved a complete change in the shape of the dies; they were now made circular or square in section and only about 2 inches deep, and they were normally encased in a collar which prevented them from slipping as the blow was struck. Such a machine could strike 30 coins or so per minute, but the work was extremely exhausting, so that it required a crew of some eight men who worked in twenty-minute spells.

The alternative methods of impressing the dies on the coins were the roller press and the rocker press. In the case of the roller press the dies were engraved on the surface of the rollers and the fillets of metal passed between them, so that these emerged bearing the

impression of a series of coins which could then be punched out
separately with cutters. Since the pressure of the rollers caused the
metal strips to expand longitudinally, the dies had to be engraved
as broad ovals if the resulting coins were to be circular in shape.
Roller presses were not very satisfactory to use, for it was difficult
to align the dies exactly with one another and, since the coins were
punched out only after striking, to ensure that the weights were
correct. The usual form of roller-working (Ger. *Walzenprägung*)
had also the disadvantage that if one of the dies were damaged all
those on the same roller would have to be scrapped. Roller presses
were invented in the sixteenth century and either in their original
or in an improved form with detachable dies (*Taschenwerkbetrieb*)

FIG. 54. Cylinders of a roller press from the mint of Hall. The dies are those of a
half-guldentaler of the Archduke Ferdinand (1566).

were widely used in Germany in the seventeenth and eighteenth
centuries, but elsewhere they were usually limited to the making
of copper coins where the weights of the individual pieces did not
matter. In England they were used for making copper farthing
tokens under Charles I, and strips of copper struck with farthings
which had not been cut out were sometimes preserved as curiosities.

The rocker press was a variety of the roller press much used in
the seventeenth century. The dies were engraved on the curved
surfaces of 'rockers' which were pivoted together and operated by
a see-saw bar attached to the upper rocker, so that a coin placed
between their faces would be forced through when the bar was
depressed. The impressions were often unsatisfactory and the
coins out of shape, since the pressure did not distribute itself
evenly over the surface of the coin, but rockers had the advantage
over rollers in that the weights of the blanks could be properly
adjusted before they went through the machine. Neither the roller
nor the rocker press could produce coins with any kind of marked
edge.

All of these machines had their disadvantages. They were very
expensive to install and operate, and were both more liable to
damage and to cause accidents to the workmen than the simpler
methods which they displaced. Their introduction into the mints
was bitterly opposed by the moneyers, partly from a natural
resistance to innovation and partly from fear of unemployment.
The good effects they were expected to have on the coinage were
often slow to materialize, for as they put into circulation new and
better coins these tended to be at once withdrawn and melted
down, leaving the old ones in circulation as before. Milled coins
could only be effectively introduced if accompanied by a general
recoinage, such as occurred in France in 1643 and in England in
1695, but governments were slow to realize this and naturally
hesitated to impose the use of mechanical techniques which, even
if they produced better coins, did so at much greater cost than
hammer-striking had involved.

The history of the various inventions and of their introduction
and spread in the various countries of western Europe is still only
imperfectly known. The earliest steps were taken in Italy: both
Leonardo da Vinci and Benvenuto Cellini experimented with
devices for cutting out circular blanks, and a machine of this kind
is believed to have been installed in the Venetian mint in 1528. It
was in Germany that the decisive implements were invented. In
1550 the ambassador of Henry II of France heard that a certain
goldsmith at Augsburg had invented machines for making coin,

and he was instructed to purchase them for the Paris mint. They comprised a rolling mill, a machine for stamping out blanks, and a screw press. These were installed in Paris against the fierce opposition of the moneyers, and after a short period of use they were limited to medals, jettons, and copper coins, which the moneyers thought unworthy of their attention. The same happened in England, where some machines on the French model were set up in 1561 through the agency of Éloi Mestrell, an employee of the Paris mint who had got into trouble and fled to England. Once again the new machines had to face the charges of expense and inefficiency, and their use was abolished in 1572. Such of Henry II's and Elizabeth's coins as were milled, however, stand out from the rest by reason of the circularity of their flans and the high quality of their striking. In France and England persistent attempts to install the new machinery had to be made by such men as Nicolas Briot, Jean Varin, and Blondeau in the seventeenth century before the old hammered coinage was discontinued, in 1643 in France and 1662 in England.

While the screw press was the machine most favoured in France and England, the roller press was more popular in Germany and in countries under her influence. The important mint of Hall in the Tyrol was using a roller press for coins of the Archduke Ferdinand as early as 1566, and its fame was so great that Philip II arranged with his cousin in 1584 for the construction of two similar machines for use in Spain. One of these, called in Spanish sources 'the Engine' (*el Ingenio*), was installed in 1587 by German workmen at Segovia, where it turned out heavy silver pieces of eight much superior to those of the mints of the American continent. In the 1620s and 1630s it produced splendid fifty-réal pieces of Philip III and Philip IV which are amongst the largest silver coins that have ever been struck.

These mechanical improvements were naturally accompanied by others intended to facilitate the engraving of dies, largely based on the use of more and more elaborate punches, and by measures taken to ensure a better control of the quality of alloys and the preparation and blanching of the flans. The next major group of changes, after those of the sixteenth century, came at the end of the eighteenth century with the introduction of steam power and in the nineteenth century with the introduction of electricity.

The pioneers in the application of steam power to coining were James Watt and Matthew Boulton. Watt was a Scottish engineer of genius who had effected great improvements in the steam engine of Thomas Newcomen, while Boulton was head of the great Soho works at Birmingham which manufactured a wide range of metal-ware, some varieties of which—buttons, buckles, and so forth—were produced in bulk from stamped dies. In 1774 they began to explore the possibilities of applying steam power to coining. Boulton's basic idea was that making perfectly circular coins which were uniform in weight would put an end to counterfeiting, while mechanization would speed up the work greatly as well as improving its quality. In 1786 Boulton met the French medallist Jean Pierre Droz, who had made a number of experiments in coining devices, and though the latter proved to be a disappointment Droz spent some years in his service and produced for him a number of admirable dies.

In the 1780s and 1790s Boulton erected a whole series of coining presses, and in 1792 he was able to give a most flattering account of his resources:

This Mint consists of eight large coining-machines which are sufficiently strong to coin the largest money in current use, or even Medals; and each machine is capable of being adjusted in a few minutes so as to strike any number of pieces of money from fifty to one hundred and twenty per minute, in proportion to their diameter and degree of relief; and each piece being struck in a steel collar, the whole number are perfectly round and of equal diameter. Each machine requires the attendance of one boy of only twelve years of age, and he has no labour to perform. He can stop his press one instant, and set it going again the next. The whole of the eight presses are capable of coining, at the same time, eight different sizes of money, such as English crowns, 6-livre pieces, 24-sous pieces, 12-sous, or the very smallest money that is used in France. . . . Mr Boulton's new machinery works with less friction, less wear, less noise, is less liable to be out of order, and can strike very much more than any apparatus ever before invented; for it is capable of striking at the rate of 26,000 écus or English crowns, or 50,000 of half their diameter, in one hour, and of working night and day without fatigue to the boys, provided two sets of them work alternately for ten hours each.

In 1798, to advertise the resources of his establishment, he struck a medal of himself, modelled on the twopenny piece of George III, on the reverse of which there were marked a series of concentric circles with the number of coins of each dimension, running from 400 to 920, which could be struck per minute. When one considers that the old screw press had struck only 30 coins per minute, it is easy to see the improvement that had been effected.

Boulton had at first to limit himself to striking private tokens, and coins for such institutions as the East India Company and the Sierra Leone Company, since, despite a sustained attempt to obtain a mint contract in 1787, the government remained deaf to his appeals. It was not till 1797 that he was authorized to strike 500 tons of copper into 2*d.* and 1*d.* pieces, and in 1805 the Mint itself admitted its conversion to the new machinery. It moved in 1810 out of its cramped quarters in the Tower to a new site on Tower Hill, and Boulton supplied it with all the machinery necessary for its work. He had also been authorized to export coining machinery abroad; in 1800 he equipped the mint of St. Petersburg with machines operated by steam, and a few years later did the same at Copenhagen. In the first quarter of the nineteenth century machinery of this kind came into general use in the mints of Europe and America.

These machines, in turn, went out of date and in the mid-nineteenth century they were being generally replaced by a new type invented by the German engineer Uhlhorn. This used steam as its motive power but the dies were actuated by a heavy fly-wheel; although slower than some of Boulton's presses, it was less hard on the dies and provided more regular coins. A modification of this press by Thonnelier was installed in 1845 in the Paris mint, which had continued up to then to use the screw press, and Uhlhorn presses were set up in the subsidiary British mints of Sydney and Melbourne in 1853 and 1859 respectively. In the 1870s several were acquired for the Royal Mint, which in 1882 went over completely to the new machinery. The presses could strike an average of about 100 coins a minute, and since there might be up to twenty in use at any one time, the total output could reach 700,000 or 800,000 in a working day. Output per pair of dies varied from about 20,000 to 70,000 according to the metal and denomination.

Modern coining presses have affected only one aspect of the mechanization of minting; they are supplemented by electric furnaces for melting the metal and preparing the alloys, by improved methods for annealing and blanching, by automatic weighing machines for the blanks and the finished coins. One important device, the reducing machine for preparing dies, requires more specific mention.

Although die-sinkers in the sixteenth and seventeenth centuries were using more and more complicated punches for whole sections of the design of the coins, the making of dies was a serious bottleneck in large-scale coin production. Early in the nineteenth century, however, a *tour à reduire* was invented in Paris to facilitate the making of dies for medals, and after Pistrucci had acquired one for his own use and found it satisfactory William Wyon had

FIG. 55. Modern coining presses at work in the Royal Mint at Llantrisant, South Wales. The presses have an automatic blank feed system from above, and each produces 200–250 coins a minute.

one installed in the Royal Mint (1824), and they are today in general use. A large plaster model about ten or twelve inches in diameter is made of the design of each face of the coin. From this either a cast or an electrotype is made. The reducing machine, working on the pantograph principle, involves a delicately pivoted arm which moves up and down over the surface of this large model as it is rotated, and since it has at its other end a cutting edge which moves shorter distances against the surface of a smaller disc of metal it will reproduce on this the design and contours of the original model but on a smaller scale. The reduction to the size of the coin is effected in several stages, till finally a punch the desired size is complete. This is used to prepare the coin dies, which are thus all identical with one another. It cannot be said that the results are artistically satisfactory, for proportion and details that may appear attractive on a design ten inches in diameter may be quite inappropriate on one of an inch or even less. The reducing machine is commonly blamed for the banality of most modern coin design, but the existence of Wyon's admirable 'young head' of Queen Victoria shows that this explanation cannot be the whole truth. In any case, since a modern coin die may be expected to strike 80,000 coins and many millions of a particular denomination may have to be struck in a year, its use is a necessary concession to the needs of modern currency.

The Issue of Coin

Once coin is struck it has to pass into circulation. How it does this depends very largely on who was the original owner of the bullion from which it was made, or at least on the conditions under which bullion is brought to the mint to be coined.

Where a private person is free to bring in bullion for minting there is obviously no problem. He will receive back an amount of coin corresponding in value to the bullion he has brought. There will probably be some delay in this, since the mint officials will have to assay the metal. In any case, the coin he receives will not normally be made from the ingots or plate he brought in, but will merely be made from metal equivalent in value. Where mints were small and output inconsiderable, however, as in medieval times, there must often have been an exact correspondence between bullion and coin. This would have been the case for the Athenian gold coins struck from the melting down of the statues of Victory on the Acropolis in 407 B.C. and the unicorns made from sixty-one links of the king's gold chain condemned to the crucible by James IV of Scotland in 1497.

Bullion provided by the government for coining will have been for the most part acquired through taxation, though occasionally it will happen that the state is either in control of gold- or silver-mines or can make a substantial levy on their exploitation. When money comes in to the government in the form of coin it may be either paid out again with the same coins, in which case the mint will not be involved, or it will be melted and re-issued as new money. Melting and re-issue are costly and troublesome, but they prevent the government being defrauded and they perform the valuable function of keeping the coinage in good condition. They have consequently often been the custom. In late Roman times the gold collected in the form of taxes was melted, assayed, and valued before being accepted by the officials of the Treasury and turned over to the Mint, and the *Dialogus de Scaccario* describes in detail how the silver pennies brought in by the sheriffs in twelfth-century England were assayed and often melted before payments were approved by the Barons of the Exchequer. At certain periods of the Byzantine Empire it seems to have been the custom that government expenses should be paid in newly minted coin, which explains both the high quality of surviving solidi and the vast amount of overstriking that is found in the bronze.

Government money can pass into circulation in a number of ways. In varying degrees a government will have a civil service to pay and a mass of daily needs to satisfy. Even under medieval conditions, when customary services might provide much gratuitous transport and food-rents supply many of the requirements of a court, there would be innumerable needs over and above these—the construction of buildings and the purchase of luxuries—which could be satisfied only by money. Most important of all would be expenses of a military character. *Point d'argent, point de Suisse* is a maxim whose relevance is not confined to the sixteenth century, and the cost of equipment has often been an even heavier drain on the treasury than mere army pay. The close association of coining with military activity is a phenomenon recorded from all periods of history.

A mint normally needs to possess a certain reserve, so that it does not run on a hand-to-mouth basis. In the Middle Ages this was effected by confining contracts to moneyers, either singly or in partnership, who had considerable means as well as technical competence at their disposal. In more modern times, and even to some extent in the Middle Ages, governments have tried to build up reserves of coined money for emergencies. A consequence of this may often be some considerable delay between the minting of a coin and its issue to the public. When a mint finds that it has overproduced a coin for which there is little public demand, it may suspend its manufacture for some years. No British pennies were struck during 1923, 1924, or 1925, since the Mint found that it had large supplies of 1922 and earlier years on hand. These coins were in consequence being 'issued' over a period of years subsequent to the dates they bear. Lower denominations tend to pass into circulation more slowly than high ones, in which government payments are made, for they serve only the needs of small-scale commerce and usually have to be applied for directly by members of the public.

6
Coin Finds and Hoards

On the night of 12 June 1667, when news came that the Dutch had broken the chain in the Medway and burnt *The Royal Charles*, Samuel Pepys discussed with his wife and father what to do with 'the little that I have in money by me'. Next morning he sent the pair off by coach with £1,300 in gold, and instructions to conceal this safely at his country estate in Huntingdonshire. Later in the day, alarmed by the growing panic in London, he dispatched his clerk with another thousand guineas to the same destination, while he himself acquired a belt in which, very uncomfortably, he could conceal £300 in gold on his person.

Not till 10 October, nearly four months later, was Pepys able to recover what had been buried, digging at night in his garden with the help of a lantern under extremely exasperating conditions. First the exact place could not be found, his arguments with his father being hampered by the fact that the latter was deaf and he dared not shout for fear of attracting the attention of neighbours. Then, when something was located by poking about with a spit, Pepys feared that the hoard would no longer be intact. The hole was only shallow and had been dug, as he learnt to his dismay, during daytime and might have been observed, for he found himself unable to take seriously his father's assurance that it was perfectly safe, since the neighbours would all have been at church. The bags holding the gold were in due course found to have rotted away, so that the coins were scattered through the soil and had to be dug for and subsequently cleaned in a pail of water. The exact total to be expected was anyhow uncertain, for one of the bags had split while on the road and not all the coins that had fallen out had been found, so that Pepys in the end thought himself lucky to emerge only some £20 short of what he had sent.

Pepys's hoard differs from the many that have come down to

us in that its owner was able to recover it. This, no doubt, was what usually happened. Most hoards buried for safe-keeping were dis-interred when the emergency was over, but some, in all periods, were not. Warfare was important not so much because it caused more hoards to be buried than during peacetime, although this was the case, but that it greatly increased the chances of their permanent loss, either because their owners were subsequently killed or because they forgot exactly where they had concealed their wealth or were not able to revisit the site owing to enemy occupation.

A hoard is by definition a group of coins or other valuables which was concealed as a unit, but hoards are not the only form in which coins are lost. Coins are being casually dropped all the time, and since metal is in varying degrees resistant to corrosion a high proportion are eventually found. Hoards and accumulations of single finds are for the most part less obviously interesting than coins in collections, since they often consist of hundreds of virtually identical objects instead of being chosen precisely because they differ between themselves. But quite apart from being the ultimate source of all the coins, other than those of the most modern period, that one sees in collections, coin finds are the numismatist's most valuable single guide to classification and dating and are virtually his sole guide to coinage in circulation.

Classification of Finds

The interpretation of coin finds depends very greatly on what can be surmised regarding the circumstances of their loss. The best clue to this is provided by the context in which they were found. There are three main categories of coin finds: (1) casual or stray finds, (2) hoards, and (3) excavation finds. The two latter can be further subdivided: hoards according to the probable circum-stances of their loss and excavation finds according to whether they are location or area finds. It is also possible to make a further distinction, to some extent cutting across those based on context, between finds of single coins, cumulative finds, and hoards, the two latter each involving a number of coins but hoards implying groups put together at the time of loss and cumulative finds implying those brought together by circumstance. Each of these types can be expected to supply the numismatist and historian with different kinds of information.

The use that the numismatist makes of find evidence raises an important question of principle. The coins in a single find are not normally of much consequence in themselves; indeed, from the moment that they were lost—though not from the moment they were concealed, if their concealment was intentional—they ceased to perform any economic function at all. They are important because they are samples of coin populations, but they are samples only at several removes. The coins whose finding is recorded are only samples of those actually found, since many others will have been melted down or disposed of to collectors without record. The coins that have been found are in their turn only samples of those that were lost, for many others will have been lost and found again in the past and others still remain to be found in the future. The coins that are lost are themselves only samples of the circulating media, and are likely to be highly slanted samples, since except in such a period as that of the silver penny in the West, when there was only a single denomination in circulation, they will in excavation finds be strongly biased in favour of low denominations and in hoards be equally strongly biased in favour of high ones. It must be accepted, in fact, that when a number of denominations existed any coin find will be a sample of only some of them. The problem is that of deciding how representative, within this limitation, it is likely to be.

In certain cases there is clear evidence that the sampling is good. Where an area site has been carefully excavated over a period of years and the date of each individual coin find recorded, it is possible to compare, decade by decade, the proportions of coins representing particular historical periods or reigns that have come to light. If these proportions remain constant, if coins of one period of Byzantine history remain consistently rare and those of another consistently common, it is fair to assume that the coins being found are reliable samples of particular levels of the local coin populations of these periods. Emergency hoards, which involve the sudden removal of samples of current coins from circulation, also reflect very closely the proportions of coins of particular denominations one would expect to be there. The classical demonstration of this was made by the Swedish numismatist Bengt Thordeman in the account he gave in the *Numismatic Chronicle* for 1948 of the huge Lohe hoard of silver coins, dating from the late seventeenth century to 1741, which was found in Stockholm in 1937. The hoard was discovered when repairing a cellar vault in a house that in 1741 had belonged to one of the descendants of Johann Lohe, who at the time of his death (1704) was reputed to be one of the richest men in Sweden. Almost all the 18,000 coins in the hoard were dated, and it happens that for these

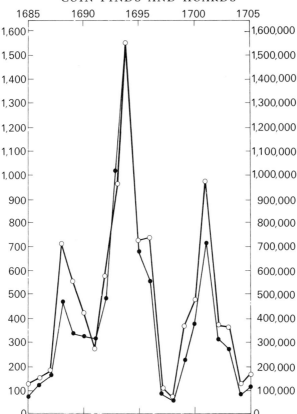

Fig. 56. Coin distribution in the Lohe hoard. Part of Thordeman's graph comparing for the years 1685–1705 the hoard content in mark-coins (thick line, figures on left) with mint output in mark-coins (thin line, figures on right).

years the records of the Stockholm mint are nearly complete and give the output of coins year by year. Thordeman drew a graph comparing annual mint output in thousands of coins with the actual numbers in the hoard, and showed that variations in high and low output were reflected in the hoard with great fidelity, the hoard numbers rarely deviating more than 5 per cent in relation to those of the coins issued by the mint. The Lohe picture was supported by that of a number of other Swedish hoards of the same period which Thordeman also examined, although since they were much smaller their correspondence with the fluctuations in mint output was necessarily less close. But they were sufficient to show that under certain circumstances an emergency hoard can reflect very accurately the pattern of certain levels of denominations in the circulating medium at the moment of burial.

If samples are sometimes accurate, however, one cannot assume that they are always so. The evidence of area excavations does not hold good in reverse, for if there are inconsistencies they cannot be assumed to imply that the sampling is unreliable; it may simply be due to the fact that other levels of a city are being dug or that the quarters involved were differently paved or inhabited by different social classes. A hoard concealed by a merchant engaged in foreign trade will reflect the latest payments he has received, and may be radically different in composition from one found no more than a few yards away, but buried by someone else, as indeed it might well be quite different from one buried by the same person a few days before or afterwards. If Thordeman's Swedish hoards reflected total mint output with great accuracy, this can only have been due to the fact that over the period in question there was little export or melting down of coin. Recent studies of actual coin populations in Great Britain and the United States show that these diverge considerably from the compositions one would expect from aggregating totals of mint output, and some of the factors lying behind these divergences will certainly have operated in the past. In any case, the Lohe evidence only holds good for sudden withdrawals from the circulating medium, not for savings hoards, where the amount of coin put away each year will vary according to the resources of the owner and not according to the output of the mint.

Casual Finds

By casual finds are meant the innumerable coins that turn up by chance and not as the result of systematic excavation. Most hoards belong to the class of casual finds, but isolated casual finds form so large a group that they have to be made a separate category of their own. They usually consist of single coins, of little interest in themselves, although if sufficiently well recorded they can sometimes provide a scholar with valuable information. A single coin found in somebody's back garden will usually tell one little unless its testimony is reinforced by records of similar finds in the same neighbourhood, in which case it is usually good evidence regarding coin circulation. An accumulation of isolated finds is in this respect more valuable than a hoard, which may have been lost by a merchant or pilgrim or some other traveller, so that its contents are not typical of the local currency. One large group of early British coins was long ascribed to the Brigantes on the strength of a hoard found in Yorkshire in 1829, and it was only the discovery of two hoards and a long series of casual site finds from Lincolnshire and other counties south of the Humber that made necessary their transfer to the Coritani. The scholar's difficulty is that except for notoriously rare series there is little stimulus to recording the find spots of single coins, and there is always the possibility of the record being contaminated by losses in modern times. It is now accepted that the few ancient Greek coins found in the British Isles, which were formerly taken as evidence of commercial relations between Britain and the Greek world, must be written off as either casual losses of the Roman period or strays from modern collections.

Cumulative finds sometimes come into the category of stray finds, for a number of people on separate occasions may lose coins over a relatively restricted area, and these for some reason may end up in the same place. One may instance the numerous coins of low value which were found in the ruins of the Campanile of St. Mark's in Venice after it collapsed in 1902 and which had evidently been dropped by visitors and collected in the stair-well, or the accumulation of fifteenth-century Scottish pennies and *Crux pellit* coins—they are better called tokens—which came to light in 1919 when cleaning out a choked-up drain once used to flush the latrines of Crossraguel Abbey in Ayrshire. These represented the casual losses of persons using the latrines over a period of a couple of centuries, and had fallen into the stream and been carried as far as the strength of the current would take them. Cumulative finds tell us little about the dating of individual coins but can be extremely important for localization. The *Crux pellit* tokens are a good example, for they bear no more than the name of a king James (*Jacobus Dei gra. rex*) and had been attributed by different nineteenth-century numismatists to a miscellany of European monarchs: James I of Aragon (1213–76), James II of Aragon as king of Sicily (1285–96), both of whom would in fact be too early for that particular type of coin, James of Bourbon (1414–16), husband of Joanna II of Naples, and James I (1382–98) or James II (1460–73) of Cyprus. Since the lettering and style of the coins is fifteenth or conceivably late fourteenth century, any of the latter would be possible as long as one had only museum material to work from, but the Crossraguel find confirmed the deduction already made by some scholars from a number of stray finds that they were really Scottish in origin.

Hoards

The essential feature of a coin hoard is that the coins composing it should have been brought together at the time when it was concealed. There is no minimum or maximum size of hoards. Strictly speaking, two coins hidden together constitute a hoard, but it is difficult to suppose that anyone would deliberately conceal only two coins, so that although these might confirm each other's evidence it is only for purposes of classification that they can be regarded as hoards. The majority of hoards probably contain between 50 and 100 coins, but a fair number exceed 1,000, and a few are much larger. A hoard of late-fourth-century Roman imperial coins of black billon discovered in 1902 at Kostolac (Viminacium) in Yugoslavia exceeded 100,000 coins, and one of thirteenth-century pennies of the British Isles and the Low Countries found in 1908 during repairs to a house in Brussels exceeded 140,000. The intrinsic value of these hoards was not very great—the Brussels hoard would have been worth the equivalent of just over £400 sterling or £1,600 Brabantine—but large hoards of gold coins, and of heavy silver coins of comparable value, are on record. The Lohe hoard has already been mentioned, but large hoards of this kind are not limited to the modern period. The Demanhur hoard from Lower Egypt, discovered in 1905, contained over 8,000 tetradrachms of Alexander the Great. A hoard of just under 3,000 sixteenth- and seventeenth-century gold coins discovered at Košice in Czechoslovakia in 1935 has as its counterpart one of 1,439 solidi of the fifth century A.D. turned up by the plough at Szikáncs-tanya in Hungary in the 1960s. The first of these had apparently belonged to some wealthy private individual, while the second is shown by the date of the coins to have made part of the huge annual tributes paid in the 440s by Theodosius II to Attila the Hun and distributed by the latter to his retainers. The largest gold hoard on record, indeed, dates from classical times. It is said to have amounted to 80,000 Roman Republican aurei, i.e. about 64 kilos or just over a hundredweight of gold, and was found in 1714 at Brescello, a village near Modena, having apparently been buried in 37 B.C. during the period of warfare that followed the death of Caesar.

Hoards can be conveniently divided into four classes: accidental losses, emergency hoards, savings hoards, and abandoned hoards. A feature of some is the way in which they include round sums of money, presumably single payments which had been kept intact or put aside for a definite purpose. The Szikáncs-tanya hoard just alluded to presumably consisted originally of 1,440 coins, i.e. exactly twenty Roman pounds, but one was inadvertently over-looked when the hoard came to light. Hoards are sometimes composite and often include sub-hoards, which are occasionally quite far removed in time from the final date of burial. The Oxarve hoard from Gotland, found in 1920, included five distinct groups of coins, Roman, Muslim, Byzantine, English, and German, of which the Roman element was a hoard of 79 Republican denarii somehow acquired by the proprietor, the Byzantine coins included what seems to have been a single sum of 100 miliaresia made up exactly half and half of two varieties of coin of Constantine IX of slightly different values, and the English and German elements totalled, with the help of a few Scandinavian additions, a sum of exactly thirty shillings. A hoard discovered at Colchester in 1959 contained what were essentially two groups of coins, one of over a thousand thirteenth-century pennies ending with issues which can be dated to 1256 and the other of nearly two thousand pennies, all struck by the same pair of dies, from ten years later. Not all hoards can be broken up in this way, but the keeping together of groups of coins is a very characteristic feature of the monetary habits of people throughout history.

Accidental losses. These usually take the form of purses or small bags of coin, the containers being sometimes found intact, although more often, having been made of cloth or other perishable material, they have disappeared. The coins involved may be of high value or low, according to circumstances, and will normally represent the currency of the day. They usually consist of uneven sums of money, since their contents will not have been put aside for any particular purpose, but there are exceptions. One of these was a small hoard of gold coins, discovered at Crondall in Hampshire in 1828, which is now, almost complete, in the Ashmolean Museum at Oxford. It consisted originally of 24 Merovingian coins, 69 Anglo-Saxon ones, one Byzantine tremissis that had been mounted and the mount later cut away, three roughly struck 'coins', evidently made by an amateur and having no recognizable type, three blanks of the same weight as the coins, and one contemporary forgery of plated copper, i.e. a total of 101 objects. The natural interpretation of this hoard is that the sum represented a payment of 100 shillings, perhaps a wergeld, that someone had to make. He managed to get together 94 coins, but since in seventh-century England coins were little used he had to make up the remaining 6 with home-made pieces of gold of appropriate sizes

and weight. When the payment came to be made, one of the coins
was discovered to be false, and a coin of the same weight, after the
mount had been cut off, was taken from a necklace to make the
sum complete.

Emergency hoards. Burials in emergency will usually have the same
kind of contents as accidental losses, for the owner buries what he
has. The most frequent cause of such permanent loss is warfare,
since while in times of peace a prudent man may keep his money
hidden, he will also be able to recover it at need. Often the sums
are large, but a poor man will on occasion have to hide his savings.
A pathetic memorial of the Thirty Years War came to light at
Bollingen (Württemberg) in 1910, when a small hoard of almost
worthless billon coins was discovered during repairs to a school.
It was accompanied by a terrified note in indifferent German on
a small scrap of paper recording how the Swedes had carried off
everything and the owner had hidden what little he had ('Der
Schwedt ist komme, hat alz mitgenomme, hat auch wolle hawe,
I habs vergrabe. 1634. Bozehartt).

   A few special types of emergency hoard may be mentioned. One
is that of official hoards, where the coins were not the property of
a private person but were of a public character, e.g. a military chest
or the receipts of a tax or customs officer. The Kostolac hoard
probably belonged to the latter category, as did a hoard of over
5,000 silver coins found in 1923 on the site of the Old Customs
House at Bristol; the date of the latest coins in it show it to have
been buried as William III was marching up from Torbay in
November 1688. Pepys's hoard is a fairly typical case of a refugee
hoard, i.e. one not buried in the spot where the coins have been
collected but in that where their owner has taken refuge. Such
hoards, whose existence greatly increases the difficulty of correct
hoard interpretation, must have been very common; examples are
a number of Cretan hoards of classical times and the large Cypriot
hoards buried in the first half of the seventh century A.D., when
the neighbouring mainland was overrun in turn by Persians and
Arabs. If islands are obvious places of refuge, however, they are
equally notorious as pirate strongholds, and the many Gotland
and Bornholm hoards of late Roman gold solidi are matched by
Viking silver hoards of the ninth and tenth centuries from the
Scottish islands. Robber hoards can often be recognized by the
presence in them of cut-up silver plate as well as coin. Many date
from the time of the Germanic invasions, two of the best-known
having been found in the British Isles, at Coleraine in Ulster and
Traprain Law in Scotland.

The value of emergency hoards to the numismatist arises from the fact that they are taken directly from the circulating medium at the moment of burial and are likely to reproduce the proportion of old coins and foreign coins in it with considerable fidelity. Emergency hoards are particularly valuable for dating. Mixed hoards of dated and undated coins will provide a basis for dating the latter, particularly if, as sometimes happens, a number of hoards of very similar composition are found together over the same area and we can be sure that they were buried on the same occasion. It was the scattered coins and hoards found by a Yale expedition amongst the burnt debris of Morgantina that supplied scholars in the 1960s with the crucial evidence for the date of the introduction of the Roman denarius, for specimens of what on stylistic and other grounds must be regarded as the earliest denarii were found in company with Syracusan coins ending with those of Hiero II (*ob.* 215 B.C.) and Hieronymus (215–14 B.C.) on a site which is known from Livy to have been laid waste by the Romans in 211 B.C. A more frequent use of such hoards for the numismatist is where a number have been found with overlapping contents, for then a comparison between them will often allow him to establish the sequence of a series of otherwise undated coinages. The thirteen types of penny issued by William I and II of England, for example, have been arranged in chronological order essentially on the basis of hoard evidence, as shown in the accompanying Table (Fig. 57), the testimony of which would be still more cogent if the exact numbers of the various types in each hoard, and not simply their presence, had been noted in the descriptions of some of the older ones. Evidence of this kind is often reinforced, as it is with these Norman coins, by conclusions drawn from moneyer sequences and type or die linkages, but it is basically on the hoards that the chronology depends.

Over and above the value of emergency hoards to the numismatist, their study can provide much incidental information to the historian. The total number of hoards is only significant in a general way, since it is impossible to make allowance for the number that were concealed and subsequently recovered, but their geographical distribution is often instructive. Coin finds in Gaul of the early fifth century A.D. can be fairly closely related to the movements of barbarian raiders of that period, and Thordeman has shown how coin finds in southern Sweden of the 1560s reflect troop movements during the Swedish–Danish War of 1562–9. Thordeman's figures also show how losses increase during a war, for only five hoards can be dated to the decade 1540–50 and one to

	WILLIAM I (1066–1087)								WILLIAM II (1087–1100)					HENRY I (1100–35)	
	I	II	III	IV	V	VI	VII	VIII	I	II	III	IV	V	I	Later types
Soberton (1851)	22														
York (1845)	1?	165													
York (1882)	Mule +	+													
Whitchurch (19th cent.)	+	+	+												
St. Mary Hill Church (1774)	+	+	+	+	Mule 1 / +										
City of London (1872)	1	2		5											
Malmesbury (1828)		1		12											
York Minster (19th cent.)					6	5									
Beaworth (1833)					31	34	11	Mule 6 / 6457							
Tamworth (1877)								30	Mule 97 / 3	164					
Shillington (1871)								1	+	+	+	+			4 or 5 (?)
Bermondsey (1820)										3	5			5	

FIG. 57. Hoards of Anglo-Norman coins. This table, adapted from one in G. C. Brooke's catalogue of coins of *The Norman Kings* in the British Museum (1916), shows how hoards can make clear the sequence of types. These are numbered across the top of the table. The earlier hoards usually contained coins of Harold and Edward the Confessor, and even of their predecessors, which are not shown. A plus sign means that the number of specimens is not recorded. The sequence is confirmed by the muling between types, whose occurrence is noted.

that of 1570–80, as against thirty-one hoards containing coins ending with dates in the 1550s and 1560s and presumably for the most part buried after 1562.

Savings hoards. Hoards in the traditional sense—savings put together by their owners over a period of years—form yet another category. 'Le sol', as a French scholar once remarked, 'était le coffre-fort de nos ancêtres', though occasionally such hoards are found not in the soil but in hollowed-out beams or hiding-places in the thickness of a wall. It is hard for a person living today to imagine the amount of precious metal which in former times any-one of reasonable means expected to have in his house, much of it in the form of plate, but some also in coin. Pepys was comfortably off, but not rich by late seventeenth-century standards, yet we have seen that he had nearly £3,000 in gold in his house and could refer to it, apparently without affectation, as 'the little that I have in money by me'. Coin would have a slight advantage over plate in that, while both represented easily mobilizable wealth, coin was already made up into acceptable units of convenient size. Savings hoards have consequently always existed, in the precious metals for those who could afford them but in billon or bronze for those who could not.

Savings hoards differ in a number of respects from emergency hoards. They will, in the first place, tend to be selective, containing high-value coins in preference to low-value ones and better specimens of such coins, unworn ones if possible, rather than inferior ones. It is the high quality of coins from savings hoards that accounts for the remarkable state of preservation of so many ancient and medieval gold coins in modern collections. Although they often cover a considerable span of years, savings hoards tend to be less useful for dating, as their contents lack the contrast between worn and unworn coins that is helpful in studying the contents of emergency hoards. Finally, but most important, under conditions of peace the vast majority of savings hoards will not have survived to modern times, since in due course they will have been put back into circulation by their owners or inheritors. We cannot therefore deduce a period of poverty from an absence of hoards. It is probably the case that savings hoards are more useful to the modern scholar in supplying him with material than for any conclusions he can draw from their structure or incidence.

Abandoned hoards. This slightly clumsy term comprises hoards whose owners have consciously disposed of their coins with no intention of retrieving them. Usually such hoards are funerary in character, involving the burial of part of a person's wealth as a kind of grandiose Charon's obol, though the latter is normally a single coin and not technically a 'hoard'. Funerary deposits sometimes include coins of value, as at Sutton Hoo, but more often, as Charon's obol often was, they are coins which are obsolete or otherwise useless, so it is difficult to draw from them firm conclusions regarding their date of deposit. The burial of coins in the foundations of buildings, which is common in many periods of history, is another example of voluntary abandonment. Some cumulative hoards have come into existence as a result of voluntary abandonment over a period of years, in the way in which visitors throw coins into the fountain of Trevi at Rome. Thousands of Roman coins, and even a few Greek ones, have been found in the holy well of Coventina at Carrawburgh (Procolitia) on the Roman wall, while the excavations of the Shrine of St. Peter at Rome brought to light thousands of early medieval coins which had formed part of the offerings of generations of pilgrims but had slipped down through spaces in the grating or cracks in the masonry and not been collected by the guardians at the time. Such cumulative finds have to be interpreted with caution, for they may easily mislead. Many of the Greek coins in Coventina's well long antedated the Roman occupation of Britain and the construction of the Wall. They must have been left there by Roman soldiers, who presumably had them as keepsakes or amulets.

Excavation Finds

Excavation finds are a type of evidence which has only begun to be exploited in quite recent times. The reasons for this are various. Single sites often produce no coins at all, and the coins which are found in the excavation of large areas of ancient cities are for the most part of bronze and in poor condition, for having lain isolated in the soil they have been subjected to corrosion and decomposition over the centuries. They are consequently of no interest to the collector and often too worn to provide evidence on metrology or privy marks. Their systematic recording is both time-consuming and costly, since it involves a meticulous sifting of the earth and the services of a competent numismatist. Many excavations have been undertaken by individuals or institutions interested in specific types of object, such as buildings, statuary, or inscriptions, and have tended to neglect anything else. The result is that the older excavations, even if efficiently conducted in other respects, often made no record of coin finds at all. Over the past half-century there has been a great improvement, though rather because excavators themselves are better aware of the contribution that coins can make to dating than out of any disinterested desire to satisfy the curiosity of the numismatist. But much room for improvement remains. Within the past decade the excavation report of a site in Apulia misdated one coin hoard by at least half a century through its author having relied on out-of-date guides to Byzantine and south Italian coins, and that of a Polish excavation in Bulgaria not only mis-identified most of the Byzantine coins that were found but wrongly linked several of the obverses and reverses in the illustrations, thus creating a number of coin types that had no real existence at all.

In discussing excavations one can make a broad distinction between what may be conveniently termed location finds and area finds. Location finds consist of the coins that come to light in the excavation of a site of limited size, such as a Roman villa or a Frankish graveyard. The coins found are likely to be few in number, since not many will have been lost in a small area occupied for a restricted period. While important for the archaeologist as providing evidence for dating, they are not likely to contribute much to the numismatist's knowledge, since unless the evidence from neighbouring sites is available, they will be too few to make possible any general deductions. Their evidence is fundamentally no different from that of stray finds, save that systematic digging will have produced more material. Area finds, i.e. the coins brought to light by the excavation of an entire inhabited area or a large part of one, are something very different, and much more important. Such excavations are only possible where the ancient site is no longer inhabited or special arrangements can be made to clear part of it, as was done for the excavation of the site of the Athenian Agora. When excavations of this kind are thoroughly done and the site has been inhabited over many centuries, the number of coins found is astonishing. The American excavations at Athens and Corinth have in each case produced over 100,000 coins, and it is believed that something approaching the same number, though they are much less well documented, have been turned up on the far smaller and much more briefly inhabited site at Richborough in this country. The types of coins that are found are basically no different from those of location finds—low denominations, coins in very poor condition—but they are important because the numbers are so large that one can draw reasonably firm conclusions from them regarding the nature of the circulating medium and the changes in it over long periods of time.

Area finds, however, have their own limitations. Hoards are only rarely found on town sites, since while towns represent places where the use of coin was concentrated, their streets and buildings will have been so frequently repaired and reconstructed over the centuries that virtually all hoards of valuable coins will have long since been discovered and found their way to the melting-pot. It is only when the occupation of a site has been brought to a sudden and catastrophic end that we can hope to learn much from it about the higher denominations in use. This has sometimes happened, as when Pompeii was overwhelmed by Vesuvius in A.D. 79 or Morgantina in Sicily destroyed by the Romans, but in general we must recognize the fact that area finds are important for subsidiary coinage only. Even here their evidence may be incomplete, and care has to be taken in interpreting it. It is tempting to compare the numbers found over different periods and draw economic conclusions from the changes one finds, but one must view the evidence critically before doing so. Small coins are more easily lost than large ones, and, despite the story of the widow's mite, their losers will worry less about their loss; one must therefore avoid direct numerical comparisons when the values or types of coin involved are very different from each other. One must also take account of the general archaeological setting; the coin population of an area may change because the character of its settlement changed—city areas go up and down—not because the currency situation changed in general. Casual losses are likely to be frequent during building operations or repairs to sewers: is the high proportion of coins of a particular ruler in one quarter of a city due to such activities during his reign? It is true that the reliability of area evidence can sometimes be checked by comparing the number and character of finds made in successive decades while a major excavation has been in progress, but this is not always possible. Excavation coins are an extremely valuable source, but not one to be used uncritically.

Recording and Preservation

In view of their importance to the numismatist, the treatment of single finds and hoards raises a number of problems. Recording and preservation have to be looked at separately. Accurate recording of where coins are found, and what they are, is in general highly desirable. It has too often been badly done, or left completely undone, in the past. Every numismatist has at some time or other been completely frustrated because some element in a hoard description, essential to his research, is missing. The names of rulers are recorded but not the mints, the identities of the coins but not the numbers present. On the other hand, hoard description is a slow business, and can take up the time of scholars who could be better occupied; many hoards are quite without importance, and it would be mere waste of time to try to record every coin that is found. Yet it is difficult to know where to draw the line between recording the finding of an Anglo-Saxon coin with a Runic inscription near Cambridge, which is important, and that of recording the finding of a denarius of Hadrian or a halfpenny of George III nearby, which may tell us nothing at all. Age by itself is no criterion: a coin of Hadrian is earlier than an Anglo-Saxon one. One has to exercise one's common sense, and hope one does not go too far astray.

Some scholars hold that the remedy for imperfect hoard descriptions is to ensure that all coins become the property of the community and are kept in local or national museums, so that they can be consulted by later scholars and the deficiencies of earlier accounts put right. This is done in Scandinavia and most of the states of eastern Europe, but it may be doubted whether it does not tend to create a greater evil. Few hoards are so important that, when they contain many of what are customarily regarded as duplicates, i.e. coins struck by the same pair of dies, their maintenance as intact units serves a useful purpose. An excellent case can be made for keeping the Crondall hoard intact, despite the presence of die duplicates in it, since it contains over half the Anglo-Saxon gold coins at present known and it is highly desirable to keep them together for purposes of comparison and study. But no object is served in keeping together accumulations of hundreds of identical Roman denarii, or thirteenth-century Wienerpfennige, or even solidi of Theodosius II. Once they have been properly recorded, and arrangements made for the retention of rarities, the others are far better made available to collectors, whether private persons or other museums. No doubt, some time in the future, scholars will find that details which they want to know will have been overlooked by numismatists of the present day, just as we deplore the deficiencies of our predecessors. But such occasional and uncertain disadvantages are outweighed by the certainty that, if the supply of coins is curtailed, we are depriving working numismatists of the material which they need for their studies.

7
Numismatic Techniques

There are a number of ways in which the numismatist can set about verifying and extending the information made available to him by a single coin. His aim, most obviously, is to discover when and where it was struck, and by what authority; what its value was in relation to the monetary system of the time; and what its theoretical weight and fineness were. Beyond these fairly immediate requirements he will wish to know more about its numismatic features—the sources of its type and inscription, the details of its manufacture—and its monetary features—the approximate size of its issue, its area of circulation and exchange value against other coins. Information on some of these points may be provided directly by the coin itself; information on others depends on further specimens of the same type of coin and of related ones being available for comparison; and some matters can be learned only from written records, although since these are not available for many periods of history the numismatist must learn to make do as best he can without them. In their absence, however, his knowledge will always remain imperfect. The study of coin types and find spots alone would allow the student of Ancient British coins to group them in a meaningful fashion and determine the areas over which each type circulated, but if it were not for the documents he would not know the name of a single one of the Celtic tribes responsible for their issue.

Inscriptions and types are the primary sources of information, for in favourable circumstances they will answer a number of the numismatist's basic questions. But their information may not go into much detail. If there is no date on a coin, he may learn that it was struck by a particular ruler, but not the exact year; worse still, if the coin is one of a republic or city and does not record either dates or magistrates' names or symbols, the inscription may give only the name of the state and leave possible a theoretical period of issue extending over several centuries. Sometimes information which is apparently precise may be misleading, for not all coins were struck under the conditions alleged by inscription and type. In some periods of history there are imitative coinages and coinages with 'immobilized' types and inscriptions, when the effigy or name of a ruler was continued for decades and occasionally even centuries after his death. Further, some designs are meant only to distinguish a coin from others circulating at the same time, not to identify it in the full sense of the word. Successive issues of Wienerpfennige of the thirteenth century have no inscriptions but only a miscellany of such types as a unicorn, a griffon, a horseman, an eagle, a crowned lion, and so forth, from which by themselves we could not hope to learn when, by whom, or in what country the coins were struck.

Dating and Localization

The amount of information given on a coin is quite unpredictable. A modern coin may bear the name of a sovereign or a country and a precise date, thus giving us information on these points directly. Coins have often been dated in the past, sometimes by particular eras, for example by the Seleucid era or from the Hijra, or by regnal years. Sometimes coins are dated indirectly. The inscription of the coin of Trajan cited on p. 21 enables us to say that it was issued in A.D. 102, but only because we know from other sources that Trajan was associated on the throne by Nerva in A.D. 97 and that the tribunician power was assumed annually, so that TR.P.VII in the inscription must mean A.D. 102. But if the coin had recorded only a consulship, as many of Trajan's coins do, we would probably have been much worse off, for while his third and fourth consulships were assumed in successive years, so that coins with COS.III in the inscription belong to A.D. 100, there was a long interval between his fifth and sixth, so that coins with COS.V may belong to any year between 103 and 110. Trajan's coinage, however, even within the Roman imperial setting, is unusual in the length and precision of its obverse inscriptions, and those of other states are normally less informative. A coin of classical Athens of the type illustrated on p. 85 may have been struck anywhere between either 490 B.C. or 480 B.C., when—or so it has been supposed—Athena's head was provided with an olive crown to commemorate the victories of Marathon or Salamis, and

322 B.C., or soon afterwards, when the city was conquered by Macedon and the Old Style coinage came to an end.

For the more precise dating of coins as vaguely labelled as those of many Roman emperors or of Athens in the fifth and fourth centuries B.C. one can formulate virtually no rules at all. Each case depends on circumstances: on what further information can be extracted from the coin, on the availability of other sources for the period in question, on considerations of type and style, on a study of die relationships. The first two require no explanation. If a ruler reigned for a number of years at a time when the convention of characterized portraiture was respected, the details of the bust may allow us to date the coin early or late in the reign. A sovereign may associate himself with one or more co-rulers, or may acquire or lose territory (cf. Edward III's noble on p. 84), or may change his title, any of which may be reflected in type or inscription or both. A coin may be datable because it alludes to a military victory or the completion of a building or the celebration of an anniversary or some similar event, though such indications have to be interpreted with caution: anniversaries are not always celebrated punctually and what are interpreted as veiled allusions to public events may really have been nothing of the kind. A stater of Delphi was for long ascribed to 346 B.C. on the assumption that its inscription *Amphiktionon* was due to Philip of Macedon's having presided in that year at the meeting of the Amphictyonic Council; the subsequent discovery of the treasurers' accounts showed that the coin was struck ten years later and the inscription had no special significance at all. The chronological order of different coin types is often determined by hoard evidence, as described in Chapter 6 (pp. 133–4), and hoard evidence is sometimes reinforced by mulings between the dies used for successive types (p. 134). Changes in weight may sometimes be of assistance. Groats of Edward IV of England are of the same type throughout his reign, but in 1464 their weight was reduced from 60 grains to 48 grains, so coins issued before this date can be readily distinguished from those issued after it.

When such aids to dating, or at least to chronological ordering, are not available, the numismatist has traditionally had recourse to considerations of style. Virtually the whole of ancient Greek coinage was originally classed on this basis, since there seemed to be no alternative. Within its limits, and when applied to large groups of coins over a long period of time, it works reasonably well. One can distinguish between coins of a primitive and rather wooden style and those showing greater maturity and suppleness:

with practice a trained eye can even distinguish the work of individual die-sinkers and discern when one is replaced by another. Over short periods it is less satisfactory, since neither within the work of a single die-sinker nor in that of successive die-sinkers is stylistic evolution necessarily uniform. Over a period of years a workman may learn how to simplify his task and to cut corners, or may develop a preference for a detail made in one fashion and not in another. But at any moment he may have to work under greater or less pressure, or under temporarily unsatisfactory conditions— the seasons vary, and with them the hours of daylight—or he may become careless because he is unwell or suffering from fatigue or has sustained an injury. Or he may suddenly feel the wish to revert to an earlier style or to an earlier way of doing things. Or he may be temporarily replaced by another man. Stylistic criteria are of use, but they are not infallible, and deductions from more objective ones must always be preferred when they are available.

The study of die relationships usually provides such an objective criterion. Since upper and lower dies are not normally linked to one another, although hinged dies are known, we often find coins struck by the same obverse die and several different reverse dies, or vice versa. Die-linked coins will usually have been struck at about the same time, since when minting is taking place on a considerable scale each single die will last only a few days or at best a few weeks. Further, since the upper dies, which took the hammer blows, wore out more quickly than the lower ones, it is often possible to work out the sequence in which dies have been used. In a small mint the sequence is sometimes very apparent, but in a large one there are often too many die linkages to provide a clear sequence. An interesting special case occurs when coins have dates on both sides, so that we may find an obverse dated one year linked with a reverse dated the next, for example Carthaginian solidi of the Emperor Maurice (582–602) with ΔΝЄ (i.e. Regnal Year 5) in the obverse and ΔΝЅ (Regnal Year 6) in the reverse inscription. Complications can occur through dies being temporarily lost and subsequently brought back into use after an interval, or through their being used only occasionally for little-needed denominations, so that a die may remain available over many years.

Die linkages are also helpful in determining the mints of coins. Many coins have no indication of where they were struck, or else they have a mint signature which with the passage of time has become immobilized and meaningless. Mint attributions, when not indicated on the coins themselves, usually rest in the main on

find evidence (above, pp. 128–9), which may show the local
occurrence of particular coins. Usually quite different types are
involved, but it may happen that coins of the same type can show
considerable regional variations—differences in the spelling or
letter forms of inscriptions, differences in the details of the types,
differences in style and fabric. These are the results of die-sinkers
and other mint personnel developing their own style and methods
of work, and often they allow us to postulate the existence of a
number of mints. Conclusions based on style can be reinforced by
the study of die relationships, for die linkages are only likely to
concur within the context of a single mint, although neither type
of evidence is absolutely conclusive. Die-sinkers and even dies can
be transferred from one mint to another and confuse the pattern.
When a new mint is set up, or when an old mint has to increase its
output at short notice, it will have to draw its skilled personnel
from somewhere, and will usually do so from other mints. The
borrowing of dies is also a familiar phenomenon. It is consequently possible to find late Anglo-Saxon coins having obverses
from one mint die-linked with reverses from another, usually but
not necessarily in the same neighbourhood, or a late-fourth-
century solidus having an obverse clearly Thessalonican in style
linked with a reverse having the mint and *officina* mark of Constantinople. Where there is a conflict between the evidence of
style and that of die signature, it is usually the latter, as being the
more precise, to which preference should be given.

Imitation and Immobilization

Erroneous information may be given by a coin at two levels. One,
normally the least important, is of a type shared with other documents of the period. A coin may ascribe to a ruler titles which he
commonly uses but which have in themselves no reality. English
sovereigns continued to call themselves kings of France on their
coins down to 1803; the Byzantine emperor John III Vatatzes is
styled *porphyrogenitus*, i.e. 'born in the purple', although he
acquired the throne through his wife. We know from other sources
that such titles in these contexts have no meaning, but in less well
documented periods one might easily be misled by numismatic
evidence. Coin titulature may in any case be out of phase with that
employed by the official chancery. Charlemagne is not entitled
emperor on his coins till some years after his imperial coronation,
and Cromwell is styled 'Protector' on some pattern farthings dated

1651, though he was not officially invested with this title until December 1653.

Minor errors also arise through conservatism in mint practice. Dies do not wear out punctually at the end of a year, and a die, even if it carries a date, may remain in use, as we have seen, into the next year. A portrait may be carried on from one monarch to the next, either because the mint has not had time to prepare a new design or sees no need for one. Alfonso II of Naples (1494–5) continued to use the bust of his father Ferdinand I during the first months of his reign; Henry VIII of England, more surprisingly, used Henry VII's portrait on his groats from 1509 to 1526. There is, in any case, an element of make-believe in the precise dates assigned by numismatists to coins in periods where there are no other records to put them right. The coinage of one ruler will normally continue unchanged during the first weeks or months of his successor's reign, simply because the preparations for a new coinage take time. Sometimes the results are surprising. George V of Great Britain died in January 1936. Coins bearing his name and portrait continued to be struck and issued throughout the year, though Edward VIII was on the throne, and Edward abdicated in December before his own coinage, which had been in preparation since July, was put into circulation. Some of the colonies were quicker off the mark, and one wonders what future numismatists, if they had no other evidence, would make of the fact that there are coins of Edward VIII for Fiji, New Guinea, and British East and West Africa, all dated 1936, while the only ones for Great Britain itself are extremely rare brass threepenny pieces, dated 1937, which somehow got into circulation.

A more serious source of potential error arises out of the twin phenomena of immobilization and imitation referred to in a previous chapter. Immobilization arises out of the fact that mints are liable to continue doing what they have been accustomed to do until they are ordered to change, and such an order, whether for reasons of indolence, indifference, or calculation, may never be issued. There are no English coins bearing the name of either Richard I or John, for although Henry II died in 1189 the mints in this country continued to strike coins of a type which he had introduced in 1180 right down to the next change of type carried out by Henry III in 1247. Feudal coinages created by usurpation were immobilized in part with the object of concealing this fact. The coins of the counts of Poitou continued to be struck in the name of King Charles the Bald (840–77) from the ninth century to the second half of the twelfth, with no reference to the name or title of the count, and they continued to bear the name of the Carolingian mint of Melle (*Metallum* or *Metalo*), although we have documentary evidence that by the twelfth century they were being struck at Niort, Montreuil-Bonnin, and other localities as well as at Melle itself.

Coin types and inscriptions can be copied as well as immobilized. Such imitations form two classes. In one the copying is as exact as possible: types and inscriptions are taken over without change, beyond such as may be made inadvertently through a lack of competence on the part of the copyist. In the second a well-known and generally accepted type is copied, but the inscription is changed and the different origin of the coin is frankly admitted, the intention being simply to secure that the imitation shall circulate on a par with the model and take advantage of its acceptability. There can also be a half-way stage when the inscription is indeed different but is arranged with intent to deceive, as was the case with many of the continental imitations of English sterlings struck by John the Blind, king of Bohemia and count of Luxemburg (1309–46). Altered or semi-altered inscriptions and types can easily be separated from originals by the numismatist, but unaltered imitations are often a problem. In some coin series they exist on a large scale. The earliest coinages of the Germanic states of western Europe between the fifth and seventh centuries were almost without exception imitated from those of the late Roman or early Byzantine empire, and although the cruder copies can be easily differentiated from the originals, especially after strongly marked local styles had developed in each state, the earlier and better ones are virtually indistinguishable from their prototypes. The same is true of some Irish or Scandinavian imitations of late Anglo-Saxon coins, of Low Country imitations of the English sterling, of some fourteenth-century imitations of the French gros tournois. Practice, and a good eye for stylistic and iconographical peculiarities, are necessary before such imitations can be separated from the originals.

Metrology

Coins can be weighed, and the weight of a single specimen is a fair indication of the intended weight of the series to which it belongs, but taken alone it may mislead. We have seen in Chapter 4 that coins were allowed to fluctuate in weight within certain limits, which in the case of copper or billon coins could often be large. A coin may also be underweight as a result of wear or cleaning, or

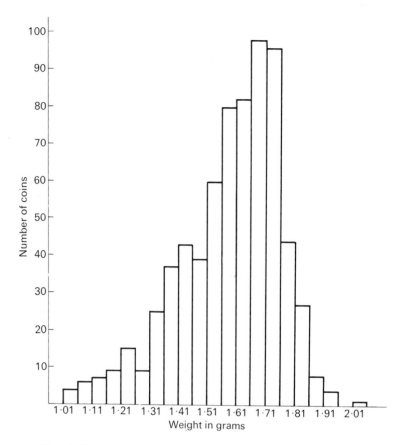

FIG. 58. Frequency table of the weights of nearly 700 Carolingian coins.

overweight through selective hoarding—the better specimens will have been set aside and tend to survive—or as a result of the adhesion of corrosion products to its surface.

Theoretical weights have sometimes been arrived at in the past by taking the weight of the heaviest specimen known or by averaging those of a number of specimens. The first proceeding is inadmissible, for accidents can happen at even the best-regulated mint and coins struck on unusually heavy flans, or even struck by error on flans intended for another denomination, can pass into circulation and be preserved as curiosities. The second method gives reasonably good results provided one is sure that one is dealing with a homogeneous issue, but it is necessary to exclude from the averaging all coins that are damaged, badly worn, or heavily patinated. A still better method, however, is to construct a frequency table of recorded weights, since this will usually bring out any heterogeneity that is present and exceptionally light or heavy coins will not distort the result.

Frequency distributions are applied to coin weights by tabulating the weights of all available specimens at conveniently spaced intervals, for example those between 3·01 g. and 3·05 g., 3·06 g. and 3·10 g., etc., and making a frequency histogram of the results. The resulting distribution is usually rather sharply skewed, since it will normally be applied to a mixed coin population whose issue will have extended over a number of years. The older coins will all be somewhat worn, and the mode of the curve, if it is plotted as one, will therefore be amongst the heavier weights. The distribution can indeed be conceived as the summation of a series of Gaussian bell-shaped curves of the weights of each year's mint output, each with an even distribution of coins on either side of the theoretical weight laid down by the mint prescription but in which, as a result of wear, the modes of the individual curves have moved into lower weight brackets as the coins recede backwards in time from the final date of the series. The object of constructing such a table is to determine the weights of the least worn specimens, i.e. those closest to the theoretical weight of the coins. Fig. 58, based on a table prepared by Paul Naster with the object of determining the theoretical weight of the Carolingian denier and employing the weights of nearly 700 specimens in the Bibliothèque Nationale, shows the method. The histogram is skewed towards the higher weights, the mode being in the region of 1·70 g., but the large number of coins over this figure suggests that although there are not two separate modes some weight change may have occurred and that replotting it reign by reign would have been a useful exercise. The coins of very high weight arouse suspicion; indeed, the only coin weighing more than 2·00 g., a Strasbourg denier which Prou believed to show that the theoretical weight of the Carolingian denier was 2·08 g., is in fact a forgery of the eighteenth century.

Once such a histogram has been constructed it can be assumed that the theoretical weight of the original issue is within or slightly above that of the most numerous group, or, as in the case of the Carolingian deniers, in the weight-span of the two heaviest groups where these are numerically virtually equal. The customary procedure is to take the arithmetical average (i.e. the mean) of the weights in the heaviest group, but exactly where it falls is a matter for estimation, not for precise analysis, since all that the curve has established is the weight distribution of the coins *in their present condition*, and an allowance has still to be made for wear. This can only be done satisfactorily if one has seen the coins themselves and can judge their condition, or if one is concerned with a single hoard where the degree of corrosion and cleaning will be uniform; it is quite impossible to estimate when one is dealing, as one frequently is, with a large number of weights drawn from museum catalogues, find reports, and other sources. Comparisons of actual results with theoretical weights known from documents, for example for late medieval English nobles and groats, suggest that the allowance for wear in gold will normally be small, perhaps only 1 per cent or 2 per cent, but that on silver it may well be up to 4 per cent or 5 per cent, and even larger for copper. If instead of using the mode of a frequency curve one takes the average (mean) of the recorded weights of coins in good condition, these figures should probably be doubled. The uncertainty over how best to allow for wear makes unprofitable such mathematical refinements as the manipulation of a frequency curve to make it fit into some well-known distribution pattern save in those rare cases where one has a large group of virtually uncirculated coins to deal with.

Coin Fineness

The original currency value of coins depended as much on their fineness as on their weight, and information regarding fineness is essential for any study of the monetary aspects of coinage. It is desirable on other grounds as well. A qualitative investigation of the range of impurities, to some extent by methods which have only become possible in very recent years, may allow the grouping together of coins of common origin, and thus throw light on place or date of minting or on sources of metal. Further, the composition of a coin is often the simplest indication of whether it is genuine or false. A modern forger may be able to make his products approximately correct in weight and fineness, but trace elements cannot be so easily manipulated, and only if a genuine piece has been used as a blank will there be present those which it should contain.

The difficulties in the way of accurate analysis are considerable. The chemical composition of coins is often far from uniform. There will usually be irregular distribution of metals in a coin from the first, since a cooling ingot tends to separate out into layers of varying composition. A billon coin which was treated with acid before striking will, if in good condition, have a higher proportion of silver near its surface than in its interior. A gold coin alloyed with silver or copper will also tend to have a higher proportion of gold near the surface. This is a consequence of the phenomenon known as surface enrichment, resulting from the dissolving away of the baser metals on the exposed parts of the coin by the action of acids during its period of burial in the earth. Corrosion and chemical or electrolytic cleaning may also have left their marks on the composition of the surface. A further problem is that coins are often objects of value and their owners are not usually prepared to allow them to be analyzed by methods that will injure them, more especially since they know that scientists may within a few years discover some quite harmless way of procuring the information desired. Finally there is the difficulty that many recently devised techniques are not within everybody's reach. They require close co-operation between numismatists who can explain what they want to know and lay hands on the material—the two do not necessarily go together—and scientists who can see how their problems may be solved and who have access to the apparatus required.

The numismatist is therefore faced with a choice of evils. Certain methods which are or may be at his disposal give satisfactory results because they estimate total composition and not just that of the surface, but they will either injure his coins or only work in certain cases. Chemical analysis is effective but destructive; gravimetric analysis and neutron activation analysis are effective but only give reliable results for particular combinations of metals. Other methods, some quite harmless and others not likely to inflict more than minor injury, only throw light on the composition of the surface of the coin. Such are the old-fashioned touchstone, microchemical analysis, ocular spectrometry, X-ray crystallography, and X-ray spectrometry. The numismatist must make his choice according to the usefulness of each particular method in his own case and the possibilities open to him. Gravimetric analysis he can learn to do himself if he has the use of a sufficiently accurate balance; chemical analysis he can usually have done for him without too much difficulty, at least if he is prepared to pay for it; for the others he will have to invoke the help of physicists who will arrive at their conclusions by means of processes and calculations which he may not even begin to understand.

The touchstone is not now employed by numismatists, though it is sometimes used by goldsmiths, and by coin dealers in the

Near East and India. A touchstone is a small slab of some smooth-grained variety of quartz or jasper, black or almost black in colour. If a gold coin or other object is rubbed firmly against it, the colour of the resulting 'strike' of metal—gold is so soft that only a trace will be removed—will vary according to its alloy, and by matching this with another made by a 'touch needle' of known alloy its composition can be ascertained. In practice goldsmiths often dispense with needles and use gold coins of known fineness as their standards. When carried out by an expert, this 'touching' is said to give results accurate to half a carat, but much practice is required to ensure that the strike of the needle and that of the object being tested are equally firmly made. A modern variation of 'touching' is to treat the 'strike' of gold with nitric acid, which dissolves the silver or copper in it and leaves a thin film of gold adhering to the stone. The colour of this will vary according to the proportion of gold which the 'strike' originally contained.

For gold alloyed with small quantities of silver, or with silver and copper in known proportions, gravimetric analysis is both satisfactory and easy to carry out. Already in the fifth century B.C. Herodotus was aware that a block of electrum was larger than one of gold of the same weight, but it was left to Archimedes to realize that the volume of an irregular mass of metal could be discovered by weighing the volume of water which it displaced. The method which he devised for determining the composition of King Hiero's crown does not differ in principle from that used in specific gravity measurements today. The coin is weighed accurately in air and then again, on a double loop or cradle made from fine wire, in distilled water. The weight of the coin in water is this second weight minus that of the wire alone in water, the figure for which has previously been determined. The difference between the weight of the coin in air and its weight in water is the weight of the water which it has displaced, and this divided into the weight of the coin in air gives the specific gravity. Where the metals composing a binary alloy are known, their specific gravities can be ascertained from any work of reference, and the figure for any specific gravity between them will be related to the amount of each metal in the alloy. Great care has to be taken to ensure that the coin is perfectly clean and that there are no air bubbles adhering to it or to the wire when it is being weighed in water. Carbon tetrachloride is sometimes used instead of water. Gravimetric analysis is extremely accurate for binary alloys of gold and silver containing a high proportion of gold (sp. gr. 19·3), but its reliability falls off rapidly as the specific gravity of the alloy approaches that of silver (sp. gr. 10·5), and is severely affected by the presence of more than traces of copper. It is virtually useless for silver coins and cannot be satisfactorily applied to very small coins of any metal, since the extreme difficulty of weighing these accurately in water makes the possible margin of error unacceptably large.

The information given by chemical or microchemical analysis is far more comprehensive than that which gravimetric methods can provide, since such analysis can be used for complex alloys and for those grades of binary gold–silver and silver–copper alloys where gravimetric analysis breaks down. A description of the preliminaries, however, is calculated to make the numismatist's hair stand on end. Where a coin can be completely sacrificed, as in the case of common coins or of specimens from a large hoard, the first step is to transform it into a disc of metal having a composition as close as possible to that of the blank before the coin was struck. This is done by filing down the surface and edges, which will get rid of the outer metallic layer and such corrosion products as it may contain, and then removing any traces of oxidized metal from cracks or crevices with a hack-saw. The clean blanks are cut into smaller pieces with a chisel and analyzed by whatever methods the probable composition of the coins may indicate. Where a coin cannot be sacrificed as a whole but the removal of a few milligrams from the surface or from the interior of a crack is possible, microchemical analysis can be substituted for straight-forward chemical methods, but the greater delicacy required for the operations and uncertainty as to how far the composition of the fragment analysed is typical of that of the coin as a whole leave a much larger margin of error. Where a coin is thin or is cracked or pierced, however, it may be possible to remove for analysis a slightly larger quantity of metal from what is in effect a cross-section of the coin. The method can only be applied by experts and is necessarily expensive.

Microchemical analysis was used by Michael Grant in the late thirties to determine the proportions of zinc, tin, and lead in the bronze and brass coins of the early Roman Empire, and has since been used for other series, for example by William P. Wallace in working on the early silver coins of Euboea, but comparative tests against modern coins whose composition is known shows that for some metals (e.g. copper) its results are not reliable. A more promising use is in the detection of trace elements, whose presence may in certain cases make it possible to identify the mints at which coins were struck or localize the region or mines from which the metal they used originally came. Further, the discovery of new sources of metal or the introduction of new methods of refining will commonly have altered the trace elements present and so may help one in dating coins. A change in copper content in 'tortoises' of Aegina from an average of about o·1 per cent in the early series (mid-fifth century B.C.) to 5 per cent in the later ones (fourth century B.C.) has presumably both a geographical and a chronological significance. But the method has to be applied with circumspection. While similarity in metallic composition where unusual trace elements are concerned is a strong argument in favour of a common origin, dissimilarity is not necessarily proof to the contrary. The same mine may produce metal of varying quality, particularly when poorer seams come to be worked, and smelting and refining processes will materially affect its composition. The identities of mints will for their part tend to be blurred by the universal practice of treating old coins as potential sources of metal or, in the Byzantine series, of actually using old coins as blanks for overstriking. Microchemical analysis, however, is a useful adjunct to gravimetric analysis, for if the latter method is applied to a large group of coins the chemical analysis of a few specimens selected at random will show what elements are present and whether reasonably reliable deductions regarding fineness can be made from the specific gravity figures.

Chemical analysis is the most satisfactory method of determining quantitatively the constituents of an alloy; it is for qualitative determinations, and especially for the detection of the presence of trace elements, that the more advanced physical methods of analysis come into their own.

Spectroscopic methods have so far received only limited application in numismatics, though they have been widely used by archaeologists for the analysis of other metal objects. They depend on the fact that when a metal is vapourized in an electric arc its light has a spectrum peculiar to itself, and that when an alloy is treated in the same way the resulting pattern can be analysed by a spectrometer and the metals identified. It is also possible, within limits, to determine the proportions as well as the nature of the various elements present, for the intensity of the blackening of the characteristic lines for each element can be measured by a sensitometer, and a quantitative estimation can be made by comparing the results with those from samples of known composition approaching that of the alloy. When used for coins it is customary to spark the edge of the coin, or rather a point on the surface which has been first cleaned by a file, as one of the electrodes. The resulting damage takes the form of a small pit or roughness on the edge and discoloured patches on the adjacent surfaces, but these soon disappear. On modern coins, with sharply cut or milled edges, the traces of sparking remain as permanent if slight disfigurements, but on the irregular edges of ancient and medieval coins they are usually barely visible.

Two methods of analysis recently developed for archaeological work which have the advantage of doing no damage at all to the objects under investigation are X-ray fluorescent spectrometry and X-ray diffraction analysis. The first of these is made possible by the fact that a substance subjected to the action of X-rays from a high-voltage tube will emit secondary or fluorescent X-rays which have precise wavelengths for each element forming part of it. These can be measured in various ways, and their relative intensity corresponds to the proportions of the elements present. The method has proved its value in the study, for example, of early glazes on pottery, but its usefulness in numismatics is limited by the fact that since X-rays are strongly absorbed by metal, the analysis is only valid for a thickness of about 1/1000th of an inch on the surface of the coin. X-ray crystallography, which has been applied to the study of the early electrum coinage of Asia Minor, suffers from the same defect. The method is based on the fact that the crystalline structure of matter can be studied by means of the diffraction undergone by X-rays when passing through it, and that for a solid solution of one element in another, as in this case silver in gold, the proportions between the two elements present can be calculated from the resulting pattern. The reliability of this method has not yet been sufficiently tested, and in any case it suffers from the disadvantage of analysing only the surface. Where a coin is of no value, however, and a section can be cut through it for examination, either X-ray spectrometry or X-ray diffraction analysis can throw light on the distribution of impurities in the metal and the phenomenon of surface enrichment. They have also an obvious utility in the detection of faked patina on bronze coins.

The final method that requires mention is that of neutron activation analysis. This depends upon the fact that elements subjected to neutron radiation from an atomic pile are in varying degrees transformed into radioactive isotopes. As these isotopes decay they emit gamma rays whose energy content is specific for the element concerned, so that they can be detected and sorted by a gamma ray spectrometer, just as a light spectrum is analysed by an optical one. Where the energy content of the induced gamma rays of one element happens to be very close to that of another also present in an alloy the spectrometer may not differentiate clearly between them, just as in specific gravity determinations it is impossible to determine the proportions of metals whose densities are virtually identical, but the difficulty may sometimes be resolved by the fact that the half-life of radioactive isotopes varies greatly from one element to another. Neutron activation analysis shares with specific gravity determinations the advantage of analysing the coin as a whole, not simply a fragment of its surface. It is quick and simple to carry out and eminently suited to the treatment of small objects—coins under examination at Harwell some years ago were irradiated in batches of a dozen at a time—so that information about statistically significant numbers of coins can easily be obtained. The coins used are rendered weakly radioactive for a time but are otherwise unharmed. On the other hand, not all metals produce isotopes that can be satisfactorily studied, and the range of sensitivity of the method, while in some cases much greater than that of ordinary spectroscopic analysis, is very variable. Gold as an impurity in silver can be detected and measured in traces as low as 1 part in 100,000, silver and copper in traces as low as 1 part in 10,000, but copper in gold coins cannot be detected or measured in quantities of less than 2 per cent, and lead, which is frequently an impurity of silver and has sometimes been used as an alloy, is very insensitive to neutron radiation—it is to this fact that it owes its utility as a 'shield'—and consequently cannot be measured at all. It is also obvious that not every numismatist has an atomic reactor at his disposal.

Mint Output

Mint and die output were matters which till recently were largely ignored by scholars, since it seemed that without written records they would have to remain unknown. If a particular coinage had survived in quantity and the number of dies involved in it was large, the original issue was evidently considerable, but the vagaries of coin survival were so great that the reverse was not necessarily the case. The Canea hoard of 1922 brought to light 586 specimens, struck from 9 obverse and 65 reverse dies, of a type of diobol of Cydonia in Crete which prior to that was entirely unknown, while the *Pax* pennies changed from being one of the rarest into one of the commonest issues of William the Conqueror (Class VIII: see Figs. 18b and 57) as the result of the finding of the Beaworth hoard in 1833. In view of the element of chance in coin survival, and even in die survival, it seemed hopeless to speculate about mint output without the assistance of written

evidence, such as we have by chance for a few years of the Amphictyonic coinage of Delphi in the early fourth century B.C. and more
regularly for many western European mints from the thirteenth
century onwards.

In recent years the picture has greatly changed. Estimates of
mint output are now fairly frequently made, although not all
numismatists would agree on the credibility of the figures proposed. Two separate estimates are involved, one of the number
of dies used for a particular coinage, the other of the number of
coins likely to have been struck per die. The first estimate is arrived
at by the use of well-established statistical procedures whose
general validity is not open to question, though their application
is not always easy. The second depends on the assumption that
die output—the number of coins struck per die—is not likely to
have varied greatly from one period to another, and that figures
obtained either experimentally or from later written sources will
be generally valid. This is something which the historian will find
it hard to accept. Average die output is no more likely to be a
constant than average family size, and can no more be identified
with maximum die output than the size of the family can be
equated with the number of children which a woman is physically
capable of bearing.

The principle of estimating the number of dies involved in a
coinage is a quite simple one. If in a random sample of a hundred
coins there are no die duplicates, the total number of dies responsible for the issue cannot be calculated but must be very large; if all
the coins were struck by the same pair of dies, it is in the highest
degree improbable that any others existed; and for any figures
between these extremes it is possible to calculate, within very
broad limits of probability, the total number of dies likely to have
been used. For the calculations to be valid, however, a number of
assumptions have to be made: the number of coins struck per die
must have been reasonably large, each die must have struck an
approximately equal number of coins, the coinage must be homogeneous, the sample available for study must be random in
character, and, finally, the die identifications must have been
correctly made, for the addition or subtraction of even a single die,
when the number of die duplicates involved is small, will substantially affect the totals. The actual calculations can be carried
out in various ways. One involves a direct estimate of the total
from the number of duplicated dies in a sample; another proceeds
from an estimate of the average minimum size of the sample in
which one would expect to find every die represented; and a third

is based on the possibility of establishing a statistical relationship between the number of dies one would expect to be unrepresented in a given sample with the number likely to be represented by only one coin. The margins of probability involved, where only a few die duplicates are present, are very wide. In a study of Offa's coinage the use of a formula based on the first method gave the total of dies as likely to be between 2,250 and 3,000, since 298 obverse dies were found amongst a total of 325 coins examined. A calculation based on the third method gave a slightly lower total, between 1,350 and 2,700 dies, but with the element of uncertainty very large.

Such totals provide a good basis for comparing the sizes of related issues, but to give absolute figures for mint output is more difficult. Output of coins per die is highly uncertain. In the *Numismatic Chronicle* for 1963 Mr. D. G. Sellwood published the results of actual experiments which showed that some 8,000 imitation Greek coins could be struck with specially made bronze dies before the upper die became unusable, and records summarized by Miss M. Mate in the same periodical for 1969, which give the number of dies used at various English mints between 1281 and 1327, suggest an average coin output per die of 30,000 over much of this period. The quality of the latter dies, however, was very variable, and in 1300 the die-sinkers had to be reprimanded for supplying ones of such poor metal and workmanship that they wore out after a few days, a complaint borne out by the fact that in that year the average output fell to 23,000 coins per die from the 30,000 it had been the year before. That die life is highly unpredictable has been shown by some observations in modern times, despite the higher quality of the metal used for both dies and coins and the efforts to secure uniformity. In 1879 it was found in the Royal Mint that the coin output of a group of four dies varied between 42,000 and 119,000, i.e. from 43 per cent above to 49 per cent below a mean of 83,000, and two dies used in Brussels for striking twenty-franc pieces struck 20,000 and 123,000 coins respectively before becoming unusable. In view of such discrepancies, and of the risks involved in using figures of one period under conditions that may be quite different—varying qualities of dies, varying size and composition of blanks, the contrast between thick coins struck in high relief and thin coins struck in low—it seems better to avoid putting forward highly problematical totals for mint output and content oneself with using such approximate figures for dies as one can obtain as a basis for comparing the sizes of related coinages.

Counterfeits and Forgeries

The preceding sections have taken it for granted that the coins that the numismatist has to deal with are genuine. Unfortunately there exist both imitations of the period designed to pass current as money and modern imitations intended to deceive collectors. It is convenient to term the former counterfeits and the latter forgeries, though modern English usage allows both words to be used in either sense.

Counterfeits, to judge by the volume and severity of the legislation against them, have been common at many historical periods, and moulds for making counterfeit Roman imperial coins have been found in many parts of the Empire. Counterfeits themselves, however, have survived on only a very limited scale, partly because it is the better coins that by Gresham's Law will have been hoarded and thus come down to our own day, partly because the materials of which they are made, usually a mixture of base metals in imitation of silver and plated copper in imitation of gold, are very susceptible to chemical and electrochemical action and have either disappeared entirely or survive only in the form of unrecognizable cores. The great majority of counterfeits are cast, and are usually easy to recognize because of their defective weight, poor metal, and—when they are not cast—their great irregularities of style. They have proliferated at periods when the state was weak or the designs of coins simple and their users illiterate, but sometimes they have been made in response to local shortages of coin and because of their usefulness have been to some extent tolerated by the public authority. The line between counterfeits and tokens becomes in such cases hard to draw.

It is also sometimes difficult to distinguish between counterfeits and imitative coins, more especially since the attitude of contemporaries towards them would not have been uniform. A Viking imitation of a London penny of Alfred the Great would be a legitimate coin in the eyes of its maker but a counterfeit in those of the king's officials in London. It is usual to regard coins produced by private persons as counterfeits and those produced by states as genuine, but even under relatively stable conditions states have sometimes counterfeited the products of their neighbours. John the Blind, as has been said already (p. 146), counterfeited English sterlings—they are the *lushbournes* against whose circulation parliaments repeatedly legislated—and in modern times governments have sometimes engaged in the same activity. The objects are not always reprehensible. The government of the

Austrian Netherlands, fortified by a written justification by two Brussels Jesuits, authorized the minting of counterfeit French gold coins in 1718 because of uncertainty regarding the values of those struck in France by the Regent for Louis XV, and Wellington, in the last stages of the Peninsular War, had gold napoleons counterfeited in order that his troops should have adequate supplies of coin for purchases after the invasion of France. In both these instances the counterfeits were of good quality, but usually this is not the case and the reasons behind them are less creditable, as with Napoleon's imitations of Austrian, Prussian, and Russian banknotes and Hitler's counterfeiting of Allied paper money, known under the code-name 'Operation Bernhard', in the Second World War. Maria Theresa dollars, although minted for some years in the present century at Brussels, Paris, and London, are not technically counterfeits, since the coins are no longer legal tender in their country of origin. The same has been held by the courts in some countries to be the case for private imitations of gold sovereigns and napoleons, much to the dismay of the British and French financial authorities respectively.

Counterfeits are of interest to the numismatist when he meets them, since they are evidence of monetary conditions in the past. Modern forgeries can do nothing but harm, though there are fortunately only a few coin series in which they are at all common. They naturally proliferate where prices are high, notably amongst ancient coins, or where imitation is easy to undertake and difficult to detect (obsidional coins, countermarked coins), but since they are not always made from motives of profit they have occasionally spread to other series. In Renaissance Italy, where ancient coins were thought of more as works of art than as objects deserving scientific study, the imitation of Roman sestertii was a quite natural proceeding, and in modern times the element of archaeological fraud has come into play, with coins being manufactured to fill in 'gaps' in the record with coins of unusual rulers or mints. Luigi Cigoi, who was responsible for some of the most dangerous forgeries of the last century, specialized in small copper and billon coins of north Italian mints, creating late Roman issues for, say, Aquileia or Ravenna, when they were only known for Rome or Milan.

Modern forgeries are made in a number of ways. The traditional method, which is also the simplest, is by casting from genuine coins. It is now back in fashion, since with modern methods of pressure casting it is possible to avoid the surface defects—the presence of air bubbles and lack of sharpness—which made older casts too easily recognizable by the practised numismatist. Actual striking, with dies either made by casting from original coins or cut by hand, gives more convincing results, but involves difficulties of its own. Forgeries can be made directly from ancient coins by partial re-engraving: a common coin of Gordian III may be transformed into a rare one of his father or grandfather, a coin of Volusian into one of Aemilian. This is something that can even happen inadvertently, for it was formerly common to 'improve' the appearance of Roman sestertii by tooling, and the touching up of details sometimes involved their unintentional alteration, owing to the original form being misread or misunderstood.

No general rules for the recognition of forgeries can be given. As the working numismatist gradually becomes familiar with the features of a particular series, some incongruity which he would at first scarcely notice will attract his attention, and he will discover after further examination that the coin displaying it is false. Familiarity and a good eye for style are essential, but only come with experience, and a person capable of detecting a forged Visigothic tremissis or a forged obsidional piece of the seventeenth century may be quite unable to identify a product of the Greek forger Christodoulos or his Italian counterpart Cigoi in the ancient Greek and Roman series respectively.

The basic criteria for identifying forgeries may be summarized as stylistic, historical, and technical. A cast is usually recognizable by its surface and 'feel'. When a forgery is struck from engraved dies the fact often becomes apparent through mere lapse of time, for an artist both brings to his work some contribution of his own and picks out for reproduction those features of his model which seem to him most significant, but which may seem quite incongruous at a later period as a result of changes in artistic perception. There may be errors in design or faults in grammar or orthography which a contemporary die-sinker would be unlikely to perpetrate. Historical criteria cover such errors as the attribution of an impossible consulate to a Roman emperor or an impossible mint to a Hellenistic or medieval ruler, although they have to be invoked with caution; old dies with inappropriate inscriptions are sometimes carried over from one reign to the next, and imitative coinages and immobilized coin types abound in apparent errors. The technical considerations arise out of the practical problems involved in the reproduction of an ancient coin. It is virtually impossible to imitate the worn, rounded edges which are a mark of antiquity. Using an old coin as a blank does not dispose of the difficulty, for the outline of the new die is apt to leave traces on the edge, and the undertype may be both recognizable and impossible. Some late Anglo-Saxon coins were discovered to be forgeries when it was found that they were overstruck on *Paxs* pennies of William I, and an important group of Bohemian forgeries came to light when it was found that a supposed seventeenth-century jetton was overstruck on a nineteenth-century Austrian kreutzer. Forgeries dating from the last century are often quite incorrect in weight, since little attention was paid at that time to metrology. It is also virtually impossible to match chemical composition exactly, though this is obviously not very easy to test. In brief, there are many considerations to be borne in mind when dealing with forgeries, but no general rules to follow. In most coin series, happily, the volume of forgery is not great, though owing to the rise in coin prices and the increased perfection of the technical methods available it has somewhat increased in recent years.

8
Jettons, Tokens, Medals, and Related Objects

When a 'coin' is dug up in a garden in Great Britain, the chances are that it is not a monetary 'coin' at all but a Nuremberg jetton of the sixteenth or seventeenth century. It is only one example of many different types of coin-like object which are peripheral to the numismatist's main field of interest but of which he has to take cognizance. Some, like medals, are in no way money, though they are stamped pieces of metal that on occasion strongly resemble coins. Others, like tokens, bridge the gap between monetary and non-monetary objects; some were made to serve as coin surrogates; others were not so intended but on occasion do so; yet others never fulfil monetary functions at all. Jettons and coin-weights were used to facilitate monetary transactions without being money themselves. The terminology of the various types of object is extremely imprecise; even jettons, which functioned primarily as calculating devices and ought therefore to form a clear-cut group, merge in the sixteenth century into the class of medalets. This chapter is intended to give a brief account of the main categories of coin-like objects which are not formally coins in the monetary sense. It does not include the two large groups of military medals and decorations, since although these have strong historical associations and are much collected, they are so unrelated to coinage in its monetary aspect that the numismatist usually regards them as falling outside his purview.

Jettons

Jettons are thin discs of brass or copper, usually between one and two inches in diameter, with types which were initially based on those of contemporary coins. They are also called 'counters' or 'reckoning counters', *Rechenpfennige* in German, which gives us a better idea of their actual function than the term 'jetton', though in medieval French *jeter* had meant 'to count' as well as 'to throw', and we still speak of 'casting up' accounts. Jettons originated in western Europe in the thirteenth century. Simple arithmetical calculations were then mainly done either by counting with the fingers—it was possible, by different combinations of finger positions, to express figures running into the thousands—or by using an abacus. We are accustomed to think of this as a frame of wires and beads, either horizontal or upright, but the medieval preference was for a flat board or cloth with a column of marks of value on the left which, reading downwards, would record thousands, hundreds, tens, and units, all these referring to pounds, and below them shillings and pence. Reckoning would be carried out by moving small stones (*calculi*, whence our word 'calculate') or jettons from line to line to express the sums required. (Our shop *counter* preserves a memory of such tables, for it could be turned into a reckoning board with a piece of chalk.) Jettons had the great advantage that even persons unable to read or write could learn to use them. Sometimes, to facilitate counting, the lines across the board were marked into squares like a chess-board or chequer-board, the origin of our *Exchequer*.

In the late thirteenth century the practice began of substituting jettons for the earlier unmarked 'counters' of stone or other materials. The practice quickly caught on, and in the later Middle Ages and during the sixteenth century the use of jettons became universal and their manufacture an important international industry, with Paris, Tournai, and Nuremberg as its chief centres. In the sixteenth century the need for them began to decline in England, as arabic numerals became widespread and people started to learn basic multiplication tables by heart, but they continued in use over much of the Continent, and as late as the eighteenth century books on commercial arithmetic still contained sections on reckoning by jettons. Most jettons are of brass or copper, but silver jettons were often made for formal use by members of city corporations and the like. Henry II of France ordered in 1557 that each town councillor in Paris should on appointment receive a bag of fifty. Gold jettons were occasionally made for the use of princes, or at least for presentation to them. Ordinary jettons were usually sold to the public in bags of fifty or a hundred, since large numbers were needed for all but the simplest calculations and, being of small value, they were easily lost or mislaid.

As long as jettons remained in practical use, their designs were

Fig. 59. Nuremberg 'token' (*recte* jetton) of Hans Schultes (*ob.* 1584). Brass. Late 16th cent. The observe type is a ship between sun and moon, with the inscription GLICK IST WALCZET, i.e. fortune is changeable, a sentiment symbolized by the ship blown hither and thither by the winds. The reverse has the arms of France and the name of the maker and city, NVREN(berg).

simple and their resemblance to coins is fairly close. They are very roughly struck with such designs as a crowned head copied from that of the king on the English sterling, a shield semée with fleur-de-lis, an Agnus Dei, the imperial orb and cross (*Reichsapfel*) in a tressure (*Dreipass*) of the kind frequently found on the reverses of German goldgulden. The inscriptions are often religious (e.g. *Joie sans fin Ave Maria*) but may be a simple motto (*Sans blâme*, that of the Golden Fleece) or consist of the name and office of the person for whom they were made (*Jehan Stanlawe escuier Trésorier de Normandie*) or, in the case of those sold to the public, that of their maker. The commonest of the Nuremberg tokens found in England are those bearing the name of some member of the Laufer or Krahwinkel families, for the business was one handed down from father to son, and having on one face the *Reichsapfel* and on the other three crowns around a rose. Occasionally the inscription warns the user that they are not money—*Je ne suis pas vrais agnel d'or* or *Je sui de laton por fer kum* (= *pour faire compter*)— but in a largely illiterate society they were often taken as such, so that 'faux comme un jeton' passed as a common expression into the French language.

In the sixteenth century jettons begin to change their character, or rather, as they ceased to have any functional purpose, the French term *jeton* comes to be loosely applied to objects that were no longer used for counting at all, but are rather medalets or souvenirs distributed on the occasion of weddings, baptisms, coronations, meetings of learned academies, and so forth. From the late sixteenth century onwards they are normally machine made, not hammer-struck, and their designs lose all contact with those of real coins, exhibiting an endless variety of emblems, rebuses, biblical scenes, allegorical representations, military triumphs, buildings, sieges, and similar topics. They were particularly popular in France and the Low Countries where such jettons continued to be made on a considerable scale down to the end of the *ancien régime*. Despite being called *jetons*, however, they are really medalets or medallic tokens, not jettons in the traditional sense at all.

Tokens

'Token' comes from an Old English word meaning to show, teach, and is frequently used in the special sense of a mark or symbol of identification (badge), allowing a person or object to represent another, as is implied by the phrase 'in token of'. Since such tokens are conveniently made of metal, there exists a vast numismatic borderland of objects representing value or coin. When the designs of such tokens are of extreme simplicity, for example one or two letters, or letters combined with numerals, their function can only be discovered where their context is known, but many of them are more specific. Some defy classification, but the majority can be considered under the three headings of monetary tokens, semi-monetary tokens, which form so to speak the underworld of money, and non-monetary tokens.

Monetary tokens. Coins of base metal have in the past been token money, in the sense that their commercial value was substantially inferior to their nominal value, so that to obtain the latter they had to be exchanged against coins of silver or gold which had a 'real' value. A copper halfpenny of George III was thought of by contemporaries as a token, not as a real coin, and this notion persists in our use of the term token money. When such tokens are made by the state they are customarily treated as full coins, and given their due place in descriptions of the coinage of a mint or period. When they are made by private persons, or by such bodies as commercial companies or city corporations which do not normally possess the right of minting, they are regarded as a separate class of object to be studied and catalogued separately from coins.

Such tokens are normally made either because no coins exist of a value low enough for small transactions or because the supply of low-value coins is insufficient for the public need. In the reign of Henry VIII the cost of mutton was three-farthings a pound and that of beef a halfpenny; veal came between them at a halfpenny and a half-farthing, i.e. five-eighths of a penny, but since there

FIG. 60. Seventeenth-century English token. Penny token issued in 1671 by Edward Bryan, grocer, in the small Yorkshire town of Gargrave.

was no official coin worth a half-farthing the need had to be supplied by tokens. Such objects are heard of in the Low Countries from the thirteenth century and in England from the late four-teenth century onwards, but their importance was to come later, when the silver penny and its fractions had become so small and awkward to handle that moneyers were reluctant to strike them and the public did not care for them because they were so easily lost. Private tokens of lead or copper, more manageable in size because of base metal, filled the gap. Thomas Platter, a German visitor to England in 1599, describes how he found merchants making tokens in their houses worth as little as a quarter or a sixth of a halfpenny, and how these would be saved up by their recipients and exchanged against real coin when their masters were agreeable. Tokens were sometimes officially authorized: the city of Bath was allowed to strike them in the 1590s. Early in James I's reign it was reckoned that tokens, mostly of lead, were being made by as many as 3,000 tradesmen in different parts of the country. It was in the hope of putting an end to this growth of a kind of sub-coinage of uncertain value that Sir John Harington was granted a patent for striking copper farthings in 1613. Harington's farthings, however, were struck in the king's name, without any reference to himself, so that most numismatists treat them as normal coin although not issued by the mint. They were in any case a failure. But England, unlike most countries on the Continent, lacked a billon coinage (see p. 33), so that periodical revivals of private tokens continued down to the nineteenth century. The two main periods were the years between the end of the Civil War (1649) and the introduction of copper halfpennies and farthings by Charles II in 1672, and the last decades of the eighteenth century, after the Mint had struck no copper coinage at all for a number of years.

The tokens of these two periods are quite different from each other. Those of the first period are crude in fabric and simple in design, bearing no more than an inscription giving the name and address of the issuer, the value of the token and sometimes the date, and at most a rather primitive type, such as a ship, a jug, a scythe, or a personal or local coat of arms. Thus a Chester token had the inscription WILLIAM SNEAD accompanying a scythe, and on the reverse OF CHESTER. 1668 and across the field, in three lines, HIS||PENNY||W.S. Many were issued by the local authorities concerned with poor relief, as the inscriptions show (e.g. SHERBORN || FARTHING||FOR||THE||POOR||1669). They are interesting records of social history, since they were issued in virtually all towns and most villages throughout the country, and sometimes even give the name of the street where the issuer carried on his business.

The interest of the later tokens is of a different character. They are in general greatly superior in design and execution to the earlier ones and were issued at a more sophisticated level, not so much by local tradesmen as by public bodies and by the entrepreneurs of the early stages of the Industrial Revolution, who had made the same discovery as Roman magistrates had done many centuries before, that coins could be used as vehicles of pictorial propaganda. The tokens of this second period exhibit a great variety of designs—public buildings, bridges, shop frontages, inn signs, landscapes with turnpike roads or canals, illustrations of industrial processes in great detail, such symbolic representations as a camel accompanying the inscription TEAS COFFEE SPICES & SUGARS—besides giving the name and address of the maker and a statement of his business. Those issued by public bodies often use the city arms and some design commemorating a well-known local event, e.g. a Coventry token on which the elephant and castle on one face is balanced by Lady Godiva on horseback on the other, with the accompanying motto PRO BONO PUBLICO alluding to the

FIG. 61. Lancaster token of 1794. Æ Issued by Abraham Seward, known from old directories to have been a brass- and bell-founder. It shows the castle and the bridge over the Lune, which at the time was regarded as one of the finest in Europe. No value is indicated, but from its size the token must have represented a penny.

purpose both of that lady's exploit and of the token issue itself. Firms whose business involved the stamping of metal took up the manufacture of tokens as a sideline, and Matthew Boulton had many years of experience in making them before obtaining the mint contract of 1797 which flooded England with 2*d*. and 1*d*. pieces from his workshop. Many tokens circulated only locally, where their makers were known, and some were indeed made for the benefit of collectors and were never truly current at all, but a few achieved a wide circulation as if they were coin of the realm. This was the case with the common penny and halfpenny tokens of the Parys Mines Co. in Anglesey, with their druid's head in an oak wreath on the obverse, and on the reverse an elaborate *PMCo*, with 1788 above, surrounded by the inscription WE PROMISE TO PAY THE BEARER ONE (HALF)PENNY which is continued on the edge ON DEMAND IN LONDON LIVERPOOL OR ANGLESEY.

The copper coinage of 1797 did not quite mark the end of copper tokens in Great Britain, where their continued circulation was only prohibited in 1817, and a shortage of silver coin in the early nineteenth century led to a brief flowering of a much rarer phenomenon, the issue of silver tokens, in particular by the banks. English seventeenth- and eighteenth-century tokens are in any case only a specific case of a much more general phenomenon, local reaction to a lack of small change. They are rarely found on the Continent, which had an abundant billon coinage, but coin shortages were a perennial source of complaint in the British and French colonies of the period, so that we find widespread creation overseas of local tokens whose study forms an essential part of the early history of all colonial coinages. In many places the use of such tokens persisted until late in the nineteenth century.

The issue of token money, in metal or paper, has often been resorted to in the present century by local authorities during times of distress and shortages, especially those occasioned by war and enemy occupation. This was done by town authorities or local Chambers of Commerce in the First World War. They are usually small pieces of cardboard or discs of base metal (zinc, lead) with simple designs and inscriptions, for example a paper disc with 5 CENTIMES in a wreath and surrounded by the inscription BANQUE D'EMISSION DE LILLE and the date, 1915, issued during the German occupation in the First World War. Another reason for the issue of tokens can be the lack of coins of suitable denomination for specific purposes, for example sales tax tokens in the United States, or the New York subway tokens introduced when the fare went up to 15 cents, or the cardboard farthing tokens issued by some Dublin bakeries when the farthing was discontinued in Great Britain (1961) and the supply ran short across St. George's Channel. Such tokens, however, rarely pass into general circulation; they remain confined to the purpose for which they were made.

Temporary tokens merge into the more general class of what is known as obsidional or siege money. The circumstances of a prolonged siege, bringing together large numbers of soldiers usually insufficiently supplied with ready cash, have often led both besieged and besiegers to issue temporary coinages which it is intended should be redeemed at their face value when the emergency that gave rise to them is over. Some of them are 'token money' in the sense in which we have been using the word, but others are of silver and of high value, since the conditions of the emergency may lead private persons to sacrifice their silver plate and authorities to lay hands on church treasures, public monuments, and the like. The 'token' character of such coins lies in their not being struck at a regular mint and in their being intended to have only a temporary existence.

(a)   (b)

FIG. 62. Obsidional coins. (a) Siege of Vienna by the Turks, 1529. Æ 3·30 g. The shields are those of Austria, Hungary, Bohemia, and Castile, i.e. the duchy in which Vienna was situated and the three kingdoms of the Emperor Charles V. Some specimens have the crowned bust of the king above the inscription. (b) Siege of Scarborough during the English Civil War. Æ 6·61 g. (102 gr.). The design shows a roughly designed castle, accompanied by the value (1s. 3d.). The piece has been cut from the edge of a bowl.

The issue of siege money is recorded on various occasions in antiquity and the Middle Ages, but its history effectively begins in the late fifteenth century, and the issue of obsidional money accompanies all the great sieges which are such a conspicuous feature of the military history of Europe under the *ancien régime*. Obsidional pieces are often square or rectangular in shape, to save the extra labour and trouble of producing circular blanks, and their designs and inscriptions are usually simple; for example

TVRCK‖BLEGERT‖WIEN‖1529 and four oak leaves on one side of an obsidional coin of Vienna during the Turkish siege of 1529, or a crowned shield between X and S(ols) and 15 and 78 issued at Amsterdam blockaded by the Estates, the silver for the latter coins coming reputedly from a statue of St. Nicholas. Where silver plate has been used it is often cut up into pieces of convenient size without re-melting, so that fragments of the original designs may still be visible. Siege money is one of the types of coin that has been most frequently counterfeited. The rough design and fabric of the originals make forgeries particularly difficult to detect, and their local and historical interest renders them especially attractive to antiquarians who are otherwise not interested in numismatics.

Semi-monetary tokens. The class of monetary tokens merges into that of semi-monetary tokens, which have no formal monetary value but are issued in recognition of work done or services rendered, and will within a very short time be redeemed for cash. They have been widely used in modern times for certain types of agricultural work, where the custom is not to pay by the hour or the day but by the amount of work done. One may instance the hop-tokens of Kent, where the hop-pickers would receive tokens corresponding to the number of baskets of hops which they turned in and would exchange these for cash at the end of the week. Such tokens have no more than the name or initial of the farmer concerned and the quantity for which they were a tally, so that except where found in a local context they are difficult to identify. The same is true of the many industrial tokens of the last century.

A historically interesting series of semi-monetary tokens is formed by the ecclesiastical tokens formerly issued in many countries, when persons assisting at religious ceremonies were entitled to a recompense that might take the form of actual money —Esquire Bedells attending a particular university sermon in Cambridge were entitled to a groat—but were often tokens (French *méreaux*) which could be exchanged against money later. Other *méreaux* were exchangeable against determined quantities of bread, meat, or ale, in which case they merge with the category of non-monetary tokens. Their designs are usually simple, the representation of a saint being the commonest, with sometimes the name of the issuing body and very rarely a date. The great majority are of the sixteenth and seventeenth centuries, though specimens as early as the thirteenth century are known and their existence is documented even earlier. They sometimes circulated locally as coins.

Gaming counters, which replace coin while a game is in progress but are subsequently converted into cash, can also be classed as semi-monetary tokens. The commonest type found in this country consists of brass imitations of the 'spade guinea' of George III which in order to evade the charge of forgery have the customary reverse inscription, surrounding the spade-like shield which gave its name to the coin, replaced by a meaningless jumble of letters or sometimes with the motto *In the Good Old Days.*

Non-monetary tokens. Many tokens give the right to goods or services of a non-monetary character, though they sometimes have to be acquired in return for payments. Theatre tickets in modern times are of paper or card but were formerly of metal, and eighteenth-century metal tickets or passes for admission to London pleasure gardens are common. Ancient tokens of this character, marked with letters and numbers, have been useful to scholars studying the designs and seating plans of ancient theatres. A large group of Roman tokens known as *spintria*, bearing designs of an indecent character, are widely believed to have served as entrance passes to brothels. Countries in which the state had a salt monopoly often made much use of salt tokens, either as authorizing the recipient to receive a distribution gratuitously or as a receipt to prove that he had taken up his quota. In the days before the Truck Act of 1831 tokens were issued by companies to employees entitling them to acquire goods at company shops or to participate in transport or other services. Communion tokens, which usually bear a biblical text and the name of a parish, used to be given by Presbyterian ministers to members of their flock whom they had examined and judged in a fit state to receive communion and which had to be produced on the occasion. They originated amongst the sixteenth-century reformers in France and England but are especially characteristic of Scotland, from where the practice spread to the colonies. All these classes of non-monetary tokens are of some antiquarian and historical interest, but do not really come within the numismatist's purview.

Medals

Medals and medalets form the group of coin-like objects which is most remote from any monetary function, but as with 'token' the term 'medal' is of vague connotation and its etymology does not help in defining it, for in the last resort it implies no more than an object made of metal. Medals resemble coins in their shape and general appearance, but are often much larger—the finest medals of Pisanello are between three and four inches in diameter—and have frequently been cast instead of being struck. They differ from coins in being largely private in origin and in not being intended to serve as a medium of exchange. Since they are not money the metal of which they are made is of no consequence, and since they are not exposed to the wear incurred by coin in circulation they can be in very high relief. From the Renaissance onwards the professions of medallist and die-engraver have often been carried on by the same persons. It is sometimes evident in such cases that the medal allows the artist greater freedom to display his talents and provides the stimulus to higher artistic achievement.

The term 'medal' in its strictest sense implies a commemorative object of a type invented in fifteenth-century Italy, initially showing the portrait of a living person and made in his honour. It was an easy step from honouring the living to commemorating the dead and to celebrating great events—the birth of an heir, the construction of a castle, a military victory, the massacre of St. Bartholomew, the defeat of the Armada. The term 'medal' was also applied comprehensively in the fifteenth century to ancient coinage, whose portraiture inspired much of that of the Renaissance, so that even today scholars still speak of Roman medallions when these are really coins of an exceptional character. Because medals commemorated events the term easily passed to awards of many kinds whether in sport or school or war. Religious medalets are in some degree commemorative, and in the sixteenth and seventeenth centuries the classes of jettons and medalets tend to merge into one another. The subject is so vast, and for the most part so unrelated to the main interests of the numismatist, that only a few main types can be noted here.

Ancient medallions. What scholars are accustomed to term Roman medallions, because of their being larger in size and often more careful in fabric and elaborate in design than the majority of Roman coins, are for the most part no more than coins of exceptional denominations made for distribution by the emperor or his representative on particular occasions: triumphs, marriages, new year celebrations, assumptions of the consulship, the inception or completion of imperial vows (*vota*) undertaken at regular intervals, and so forth. Usually they are multiples of coins in normal use, but some reproduce denominations which were current at the period when the norms for particular distributions were established but had since disappeared, in much the same fashion as maundy money does in England. In the main they are pieces of

Fig. 63. Medallion of Constantine II. AV 13·50 g. A three-solidus medallion struck in 326 for the tenth anniversary (*decennalia*) of Constantine's nomination as Caesar. The reverse type, two winged Cupids holding a garland, symbolized the rejoicings on the occasion. The SMTS in the exergue stood for *Sacra Moneta* and the mint initials (TS, for Thessalonica).

high value—gold medallions weighing as much as a pound are known to have existed—and were intended for presentation to high officials, but at the other end of the scale coins of low denominations not usually struck were occasionally issued for throwing to the crowd during consular processions. The larger medallic pieces were often mounted and used as ornaments, either directly by their recipients or by those into whose hands they eventually passed. Some are known to have served as gifts to Germanic chieftains, and a number of crude copies of these, evidently made by local goldsmiths in central Europe, shows how acceptable they were.

Whether other medals existed in antiquity is a matter of definition. Prizes usually took the form of wreaths (crowns), sometimes of thin gold leaves, but a very splendid group of gold medals found at Abukir in 1902, which are Roman in date but Hellenistic in design, are generally assumed to represent awards of some kind and thus are comparable to one group of modern medals. The rarely issued decadrachms of Athens and Syracuse, like the twenty-stater gold multiple of Eucratides of Bactria, may have had some kind of medallic function. Later the built-in medallic quality of so much of the everyday coinage of the Roman Empire would have tended to prevent the emergence of a special class of non-monetary medals like those of modern times.

Modern medals. Medallions of the Roman type were occasionally made in the later Middle Ages—there are huge gold pieces of 10 and 20 doblas struck by John II and other kings of Castile—and Charles VII of France devised elaborate medals, usually having a central coin type surrounded by several circles of inscription, to celebrate the expulsion of the English from France at the end of the Hundred Years War (1453). Francesco II of Carrara struck bronze medals with his portrait to celebrate the recovery of Padua from the Milanese in 1390, and also invented a type of foundation medal which subsequently became very popular, since to men of the Renaissance, anxious above all for their future fame, it seemed to offer a guarantee of being remembered by a distant posterity excavating in the ruins of the buildings they had constructed in their lifetime. An enterprising French goldsmith, early in the fifteenth century, struck large copper and silver medals with supposed 'portraits' of Constantine the Great and Heraclius which have survived in some quantity.

FIG. 64. Medal of John VIII Palaeologus by Pisanello (1438). Lead (cast). Obverse only. The strange design of the emperor's hat was much commented upon by contemporaries, and the bust subsequently made to do duty as a model for any 'oriental' sovereign. The exact significance of the reverse type (not shown), which exhibits Pisanello's mastery of animal forms but is too crowded to be satisfactory as a design, is unknown. The imperial titulature on the obverse follows the correct forms of the Byzantine chancery.

None of these, however, filled exactly the roles which were to make the medal one of the most characteristic art forms of the Renaissance. The true modern medal was invented by Vittore Pisano, better known as Pisanello, a Veronese painter, who in 1438 made one in cast bronze of the Byzantine emperor John VIII Palaeologus, who was visiting Italy in the hope of obtaining aid against the Turks. The striking portraiture of this object had an immediate appeal and within the next few years—he died in 1455 —Pisanello made similar portrait pieces of a number of princes and private persons: Sigismondo Malatesta, Leonello d'Este, Alfonso V of Naples, Vittorino da Feltre, Iñigo d'Avalos, and others. These medals, admirable above all for their portraiture, have reverses of various types, sometimes naturalistic representations of their subjects on horseback, sometimes complex allegorical devices which for the most part remain unexplained. Evident throughout is Pisanello's pride of workmanship, with his signature OPVS PISANI PICTORIS displayed as prominently as the inscriptions giving the names and titles of the persons in whose honour the medals were made.

Pisanello was the earliest and in the eyes of most connoisseurs the greatest of fifteenth-century Italian medallists, but already before his death a number of excellent artists were following in his footsteps, and the products of such men as Matteo de' Pasti, Enzola, and Sperandio were little if at all inferior to those of his hand. Medals were easy and relatively cheap to reproduce, so that they have been described as the photographs of the Renaissance, and persons of means were anxious to be portrayed in this fashion. The taste was at no time restricted to princes. Pisanello's medals were cast, but struck ones were soon being produced. The taste for them quickly became universal, and has continued down to our own times, providing a medium for much of the finest portraiture that exists. Leone Leoni's medals of Charles V are of the same quality as his splendid bronze bust of the emperor and can bear comparison with the two great paintings by Titian; Catherine de Medici's character is nowhere so penetratingly observed and recorded as in a medal by Germain Pilon. Guillaume Dupré's medals of Henry IV, Jean Varin's and Jérôme Roussel's medals of Louis XIV, Andrieu's marriage medallion of Napoleon and Marie Louise are all outstanding works of art. The reverses of the earlier medals were usually symbolic, consisting often of a personal device, but later they usually refer to specific circumstances and events.

Medals are of limited interest to the student of coinage, despite the quality of their portraiture and sometimes their technique, but are of great interest to the modern historian, both iconographically and as a commentary on public events. Many are official in character, like the series intended to commemorate the achievements of Louis XIV, but satirical medals came into vogue with the Reformation and a large efflorescence of popular medals has accompanied outbursts of popular excitement down to almost our own day. Often the events that provoked them have seemed to posterity of little consequence, which makes it the more valuable to be able to see them through the eyes of contemporaries. Admiral Vernon's capture of Porto Bello in 1739, with the loss of only seven British lives, is now only remembered because its hero provided George Washington's father with the name of what subsequently became the most famous private house in America, but at the time it rocked the nation and resulted in the largest series of antiestablishment medals to be struck in the eighteenth century. The French Revolution of 1848, an event of somewhat greater importance, was likewise accompanied by an enormous output of popular medals, for the most part cast, of base metal, and of execrable design and execution. They were hawked round the streets of Paris and reflected every facet of popular feeling, for as many as half a dozen might appear in the streets or shops in the course of a single day. Although their artistic value is nonexistent and a number were certainly produced for the benefit of

FIG. 65. French Revolutionary medalet of 1848. Lead. The obverse inscription embodies the rallying cry of the workers during the June Days, *Du travail, du pain, ou du plomb*, when the National Workshops were closed and thousands were thrown on the streets. Armand Barbès was one of the leaders of the Left. The allusion on the reverse to bullets being supplied from overseas reflects the popular belief that the Right was financed by English gold.

collectors, the explicitness of their inscriptions makes them an absorbing commentary on events. Specimens were assiduously bought and published by Félicien de Saulcy, a distinguished French numismatist, who rightly defended his *Souvenirs numismatiques de la Révolution de 1848*, which he began to compile early in the year, against the charge that he was wasting his time and lowering the dignity of his subject. 'Aux yeux de beaucoup de gens, cette publication pourra paraître futile; pour ceux qui sont destinés à écrire l'histoire des temps étranges où nous vivons, elle sera d'un si puissant secours que nous ne saurions hésiter à l'entreprendre.' The modern historian neglects the study of popular medals at his peril.

Coin-weights

Coin-weights are a well-defined group of objects whose relationship to coins is obvious although their actual resemblance to them is variable. They have no continuous history, being extremely common in some periods and completely absent in others. Their normal function is that of verifying the weights of coins, especially those of gold, and they were needed partly because ordinary weights were not usually made with the necessary degree of precision and partly because the weights of coins do not always correspond to any single unit in normal use. In the nineteenth century the French silver franc and five-franc piece weighed respectively 5 g. and 25 g., but the gold twenty-franc piece weighed 4·615 g. Occasionally coin-weights could be used for other purposes. In early Muslim Egypt the copper coins (felous) were struck to no specified standard, so glass weights were made, stamped 'fels of [30] kharroubahs', the number being variable, and the copper coins were accepted by weight against these. Since coin-weights should in theory have been made with great precision, as gold coins were often expected to be accurate to within half a grain, one would expect them to be very useful to the numismatist in determining the theoretical weights of coins, but in practice they are of little value in this respect. Surviving specimens have often been damaged either by wear or by the loss of inlays which once filled in details of design or lettering, and many were of private manufacture and inaccurate from the start. Their existence in some periods of history and not in others is useful in interpreting the monetary practices of the past, and one can learn a great deal from the areas over which they are found. Eighteenth-century brass weights stamped A MOIDORE OR 27 SHIL[S], which are quite commonly found in England, provide evidence for the common use of Portuguese gold coin (*moeda de oiro*) in Great Britain—this is known also from the written sources—and the rate at which it passed.

Coin-weights are rare in classical antiquity and for the main period of the Roman Empire, but from the second half of the fourth century down to the seventh they are very common. This was apparently a result of an undated constitution of Constantine regarding the verification of the weights of gold coins used in commercial transactions. The typical weights of this period are circular or square pieces of bronze stamped N (for *nomisma*) or SOL(idus) for weighing either single solidi or, when a numeral is added, groups of solidi, and sometimes bearing imperial busts, or a figure of Moneta with a pair of scales, or the monogram or title of the public official responsible for verification. In the sixth century bronze weights were in many places, and particularly in Egypt, supplanted by glass ones, since glass is more resistant to wear, and it was these that were particularly favoured by the Arabs. Early Arab glass weights (seventh and eighth centuries) are extremely common and were used for verifying the exactness of silver dirhems as well as that of gold dinars, while the earlier Romano-Byzantine ones had been used only for gold. It was formerly thought that these glass weights actually served as money, since their inscriptions (e.g. 'a dinar of good weight') were taken too literally. It is now recognized that this was not the case, though it is possible that very similar glass objects, bearing inscriptions of a different kind, were used as small change in Egypt under the Fatimids.

The use of coin-weights disappeared in the West in the period of the penny, though larger weights were used for verifying those of sums of money (one shilling, five shillings, a pound). It was the 'poises' used in the Tower of London for verifying the weight of £1 in coin that gave rise to the Tower pound of 5,400 grains, lighter by 360 grains than the troy pound of 5,760 grains because the penny sterling weighed only $22\frac{1}{2}$ grains, as against the 24 grains of the nominal pennyweight. King John is known to have instructed the Mint to issue penny 'poises' lacking one-eighth of a pennyweight to mark the limit under which the penny would not be legal tender. With the reintroduction of gold coinage in the second half of the thirteenth century, coin-weights again came into common use. Many of the earlier ones were made by merchants or bankers, as some inscriptions make plain (e.g. *Bertelin Lombart*). Their use was officially disapproved of by the govern-

(a)   (b)

FIG. 66. Coin-weights. (a) Brass weight (9.44 g.) for a teston of Henry II of France (1547–59). The obverse shows the royal bust, while the reverse gives the name of the coin and the official weight, 7 deniers 10 grains. (b) Brass weight (6·78 g.) for an English noble. The type is that of the noble (above, p. 84, Fig. 47b), but the Roman H (for *Henricus*) shows that the weight dates from the 16th cent. The reverse is blank. This type of thick square weight was intended for the boxes of weights described in the text.

ment, which was anxious that its gold coin should be accepted at face value with no allowance for wear or maltreatment, but they were soon made by mints and sold to the public. They often bear on them the design of the coins they were meant to weigh, but in order to differentiate them from these they were usually made small and thick instead of large and thin, a change in module which occasionally led nineteenth-century numismatists into supposing that fifteenth- and early-sixteenth-century examples were early copper coins of, for example, Utrecht or Barcelona. Later they were more often made small and square, to reduce still further the danger of their being confused with coins. From the late sixteenth to the late seventeenth century the professional coin-weight manufacturers in the Low Countries put on the market beautifully made wooden boxes of such weights, containing a pair of folding scales, several sliding trays with compartments for between thirty and fifty weights, and a selection of small squares of metal stamped from a half-grain to 10 grains which made it possible to determine how far short of the correct weight any individual coin might be. Only in the eighteenth century, as the variety of gold coins likely to be in general circulation diminished, did these boxes go out of fashion. The nineteenth-century businessman usually contented himself with pocket scales allowing him to verify the weight of a guinea and half-guinea or a napoleon and a half-napoleon. These scales have at one end of a brass bar a single counterweight and at the other two circular depressions to take one or other coin, the distances between them and the fulcrum being carefully adjusted so that the one counterweight will do for both denominations.

Miscellaneous Objects

At the end of this survey there must be mentioned a few coin-like objects whose purposes are known but which do not fit into any of the categories so far considered, or whose purposes are at present obscure but which may have to be classed as tokens when they are better understood.

The first group includes coin ornaments, which range from very close imitations of real coins to stamped roundels of metal only related to coin types in a quite distant fashion. Imitations of coins also include the very common 'To Hanover' tokens, brass copies of the 'first' sovereign of Queen Victoria but having as obverse inscription VICTORIA REGINA and on the reverse a crowned horseman and a three-headed dragon with the inscription TO HANOVER. These were originally satirical medalets issued at Victoria's accession to celebrate the departure of the unpopular duke of Cumberland to be king of Hanover, but because they could be easily passed as genuine sovereigns they were manufactured and widely used by card-sharpers and other denizens of the Victorian underworld. Coin ornaments include many varieties of amulets and charms, which are often of metal and vaguely coin-like in appearance. Pilgrims' badges are likewise objects of known function but difficult to classify, unless they be treated as tokens on the ground that they provided evidence of their owners having accomplished their vows. Most of those current in Great Britain, however, are not genuine. They are what are known as 'Billies and Charlies', grotesque pseudo-medieval objects with designs and inscriptions derived from illustrations in books on Gothic art which were made by two dealers in curios and sold by them to the labourers working on the construction of the Shadwell Docks in 1857. Since they were apparently dredged up in the course of the work they were assumed by many to be genuine, and found a ready sale amongst lookers-on. They have a kind of Indian equivalent in the equally common class of Ramatankas, discs having on one side the standing figures of Rama and Lakshma surrounded by a Tamil inscription, and on the other the same deities enthroned with courtiers in attendance, and in the exergue the figure of Hanuman, the monkey god. Such pieces of 'temple money' go back to a genuine accession coin of a south Indian king, but are now made of brass and distributed to pilgrims and those attending ceremonies on festal occasions.

Coin-like objects of uncertain function include the great number of objects of base metal, usually bronze or lead, which classical archaeologists are accustomed to call *tesserae*, despite the fact that they are round and not square in shape. They have on them quite simple designs (a letter, a wreath, a jug, a loaf of bread, a letter, an imperial bust, and a numeral), and some may have served to facilitate distributions of bread and wine, to serve in the docks as receipts, etc., while others were probably no more than dice for board games or objects for children to play with. A group of considerable historical interest consists of what scholars since the eighteenth century have been accustomed to call contorniates. These are large bronze discs, about two inches in diameter, which have on one side the head of an emperor, sometimes living but more usually dead—Nero is particularly common—or that of some well-known personage (e.g. Homer, Alexander, Apollonius of Tyana, the historian Sallust) and on the other a variety of types, a pagan deity, representations of such events as the rape of the Sabines or the adventures of Ulysses, scenes connected with the circus games and gladiatorial combats. They all date from the fourth and fifth centuries A.D. and derive their name from a deep groove round their edges (It. *contorno*) whose function is unknown. So is their actual use, but their production was localized in Rome itself and they were probably connected with the games. It has been argued that they were issued as propaganda by the late Roman senatorial aristocracy, which was for the most part strongly pagan in its religious outlook, but this theory has not won general acceptance. A high proportion are countermarked with a monogram which includes the letters PE but has not yet been satisfactorily explained.

Fig. 67. Contorniate with head of Nero. Æ Late 4th cent. The reverse shows a distribution of loaves of bread, or perhaps of money.

9
Numismatic Scholarship

The status of numismatics as an auxiliary science to history has been recognized since the eighteenth century, but the provisions made for its teaching and study are usually meagre. Even when it forms part of prescribed courses for students of the classics at a university, its teaching has in general to be provided by scholars who happen to find it a congenial field for research but who are formally professors or lecturers in some related subject. The only professionals are normally to be found amongst the curatorial staffs of the great museums, and in every country these are few in number. Fortunately, numismatics, like some aspects of astronomy and natural history, remains a branch of learning in which the amateur can still do valuable work, and it is on the great collecting public, or rather on that part of it which is interested in the subject at a scientific level, that the progress of numismatic science largely depends.

Coin Collecting

Coin collecting has always been popular, and in recent years, partly as a result of skilful publicity by dealers, partly as a consequence of greater general affluence and perhaps wider educational opportunities, the number of collectors has greatly increased. This rapid expansion has had fringe consequences that are far from happy: a spectacular rise in coin prices, an increase in the proportion of collectors interested in coins primarily as an investment, the invasion of the market by banks for purely financial reasons. The last is particularly unfortunate, for banks can always outbid private purchasers and many of them, regarding their acquisitions simply as a hedge against inflation, are either unable or unwilling to provide inquirers with information about coins in their possession or with facilities for their study. It is only in exceptional cases that they put their treasures on show to the public, as is done by the Chase Manhattan Bank in New York. Private investors also make life more difficult for those who collect for study or pleasure, and it is small consolation to know that their activities are not always as profitable as they think. Price changes do not affect all coin series equally or operate uniformly at all levels, and the highly prized rarities of one generation may be quite out of fashion only a decade or two later. Banks and numismatic investors, however, are no more than a minority, even if the disturbance they create in the coin market is out of proportion to their number. The majority of those who collect do so because they have a genuine interest in coins, and wish to acquire them partly from the pleasure of ownership, partly because in handling them they feel that they are brought into direct contact with times other than their own.

Private collections are so varied in size and scope that they cannot be covered by any single formula. Most collectors start by interesting themselves in everything that comes their way, and gradually narrow themselves down to coins of a single country or mint or reign. It is sometimes said that no general collection in private hands can be of importance, since no single person has either the money or the knowledge to collect intelligently over a wide field. This is not quite true. The Lord Grantley Collection, dispersed in London in eleven sales between 1943 and 1945, ran to over 50,000 coins, all carefully labelled in the owner's legible if untidy hand, and the Karl Hollschek Collection, dispersed at Vienna in twenty sales between 1956 and 1964, exceeded 200,000 coins and was larger than all but the very greatest national collections. But the owners of such huge collections have rarely been productive as active scholars; their services to numismatics have lain rather in their generosity in placing the material they have acquired at the disposal of others. Active scholars have always contented themselves with much smaller collections, and indeed have sometimes made several collections in the course of their career, disposing of each group of coins when they have finished with it before embarking on the study of another. The exact size of a collection is no measure of its importance. The student of eighteenth-century tokens can put together a collection of several thousand with no serious difficulty, while a scholar interested in Visigothic coins will be lucky if he can acquire fifty in a lifetime.

Coins are stored in various ways. The traditional method in this country has been to use coin cabinets, which are commonly made of walnut and vary greatly in size, ranging from small boxes some eight inches square and six deep to substantial articles of furniture three or four feet high and capable of holding between 5,000 and 10,000 coins. A medium size, however, is generally preferred, since it is convenient to have something which can be easily moved to the table where one is working. A cabinet a little over a foot wide and something like a foot high and a foot deep can be fitted with twenty to twenty-five shallow trays pierced with rows of circular holes and will have a capacity of between 800 and 1,500 coins, the exact number depending on the size of the holes. Each hole is fitted with a felt roundel to protect the coin from any damage that might accrue through contact with the wood, and information about the coins—identification, a note of particular features, date of acquisition and provenance, and sometimes, but usually in a privately devised code, the price—is written on circular tickets which go under them. Some collectors nowadays prefer to use albums, which the invention of strong transparent plastic has rendered possible. Each double sheet of plastic is divided into about twenty pockets into which the coins and their tickets can be slipped, the sheets being held together in a ring binder. Albums are cheaper and more easily transportable than the traditional cabinets, but they are less elegant—cabinets made by good nineteenth-century craftsmen can still sometimes be bought at quite reasonable prices—and some early types of plastic are said to have contained chemicals which over a period of years could injure the coins. For many purposes coins can be filed away in long boxes containing small envelopes on which information about their contents can be written, but while convenient for transport such storage in envelopes is unlikely to satisfy an owner who takes any pride in his collection.

Numismatists do not exist in isolation. In 1836 a group of English collectors came together to form the Numismatic Society of London, which subsequently (1904) acquired a charter and became the Royal Numismatic Society. For its first three years (1836–9) its publication was known as the *Numismatic Journal*, but in 1839 it became the *Numismatic Chronicle*, under which name it still flourishes today. Also in 1836 two French scholars founded at Blois the *Revue de la numismatique française*, renamed in 1838 the *Revue numismatique*, and in 1841 their Belgian counterparts founded the Société (royale) belge de numismatique, with a periodical which began to appear at Tirlemont in 1842. Since that time societies have multiplied. Virtually all countries have one or even two national ones—in this country the British Numismatic Society broke away from the Royal Numismatic Society in 1905, partly owing to personal difficulties and partly because its founders thought that insufficient attention was being paid to the study of English coinage—and many local ones. The function of local societies is primarily to bring together collectors so that they can discover each other's interests and read papers; occasionally, though only rarely, they indulge in publication. The national societies also have regular meetings, but their main function is to finance the publication of a journal: the *Numismatic Chronicle*, the *British Numismatic Journal*, the *Revue numismatique*, the *Rivista italiana di numismatica*, and many others. It is in the pages of these journals that most important work in the numismatic field first appears. The publication of preliminary studies in such a form serves the double purpose of bringing to light fresh material, which may until then have laid unregarded in museums and private collections, and of allowing new attributions or theories to run the gauntlet of criticism before being incorporated in monographs or other publications of a more permanent character.

Public Collections

Public collections are a necessary adjunct to private collections, for they form, in a sense, the reference libraries of the numismatic world. They fall into two classes. There are, on the one hand, the great national or near-national collections: the British Museum, the Bibliothèque Nationale, the Staatliche Museen at Berlin, the Ashmolean Museum at Oxford, the Museum of the American Numismatic Society at New York. There are, on the other, local museums. The two categories differ in aim as much as in size. The great collections try to obtain as large a coverage as possible of the world's coins, though in practice they necessarily fall short of this ideal. Local museums accept the impossibility of such a goal. They are usually content to exhibit such coins of a general character as may come to them by gift. Beyond this they interest themselves only in the coinage of the region in which they are situated, acquiring coins of local mints, or others which are found locally, when from time to time they have the opportunity to do so.

The great coin cabinets for the most part grew out of the private collections of objets d'art made by seventeenth- and eighteenth-century princes, often as annexes to their libraries. This explains why the Cabinet des Médailles at Paris forms part of the Bibliothèque Nationale, not of the Louvre, and why it contains ancient cameos, gems, ivories, and jewellery as well as coins. The basis of each was usually a collection of Roman coins, whose portraiture appealed to the artistic taste of the period and whose historical background was familiar to a society brought up on the classics. Greek coins began to be added on an appreciable scale only in the eighteenth century, though the full flood did not come till later, and an attempt was usually made to acquire as representative a collection as possible of the coins of the country itself. Beyond this everything would depend on the interests of individual curators and the occasional gift or purchase of important private collections or notable rarities. The acquisition of other coin series has rarely been systematic. It often happens today that a great national collection will be found to lack quite common coins of a neighbouring country while possessing a fair selection of its rarities.

A small proportion of these coins is usually on exhibition to the public, but coins are not easy to display satisfactorily and the great bulk of every collection is not on view, though it can be seen by any serious student on request. There is, indeed, a certain conflict of interest between public and student, since a coin on exhibition can be easily overlooked by a scholar working with the trays, and even if it is not forgotten it is not always very easily extracted from a showcase for closer inspection. Coins not on exhibition are either kept in small cabinets of the type already described—this is the practice in England—or in large wall cabinets of wood or metal furnished with shallow drawers, in which the coins lie either in separate compartments or in small plastic or cardboard boxes. In the last case all necessary information about the coins can be written on the boxes themselves instead of on separate tickets. Built-in cupboards are cheaper than separate cabinets and allow the storage of more coins for the same cost, but they are less attractive to the eye and they allow the user to use only a single tray at a time, and one of rather inconvenient dimensions, instead of having an entire cabinet in front of him with which to work.

The arrangement of all large collections is a problem, since historical considerations have to be sacrificed to those of easy finding. 'Greek' coins, using the word in the large sense described in Chapter 2, are arranged geographically by mints, with some criss-crossing under rulers during the Hellenistic period, and the mints themselves are grouped regionally. The regions are taken in the order in which they are described in Strabo's *Geography*, but with some hesitation as to whether one starts with Britain, Spain, and Gaul or whether one leaves these to the end. In the latter case one starts with Italy, proceeds eastwards through Greece and Asia Minor till one arrives at Persia, and then turns westwards, along the south of the Mediterranean, until one ends in Mauritania, Spain, and Gaul. Roman Imperial coins are arranged partly under emperors, partly under mints, with sometimes one being given the precedence and sometimes the other. Much the same is done with the coinages of medieval Europe, though here there is the added complication that since modern and medieval frontiers rarely coincide one is often in doubt as to the country in which a particular coin series must be sought. Will coins of Merano, the chief medieval mint of the counts of Tyrol, be classed under Italy, under Austria, or under Germany as representing the Holy Roman Empire? Will coins of Avignon be treated as French or as Papal, medieval coins of Basel as German or Swiss? May there not be, at the bottom of a cabinet, some trays of supposed counterfeits or imitations which in fact are genuine and of the highest interest? The inquirer has always to keep possible alternatives and pitfalls in mind, to remember that it is better to ask for too much than too little.

The contents of the great museum collections are made most widely available through publication, and here the record of many museums is a sorry one. Publication programmes depend on the drive and availability of individuals, as well as on their competence, and after initial spurts of energy are apt to slow down and eventually stop altogether. They are also the victims of ambitious scholars, who realize that the collection which they are cataloguing is incomplete and attempt to fill in the gaps by drawing on the resources of others. The result, when it appears, is a more useful book, but the hopeful reader may have a long time to wait. In the 1870s the authorities in the British Museum embarked on the publication of their great collection of Greek coins, and the first volume, R. S. Poole's *Italy*, was published a hundred years ago (1873). Twenty-nine volumes have by now been published, but of these twenty-five appeared in the first half-century and only two since 1914; none has been published since 1927. Those covering Africa, Numidia, Mauritania, Gaul, and Spain are still to come, and by now the first volumes are almost completely out of date. The cataloguing of the Roman series was started much later and has made good progress in recent years, but the national series has been sadly neglected, with medieval English coins not catalogued beyond 1180 and the two volumes dealing with the Anglo-Saxon period by now largely out of date. France is better off, with good catalogues of the Merovingian, Carolingian, and medieval royal coins in the Bibliothèque Nationale, but after 1515 there is nothing, and the cataloguing of the museum's vast holding of feudal coins has not yet even begun. Nor has it anything to compare with the British Museum catalogues of Roman Imperial coins. The gigantic collection of German coins at Berlin is completely uncatalogued.

In place of catalogues of the old type, with elaborate introductions and descriptions of every coin but with highly selective illustration, a type of publication known as a *sylloge* has met with much favour in recent years. In it the descriptions are reduced to a minimum but every coin is illustrated. Intended initially to facilitate the die study of Greek coins and applied under the auspices of the British Academy to a number of private or semi-private collections not always easy of access, it has been extensively adopted abroad for Greek coins, notably for the publication of the Royal Danish Collection and the Von Aulock Collection, and has been extended in this country to English (mainly Anglo-Saxon) coins. Although its advantages are many, it does not provide the solution to all a museum's problems. Sylloge volumes can be produced more quickly and perhaps more cheaply than can the old-fashioned catalogue, but if the coins are to be satisfactorily arranged and classified the basic study that would be involved in the preparation of a catalogue must already have been done; in which case, if it involves important novelties, it should be published for the benefit of other scholars. This would imply the reservation of sylloge format for series that already have been fairly well studied, but even here one must pick and choose. All collections include large numbers of billon and copper coins in poor condition, from whose illustration a reader can learn little, and even where the coins are sufficiently well preserved for their reproduction to make die study possible, the results emerging from this are not always of sufficient consequence to justify the high cost of illustrating them on so comprehensive a scale. The provision of more adequate museum staffs, and the attachment of a higher priority to cataloguing than is possible under present conditions, would form a better solution to the problem.

For unpublished coins the student can work on the coins himself or ask for the information he needs, to be supplemented with photographs or plaster casts. The latter are made from impressions of the coins in wax or plasticine, and in large museums are supplied either gratis or at a small charge. For many purposes they are more satisfactory than photos, besides being cheaper, but they are slower to make and delays in fulfilling orders are sometimes considerable. The student who can actually visit the museum will be well advised to learn the art of making casts himself. Photos have the disadvantage of sometimes distorting shapes, since the coins have to be lit from the side to bring out details in the relief, and discolorations on the surface may easily appear to be part of the design or inscription. The plates of the different fascicles of the *Sylloge of Coins of the British Isles*, some of which were made by direct photography and others by photographing casts, provide very clear evidence of the superiority of the latter. For some purposes, notably for studying countermarks, neither photos nor casts are really satisfactory. One has to handle the coins oneself.

Local museums, in so far as they possess and exhibit small general collections of coins, render a great service to numismatics through interesting young people in coins. In so far as they specialize in local coinages their activities are sometimes open to criticism. It is natural and inevitable that they should try to form collections of coins from local mints—this includes, for this country, seventeenth- and eighteenth-century tokens—and that they should try to acquire, in whole or in part, hoards discovered locally. It is also natural that collectors of local coins should bequeath their collections to such museums. The disadvantages of such proceedings are many. The objections to the indiscriminate accumulation of hoard material have been set out in Chapter 6. Donors are apt to impose unreasonable conditions, such as the obligation to exhibit or a ban on the disposal of duplicates. The museums themselves are often too small to have a staff capable of looking after the coins properly, or, rather, they cannot guarantee the presence of such a staff in the future. One curator may be an ardent numismatist, but his successor's interests may be flints or seventeenth-century pottery. When this happens the coins can easily fall into neglect; their weights cannot be ascertained and casts cannot be provided; they may be tidied away to make room for other exhibits and cannot be found when asked for; when found, they may have had their tickets interchanged. These conditions are naturally not universal and many local museums are admirably run, but there can be few working numismatists who have not occasionally come up against cases where the very existence of such museums seems almost to have been designed to impede research.

Coin Dealers

Private and public collections have to be provided with material, and for this they rely on the third element in the numismatic establishment, the dealers. At the summit of the hierarchy are one

or two firms in most capital cities which either trade in coins and
medals exclusively or are general antique dealers—or, in a few
cases, banks—with well-staffed numismatic departments. Such
firms expect to hold large permanent stocks of coins and in some
cases issue regular price lists to their clients. These lists are often
prefaced by a short series of articles, some popular in character
but others publishing new material or otherwise involving original
research. They thus become useful adjuncts to the larger and
better-known numismatic journals, and have the advantage of
appearing at more frequent intervals. The relation between coin
dealers and their clients is often one of close friendship and trust:
dealers will reserve coins for clients to whom they know they are
of particular interest and let them have them on favourable terms,
scholars will help such firms with information or identify and
label coins in return for being given first refusal of those they want.
It is through such central dealers that coins are mainly distributed. Local antique dealers who keep dishes of miscellaneous
coins through which clients can rummage or lay out rows of priced
and identified coins to attract the eyes of tourists are usually of
little importance. Such coins, indeed, are rarely of local vintage;
they have been supplied by firms from the capital and are often
simply being sold on commission.

Coin auctions are an important aspect of the coin trade, besides
providing an essential element in the literature of numismatic
scholarship. Some are conducted by dealers themselves, others by
professional auctioneers who develop coin auctions as an important element in their business. The more important ones are
usually those of single specialized collections, or parts of such, for
it is a melancholy fact that most private collections are not
catalogued till they are on the point of being broken up. Where
auctions are frequent they are often no more than accumulations
of separate consignments, the more valuable coins being sold
singly and others in lots of anything between five and fifty coins,
or even more. Customs in this respect vary from one country to
another. The earliest coin auction catalogues go back to the end
of the seventeenth century, but it was only in the nineteenth that
they became of real importance, with descriptions of the coins
sufficiently detailed to permit their identification with specimens
in present-day collections. Photographic illustrations have been
usual since the 1890s, a new standard having been set by the
catalogues of the various parts of the Montagu Collection sold in
London and Paris over the years 1895–7. Catalogues are issued
regularly to subscribers and potential clients, and where im-

portant collections are sold they are now handsomely illustrated, with anything from fifty to a hundred plates and all the coins described in detail. Such catalogues form part of the standard reference literature of the subject. Some are so important as to have been subsequently reprinted for general use, and every scholar tries to have on his shelves those most closely related to his field of study. The catalogue of the Pozzi Collection, sold by the dealer Lucien Naville at Geneva in 1921, is one of the best general reference books on ancient Greek coins (101 plates), while that of the Marchéville Collection, sold in Paris by Florange and Ciani in 1927–9 and running to three volumes, gives the fullest coverage of the coinage of the French monarchy from the accession of Hugh Capet (987) to the death of Henry IV (1610).

Coin auctions, however, are largely devoted to keeping in circulation the coins already in the market. The market itself has to be supplied. Here, in the last resort, one has to take account of coin finds, and in doing so one enters a semi-legal world in which too many questions are not asked, or at least, the answers given to them are not published. Many countries, it is true, have no legislation pre-empting coin finds for the state. In France, and in other countries governed by the Code Napoléon, the law concerns itself only with questions of immediate possession, the allocation of ownership between the finder and the owner of the land on which the coins are found. All coins which are found can thus be legally sold to dealers. At the other extreme are countries where the state lays claim to all, often without offering adequate compensation to the finder or at least making it generally known that compensation will be available if the find is declared. Usually, in such cases, it gets very little: most coins are sold by finders to local dealers who ask no questions but dispose of them gradually to clients, or in some cases send or take them abroad and sell them in countries where the coin market is free. Other countries, like our own, fall between the two extremes, with legislation that is monumentally illogical, treating objects of gold and silver—but not of copper—as potentially treasure trove, but as being such only if a coroner's court decides that they were originally hidden with a view to recovery at some future date. Casual losses cannot in consequence be classed as treasure trove, nor can objects of gold and silver which are deliberately abandoned by their owners. Grave goods fall into this category, with the result that the gold and silver treasures of Sutton Hoo became the property of the nation through the generosity of Mrs. E. M. Pretty, the owner of the land on which they were found, and not by the operation of the law. Even where coins are adjudged to be treasure trove, the authorities will normally claim for public museums only the more important items, for which the full market value will be paid, while the rest are returned to the owner to be disposed of as he pleases. The system in practice works reasonably well, for it ensures that the great majority of coin hoards are properly recorded and at the same time saves museums from being cluttered up with material that they do not want and which would be far better in the hands of private collectors, serving the useful purpose of maintaining an interest in the subject. In most countries with strict legislation the situation is less satisfactory, for, unless finders can rely on adequate compensation, hoards will naturally be dispersed and find spots not revealed. In this fashion information that is vital to scholars may be irretrievably lost.

Glossary

accessory symbol A minor mark or device in the type or inscription.

anvil die (also **pile, staple,** or **standard**) The lower of the two dies between which a coin was struck.

area The central space of an Islamic coin, corresponding to the **field** (q.v.) of Western coins.

billon A silver–copper alloy containing less than 50 per cent silver. Sometimes extended to cover subsidiary coinage in nickel, aluminium, etc.

black money Coins of very low quality **billon** (q.v.), containing less than 10 per cent silver and dark brown or black in colour, since the silvery surface such coins usually had when originally struck (see p. 107) quickly disappeared through wear or corrosion.

blank The disc of unstamped metal used in making a coin. In America the term **planchet** is more usual.

bracteate A very thin silver coin struck on one face only. Refers mainly to such coins struck in Germany and neighbouring countries in the twelfth and thirteenth centuries.

brass A term applied loosely, by seventeenth- to nineteenth-century scholars, in such phrases as First Brass, Second Brass, etc., to the **orichalcum** (q.v.) and copper coinage of the Roman Empire.

brassage The profit made by a moneyer, as opposed to **seigniorage** (q.v.).

brockage Properly speaking, any coin which is mis-struck, but particularly applied to coins on which the same design is found in relief on one face and **incuse** (q.v.) on the other as a result of the preceding coin having remained on the die and left its impress on the next coin struck.

bronze Strictly speaking, an alloy of about 95 per cent copper and 5 per cent tin, with perhaps traces of zinc, but applied loosely to all coins consisting predominantly of copper.

carat Originally a weight (about 0·19 g.), but most commonly used as a fractional term (1/24th) for expressing the fineness of gold.

contorniate Bronze coin-like objects of the late Roman Empire which are characterized by a deep groove around their edges.

countermark or **counterstamp** A small letter or device punched on the face of a coin, usually with the object of changing its value.

denomination Strictly speaking, the name of a coin, but by extension its legal valuation.

die The stamp used in coining, formerly often called an **iron.**

die axis The relation between the position of the reverse type of a coin and that of the obverse.

die link Two or more coins are said to be die-linked when their obverses or reverses share a common die.

double-striking A blurring of the design occasioned by the die or coin having slipped between successive hammer blows.

electrum Originally a natural alloy of gold and silver employed in Asia Minor for the earliest coinage, but now used of any alloy of gold where the proportion of silver or copper is large enough to affect the colour.

emission *see* **issue.**

exergue The lower segment of a coin design, marked off from the rest by a horizontal line.

field The central space of a coin, more especially that left blank on either side of the head or other main design.

flan Originally an alternative term for **blank** (q.v.), but now applied to the surface of a coin, e.g. in the phrase 'off flan', when part of the design has failed to register owing to imperfect centring of the dies.

fleur de coin Mint condition, uncirculated.

graining The technical term for what is popularly termed the 'milled edge' of coins.

hammered coinage Coins made by hand, the upper die being struck by a hammer, as opposed to 'milled money' made by machinery (*see* **mill**).

hoard A group of coins lost or hidden as a group, as distinct from coins lost separately even if sometimes found together.

hybrid *see* **mule.**

immobilization The retention of a coin design long after its details (e.g. name or bust of a ruler) have ceased to be appropriate.

incuse The reverse of a coin having a deeply impressed punch mark without design, and by extension a design in intaglio. This is usually the result of an error of striking (*see* **brockage**), but was a normal feature of some early coins of Magna Graecia.

initial mark A term sometimes applied to a **privy mark** (q.v.) where it is placed at the beginning of the inscription.

inscription or **legend** The lettering or wording on a coin.

iron Old term for coin die.

issue or **emission** Coins issued in accordance with the terms of a specific mint indenture; loosely, any related group of coins.

jetton A counter, usually of brass, formerly used to facilitate arithmetical operations.

legend *see* **inscription.**

mill The name formerly given to all machinery used in the making of coin, whence 'milled' (or 'mill') coinage in opposition to 'hammered' coinage.

mint A place where money is coined.

mint-mark Letter or symbol placed on a coin to indicate where it was struck.

module The diameter of a coin after striking.

mule or **hybrid** A coin produced from two dies not intended to have been used together. The term **hybrid** is the more usual in the field of ancient numismatics.

mutatio monetae *see* **renovatio monetae.**

obsidional money or **siege money** Emergency coins struck by besiegers or besieged (usually the latter) when normal coin is in short supply during a siege. By extension, any coins struck during military operations.

obverse The side of the coin which bears the more important device or inscription. Since these are not always identical, some numismatists use it of the side of the coin struck by the lower (anvil) die.

officina A subdivision of a Roman or Byzantine mint.

orichalcum A brass alloy used for the sestertius and dupondius under the early Roman Empire.

overstrike A coin for which the blank was an older coin, traces of the earlier impression being still visible.

patina The film or incrustation produced by oxidation on bronze coins, especially those of the Roman Empire.

pattern A proposed coin design which may or may not be approved.

piefort or **piedfort** A coin struck on an unusually thick flan as a pattern or proof, not for circulation.

pile One of several terms used for the **anvil die** (q.v.).

planchet *see* **blank.**

privy mark Letter or symbol placed on a coin as an element in mint administration or control, without its meaning being immediately evident to the public.

proof A coin of high quality struck by specially cleaned and prepared dies, e.g. for presentation purposes.

punch die *see* **trussel.**

remedy or **tolerance** The extent of deviation permitted by mint ordinances on either side of prescribed standards of weight and fineness.

renovatio (or **mutatio**) **monetae** The withdrawal of the coinage in circulation at regular intervals and its replacement by a new coinage.

restrike A later impression from original dies. The term is often improperly applied to an **overstrike** (q.v.).

retrograde An inscription reading backwards instead of forwards.

reverse The opposite face of a coin to the **obverse** (q.v.).

scyphate A term applied to the Byzantine concave coins of the eleventh to fourteenth centuries. It is best avoided, since the term *scyphatus* of eleventh-century Italy, with which these coins were identified, referred not to their concavity but to their prominent border.

segmented collar or **virole brisée** A device invented in the sixteenth century for marking the edges of coins.

seigniorage The charge exacted by a political authority for the exercise of minting rights, in contrast to **brassage** (q.v.).

siege money *see* **obsidional money.**

standard (1) the prescribed fineness and weight of coins, or (2) the lower (anvil) die.

staple One of several terms for the lower (anvil) die.

stater The term used in Greek numismatics for the principal denomination of a coinage, either in gold, electrum, or silver.

stop The term applied to the punctuation marks sometimes used to separate letters or words on coins.

tolerance *see* **remedy.**

tressure The ornamental frame around the type which is a feature of many late medieval coins.

trussel (or **punch die**) The upper die.

type The main design on each face of a coin; also a class or group of coins united by their design.

uniface coin A coin struck on one face only.

virole brisée *see* **segmented collar.**

Weights of Some Typical Coins

The left-hand column gives the weight of a specimen in good condition or, where it is known, the theoretical weight. The 'Specified Weights' in the second column are expressed in terms of the weight standard of the country and period. A date following the name of a coin shows when the denomination of that weight was introduced. The weights indicated are not necessarily limited to coins of the ruler whose name is given; they often became typical of the denominations as a whole.

GOLD COINS

Wt. in grams	Specified Weight	Country	Name, etc.
10·89	Babylonian stater	Lydia	Stater of Croesus (561–546 B.C.)
8·42	1/50th gold mina	Persia	Daric, 5th century B.C.
8·62	stater	Macedon	Philippus of Philip II (359–336 B.C.)
7·80	1/42nd lb.	Rome	Aureus of Augustus (27 B.C.–A.D. 14)
4·55	1/72nd lb.	Rome	Solidus (309) of Constantine I (A.D. 306–37)
4·25	mithqal	Syria	Umayyad dinar (A.H. 77 = A.D. 696/7), early 8th century
3·54	1/96th lb.	Florence	Gold florin (1252), late 13th century
3·56	1/67th marco	Venice	Gold ducat (1284) of Giovanni Dandolo (1280–9)
4·53	1/54th marc	France	Écu à la chaise (1337) of Philip VI (1328–50)

7·80	120 grains	England	Noble (1351) of Edward III (1327–77)
3·50	1/70th marc	France	Écu au soleil (1475) of Louis XI (1461–83)
15·55	240 grains	England	Sovereign (1489) of Henry VII (1485–1509)
6·75	1/34th marco	Spain	Pistole or doubloon (double escudo: 1566) of Philip II of Spain (1556–98)
6·75	1/36¼ marc	France	Louis d'or (1640) of Louis XIII (1610–43), earliest type
8·42	129⁴⁄₉ grains	Britain	Guinea (1662) of Charles II (1660–85)
7·99	123¼ grains	Britain	Sovereign (1817) of George III (1760–1820)
6.45	1/155th kilo	France	Napoléon d'or (20 franc piece: 1803) of Napoleon I (First Consul 1799–1804, Emperor 1804–14, 1815)
16·72	258 grains	United States	Eagle 10 dollar piece: 1837, 19th century
11·02	—	India	Mohur (1562) of Akbar (1556–1605)
c. 165	—	Japan	Oban (10 ryo), late 16th century

SILVER COINS

Wt. in grams	Specified Weight	Country	Name, etc.
5·60	1/100th silver mina	Persia	Shekel (*siglos*), 5th century B.C.
17·50	1/25th light mina	Athens	Tetradrachm, 5th century B.C.
3·90	1/84th lb.	Rome	Denarius of the late Republic, 1st century B.C.
3·41	1/96th lb.	Rome	Denarius (A.D. 63) of Nero (A.D. 54–68)
2·27	1/144th lb.	Rome	'Siliqua' of Valens (A.D. 364–78)

6·82	6 scripula	Byzantium	Hexagram (615) of Heraclius (610–41)
c. 3·03	1/108th lb. (?)	Byzantium	Miliaresion of Basil I (867–86)
1·70	32 grains	Francia	Denier (reformed: 793/4) of Charlemagne (768–814)
c. 1·43	c. 22 grains	Mercia	Denier (reformed) of Offa (759–96)
1·46	22½ grains	England	Penny (sterling) of Henry I (1100–35)
0·36	?	Venice	Denaro (very base) of Enrico Dandolo (1195–1205)
2·18	1/109⅓rd marco	Venice	Silver ducat (grosso: 1202) of the same doge
4·22	1/58th marc	France	Gros tournois (1266) of Louis IX (1226–70)
4·67	72 grains	England	Groat (1351) of Edward III (1327–77)
9·62	1/24th marco	Milan	Lira (testone: 1474) of Galeazzo Maria Sforza (1466–76)
31·70	1/8th mark	Tyrol	Guldengroschen (1486) of Archduke Sigismund (1446–90)
29·30	1/8th mark	Bohemia	St. Joachimstaler (1519) of the Counts of Schlick
31·10	480 grains	England	Crown (1552) of Edward VI (1547–53)
26·73	412·5 grains	United States	Silver dollar (1837 reduction from 416 gr.), late 19th century

BRONZE, BRASS, AND COPPER COINS

Wt. in grams	Specified Weight	Country	Name, etc.
327·45	1 lb.	Rome	Libral as (c. 280 B.C.)
13·64	½ oz.	Rome	Semi-uncial as (91 B.C.)
27·29	1 oz.	Rome	Sestertius (c. 19 B.C.) of Augustus (27 B.C.–A.D. 14)
10·92	⅖ oz.	Rome	As (c. 19 B.C.) of the same emperor
c. 10	1/32nd lb. (?)	Rome	Earliest 'follis' (recte nummus: A.D. 294) of Diocletian (A.D. 284–305)
c. 16·7	1/20th lb. (?)	Byzantium	Follis (heavy series) of Anastasius I (491–518)
1·77	1/180th lb.	Naples	Cavallo (1472) of Ferdinand I (1458–94)
11·34	1/40th lb.	Britain	Halfpenny (1672) of Charles II (1660–85)
56·70	2 oz.	Britain	Twopenny piece (1797) of George III (1760–1820)
9·45	1/48th lb.	Britain	Bronze penny (1860) of Victoria (1837–1901)

Suggestions for Further Reading

The best guides to further reading are provided by two bibliographies which appeared independently and almost simultaneously, E. Clain-Stefanelli's *Select Numismatic Bibliography* (New York, 1965) and my own *Bibliographie numismatique* (Brussels, 1966). The first is the larger of the two, and takes more account of the special interests of the collector. The second is primarily concerned with the use of numismatics to the historian, giving a better coverage of articles and containing the only general guide available to sale catalogues. Current publications (books and articles) are summarized in *Numismatic Literature*, published by the American Numismatic Society (New York, 1947 ff.) and now appearing half-yearly. Good up-to-date surveys of the various fields have been published by the International Numismatic Commission on the occasion of the last four International Numismatic Congresses (Paris 1953, Rome 1961, Copenhagen 1967, New York 1973). Indications of current literature can also be found in the monthly coin lists of two London dealers, Spink's *The Numismatic Circular* and *Seaby's Coin and Medal Bulletin*, which also contain short articles and notes on the activities of numismatic societies.

The only convenient work covering the whole field of coinage is R. A. G. Carson, *Coins, Ancient, Mediaeval and Modern* (2nd ed. London, 1970), now available in paperback as three separate volumes dealing respectively with ancient, European, and extra-European coinages (London, 1971).

The fullest one-volume reference book on Greek coinage is B. V. Head, *Historia Numorum* (3rd ed. Oxford, 1911; reprinted, London, 1963), though much of the detail is now out of date. The same is true of what is still the best short textbook, C. T. Seltman, *Greek Coins* (2nd ed. London, 1954). The most recent general books by G. K. Jenkins, *Ancient Greek Coins* (London, 1972), and C. M. Kraay and M. Hirmer, *Greek Coins* (London, 1966), are more up to date and are splendidly illustrated, but are less systematic in their coverage. A work that can be strongly recommended is a British Museum publication, *A Guide to the Principal Coins of the Greeks* (1932; revised ed., 1959), which is copiously illustrated and includes a brief commentary on each coin shown on the plates. For collectors there is a brief work by H. A. Seaby, *Greek Coins and their Values* (2nd ed. London, 1966).

The best general book on Roman coinage is H. Mattingly, *Roman Coins* (2nd ed. London, 1960), but M. Grant, *Roman Imperial Money* (London, 1954), if less systematic, is more readable and generally informative. Despite the title, it deals with coins rather than money. The standard reference books are by M. H. Crawford, *The Coinage of the Roman Republic* (Cambridge, 1974), and H. Mattingly and E. A. Sydenham, *The Roman Imperial Coinage* (10 vols. London, 1923 ff.), though some volumes of the latter are in need of extensive revision and vols. VIII and X, covering the years 337–64 and 395–480, have not yet appeared. The best introductions for collectors are R. Reece, *Roman Coins* (London, 1970), and D. R. Sear, *Roman Coins and their Values* (3rd ed. London, 1974).

The only general reference books on medieval and modern coinage are the three volumes of A. Engel and R. Serrure, *Traité de numismatique du Moyen Âge* (Paris, 1891–1905), and the two volumes of their *Traité de numismatique moderne et contemporaine* (Paris, 1897–9), both works now reprinted by Forni (Bologna, 1970). An excellent general survey, covering the period from the end of the Roman Empire to the nineteenth century, is J. Porteous, *Coins in History* (London, 1969). Coins of the past century are most easily identified in R. S. Yeoman, *A Catalog of Modern World Coins* (11th ed. Racine, Wisconsin, 1974) or G. Schön, *World Coin Catalogue : Twentieth Century*, English translation by G. Muller (London, 1972).

Coins of the British Isles are conveniently covered in H. A. Grueber, *Handbook of the Coins of Great Britain and Ireland in the British Museum* (revised ed. London, 1970). For English coins, the standard work is G. C. Brooke, *English Coins* (3rd ed. London, 1950), but C. H. V. Sutherland, *English Coinage 600–1900* (London, 1973), is easier to read and takes account of more recent work. The handiest catalogue for collectors is H. A. and P. Seaby, *Coins of England and the United Kingdom* (12th ed. London, 1973). On Scottish coins the standard work is I. H. Stewart, *The Scottish Coinage* (2nd ed. London, 1966), and there is a collectors' catalogue by P. F. Purvey, *Coins and Tokens of Scotland* (London, 1972). On Irish coinage the only modern survey is M. Dolley, *Medieval Anglo-Irish Coins* (London, 1972), although A. Dowle and P. Finn, *A Guide Book to the Coinage of Ireland* (London, 1965), and P. Seaby, *Coins and Tokens of Ireland* (London, 1970), should be consulted for details of the coins.

The standard guide to American coins is R. S. Yeoman, *A Guide Book of United States Coins* (27th ed. Racine, 1974), which is intended for collectors. The best historical studies are by A. Nussbaum, *A History of the Dollar* (New York, 1957), and N. Carothers, *Fractional Money : a History of the Small Coin and Fractional Paper Currency of the United States* (New York, 1930). D. Taxay's *The United States Mint and Coinage : an Illustrated History from 1776 to the Present* (New York, 1966) is well illustrated and very readable. Various volumes by Sidney P. Noe, Eric P. Newman, Kenneth Scott and others, in the series *Numismatic Notes and*

Monographs published by the American Numismatic Society, deal authoritatively with various aspects of the coinage of the colonial period.

The standard works on jettons and coin-weights are F. P. Barnard, *The Casting-Counter and the Counting-Board* (Oxford, 1916), and A. Dieu-donné, *Manuel des poids monétaires* (Paris, 1925). The most recent general work on medals is T. Kroha's 3rd ed. of M. Bernhart's *Medaillen und Plaketten* (Brunswick, 1966), but it omits the excellent bibliography of the 2nd ed. (Berlin, 1920). The most valuable introduction to the subject, and the most important single work in the field, is G. F. Hill, *Medals of the Renaissance* (Oxford, 1920), best read in conjunction with G. F. Hill and G. Pollard, *Renaissance Medals from the Samuel H. Kress Collection at the National Gallery of Art* (London, 1967), where the elaborate annotation of Hill's original edition (1931) has been brought up to date. The standard reference works on the tokens of the British Isles are W. Boyne and G. C. Williamson, *Trade Tokens Issued in the Seventeenth Century in England, Wales, and Ireland* (2 vols. London, 1889–92), R. Dalton and S. H. Hamer, *The Provincial Token Coinage of the Eighteenth Century* (14 fasc. Privately pr., 1910–18), and W. J. Davis, *The Nineteenth Century Token Coinage of Great Britain, Ireland, the Channel Islands, and the Isle of Man* (London, 1904), all recently reprinted (London, 1967–70). There is a brief general survey by J. R. S. Whiting, *Trade Tokens: a Social and Economic History* (Newton Abbot, 1971), and a summary listing by P. Seaby and M. Bussell, *British Tokens and their Values* (London, 1970).

General works on numismatic techniques are largely lacking, since they are normally developed in studies of individual series. Recent advances in coin analysis, however, are comprehensively covered in a symposium publication, *Methods of Chemical and Metallurgical Investigation of Ancient Coinage*, ed. E. T. Hall and D. M. Metcalf (London, 1972).

Index